T0344982

WISCONSIN AGRICULTURE

WISCONSIN AGRICULTURE

A HISTORY

JERRY APPS

WISCONSIN HISTORICAL SOCIETY PRESS

Published by the Wisconsin Historical Society Press
Publishers since 1855

© 2015 by Jerold W. Apps

Publication of this book was made possible in part by a grant from the John C. Geilfuss fellowship fund.

wisconsinhistory.org

Front cover image: acrylic painting by Richard W. Patt

Frontmatter photo credits: page ii: Stephen Moulton Babcock and cow at the University of Wisconsin, 1928, WHi Image ID 104256; page v: farm couple in Cross Plains, Wisconsin, circa 1920, WHi Image ID 25029; pages vi–vii: art installation at Fermention Fest in Reedsburg, Wisconsin, art by Brenda Baker of Madison and photo by Jeremy Mundth; page viii: maple syrup for sale at Blue Vista Farm, Bayfield, Wisconsin, Travelwisconsin.com, courtesy of the Wisconsin Department of Tourism; page ix: sorghum harvest near Osceola, Wisconsin, 1895, WHi Image ID 24505; page x: courtesy of Ruth McNair, UW–Madison Center for Integrated Agricultural Systems

Part opener photo credits: Part I, pages xii–1: © JenniferPhotographyImaging; Part II, pages 40–41: © kschulze; Part III, pages 62–63: © Lynn Bystrom; Part IV, pages 128–129: © YinYang; Part V, pages 196–197: © stu99

Printed in the United States of America
Designed by Steve Biel

19 18 17 16 15   1 2 3 4 5

Library of Congress Cataloging-in-Publication Data

Apps, Jerold W., 1934–
  Wisconsin agriculture : a history / Jerry Apps.
     pages cm
  Includes bibliographical references and index.
   ISBN 978-0-87020-724-2 (hardcover : alk. paper) — ISBN 978-0-87020-725-9 (e-book)
1. Agriculture—Wisconsin—History. I. Title.
  S451.W8A67 2015
  635.09775—dc23

                              2015005539

To the farmers of Wisconsin

CONTENTS

INTRODUCTION

Wisconsin has been an agricultural state from its very beginnings. And while it has long been known as a dairy state, Wisconsin produces much more than cows, milk, and cheese, though those remain vital to its economy and identity. In fact, Wisconsin

is one of the most diverse farming states in the nation. It is the number-one producer of cranberries, ginseng, and mink pelts and is a leading producer of vegetable crops—peas, sweet corn, green beans, onions, carrots, cabbage, cucumbers, and potatoes. Wisconsin produces ample fruit crops, along with maple syrup, Christmas trees, and honey. And the state excels in the production of corn, oats, and forage.

The story of agriculture in Wisconsin is rich and diverse as well, and the various threads of that story are related and intertwined. To understand and appreciate the state's agricultural heritage, it is necessary to examine the various factors in its evolution not as isolated entities, but *as they relate to one another.* Those factors include everything from the fundamental influences of landscape and weather to complex matters of ethnic and pioneer settlement patterns, changing technology, agricultural research and education, and government regulations and policies. For instance, the emergence of a dairy industry in Wisconsin resulted from a combination of forces that included the rapid growth and demise of wheat growing, the particular skills and traditions of immigrants, the favorable climate, and the demands of the marketplace.

People often ask me what I find so fascinating about agricultural history. As a longtime professor of agriculture at the University of Wisconsin–Madison, I believe the history of our state, especially its farming history, is something we all have a

responsibility to know. I tell my students that as we learn our history we become more whole, more human, more aware of who we are as a people. The story of Wisconsin's agriculture is in many ways the story of our nation. Food and fiber are necessities of life, and agriculture is the provider of both.

Knowing our history can also help us wrestle with today's local, national, and global challenges. Such hot-button issues as environmental protection, land-use policy, and ensuring an adequate food supply are not new debates. They've arisen in other times and other forms. A solid understanding of our agricultural history provides a foundation for decision making about today's farming policies.

A full history of Wisconsin agriculture has not been published since 1922. In that volume, *A History of Agriculture in Wisconsin,* author Joseph Schafer wrote: "I desire to make emphatic my description of the present volume as a *sketch* of the history of agriculture. No claim of finality in the study of that subject is made, and I am well aware that the rigorous exclusion of many sub-topics which others would have stressed in writing a similar work would subject this book to criticism, were its claims less modest."[1] Now, more than ninety years later, I say the same thing. A comprehensive academic study of the topic would surely fill several volumes; for this book, I present a thorough but concise discussion covering the past 150 years.

The conversation must begin, however, with the glaciers that formed Wisconsin's hills and valleys, lakes and rivers, marshes and highlands and that left behind our variety of soils. Wheat and dairy farming are examined in depth, of course, but I also tell the stories of the state's cranberry and vegetable canning industries; beef cattle and dairy goats; fur farming; the cultivation of grapes and other fruits for wine; and other specialty crops, including ginseng, hemp, cherries, sugar beets, mint, sphagnum moss, flax, and hops. I explore new and rediscovered farming endeavors, from aquaculture to urban farming to beekeeping, and I briefly discuss recent political developments, such as the 2014 Farm Bill and its ramifications.

When I began research for this book, I put out a call for first-person accounts of our state's farm history. People responded in droves, not only with their stories but with wonderful photographs, many of which appear on these pages. These memories breathe life into the facts and figures of Wisconsin farming history. I've also included an extensive bibliography for those who wish to go further in their quest to better understand Wisconsin's agricultural past, present, and future.

PART I

EARLY HISTORY

LAND AND CLIMATE

Most of Wisconsin's landscape was formed by the glaciers that pushed out of the north from east of Hudson Bay in Canada, arriving in what is now Wisconsin some twenty-five thousand years ago. Over a period of more than ten thousand years, sheets of ice hundreds of feet thick ground relentlessly southward, tearing, ripping, and gouging the landscape. Propelled by gravity and the pressure of their own weight, the glaciers advanced, retreated, and advanced again, moving just a few feet in some years, several hundred feet in others. They brought with them boulders and gravel, material that was too sturdy to be crushed but light enough to be engulfed and carried along by the ice.

During the most recent glacial period, the ice that covered what is now Wisconsin took the form not of a single sheet but of six main sections, or lobes: the Superior Lobe, the Chippewa Lobe, the Wisconsin Valley Lobe, the Langlade Lobe, the Green Bay Lobe, and the Lake Michigan Lobe.[1]

The glacier sculpted Lake Superior, the largest freshwater lake in the world (comprising 31,690 square miles of surface area), and Lake Michigan, the world's fourth-largest freshwater lake (22,290 square miles). It gouged a huge hole in what is now Green Lake County, creating Green Lake, at 239 feet the deepest natural lake in Wisconsin. It carved the Mississippi, Wisconsin, Fox, and Rock Rivers and a host of smaller rivers and streams.[2]

The advance and retreat of the ice sheet also formed eskers, long and narrow ridges of sand, gravel, and boulders deposited by meltwaters; and drumlins, low oval hills consisting of left-behind glacial drift material. When buried chunks of glacial ice melted, they created thousands of kettle lakes, most without inlets or outlets.

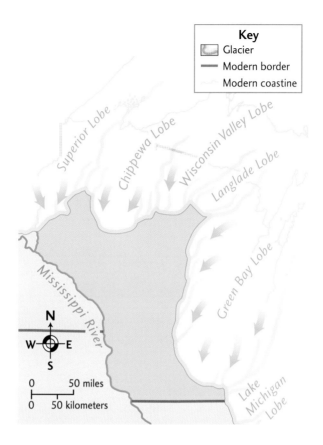

Key
- Glacier
- Modern border
- Modern coastine

Superior Lobe

Chippewa Lobe

Wisconsin Valley Lobe

Langlade Lobe

Green Bay Lobe

Mississippi River

N
W E
S

0   50 miles
0   50 kilometers

Lake Michigan Lobe

MAP BY
EARTH ILLUSTRATED, INC.

As the Green Bay Lobe melted, it formed an immense glacial lake in central Wisconsin that was up to 150 feet deep in places and covered as many as 1,825 square miles, larger than the bay of Green Bay.[3] The Baraboo Hills—a twenty-five-mile range of exposed metamorphic rock as much as 1.5 million years old—formed a dam for the glacier's meltwater, creating this glacial lake that stretched north to current-day Stevens Point, west to Tomah, and northwest almost to Eau Claire. When Glacial Lake Wisconsin drained, it left behind a flat, sandy plain studded with occasional high mounds and buttes.[4] Several of these sandstone pillars, onetime islands in the massive lake, can be seen at Mill Bluff State Park near Camp Douglas. Geographer Lawrence Martin wrote, "The craggy sides of the mounds often look, from a distance, like ruined castles and towers. . . . Their white battlements punctuate the monotonously-even, green plain which stretches eastward to the terminal moraine of the Green Bay lobe and westward to the escarpment of the Western Upland."[5]

Early settlers in central Wisconsin declared the vast plain nearly worthless as far as agriculture was concerned. The soil was sandy and poor in nutrients, and there

In 1948, Wisconsin State Fair officials commissioned a massive set of murals. This section depicted Wisconsin's natural resources—trees, water, and wooded hills—as they looked before settlement. The exposed bluffs with horizontal striations are similar to formations found along the Wisconsin River, while the diversity and density of the plant species represent a composite of the region's native grasses, plants, and trees. (For more on the state fair murals, see page 76.)

WISCONSIN HISTORICAL MUSEUM 2010.156.1.1

never seemed to be enough rainfall to sustain a decent crop. As the old joke went, if you bought forty acres of this sandy land, the seller insisted that you take another forty. (Today, however, with irrigation and modern-day fertilization strategies, thousands of acres of this old lake bottom produce tons of vegetables, including sweet corn, peas, green beans, cucumbers, and potatoes.)

But in southern, north central, and eastern Wisconsin, the glacier left behind fertile soils. As geologist David M. Mickelson pointed out, "Our agricultural land is rich because the grinding action of glaciers produced silt-sized particles that weather easily, releasing nutrients for plant growth."[6]

As they melted and retreated to the north, the glaciers left another gift in their wake: stones that range in size from a marble to a small automobile. Wisconsin's early settlers, especially in the northern reaches, encountered these impediments to cultivation when they first broke the land. Those pioneers found many uses for the stones, building fences, barn walls, silos, and even entire houses from the colorful rocks. As Wisconsin writer Charles D. Stewart recalled in 1909,

My fence was eight to ten feet in thickness and shoulder high; and similar windrows of rock ran over the moraine in all directions, like a range

Wisconsin farm children played on ubiquitous rocks, circa 1900.

WHI IMAGE ID 108535

upon a range. It is, of course, valuable land that warrants a wall like that. The barley-field might easily have defied a siege-gun on all four sides, for it had had so many bowlders on it that they had been built up into more of a rampart than a windrow. On a near-by field from which the timber had been removed, but which, notwithstanding, was far from "cleared," it looked as if it had hailed bowlders. You could have forded your way across it without putting a foot to ground.[7]

Even after newly arrived settlers cleared the land for their first plantings, there was no shortage of fieldstones in Wisconsin's glaciated areas, as the cycle of freezing and thawing brought a new batch of stones to the surface each spring. Indeed, as some Wisconsin farmers still say, "If nothing else grows this year, we can depend on a new crop of stones."

The southwestern corner of Wisconsin evaded the glacier's reach and today is known as the Driftless Area: fifteen thousand square miles of steep hills, long valleys, and good agricultural soil.[8] Edward Daniels, Wisconsin's first state geologist, described the Driftless Area in this way in 1854: "About one-third of the surface is prairie, dotted and belted with beautiful groves and oak-openings. The scenery combines every element of beauty and grandeur—giving us the sunlit prairie, with its soft swell, waving grass and thousand flowers, the somber depths of primeval forests; and castellated cliffs, rising hundreds of feet, with beetling crags which Titan might have piled for his fortress."[9]

While the last glaciers can be credited with having forged Wisconsin's landscape and soil, ask any farmer in the state about the greatest influence on farming success or failure, and you'll get a one-word answer: weather. Wisconsin has a relatively short growing season, and thus no cotton, sugarcane, oranges, or grapefruit grow here. But forage crops such as alfalfa and clover flourish in the cooler climate, along with other cool-weather crops like potatoes, cranberries, and cabbage. In addition, the cool summers and cold winters make Wisconsin a prime place for producing maple syrup, growing Christmas trees, and raising mink for pelts.

Wisconsin sees considerable diversity in its climate from north to south, a distance of about 320 miles at its greatest. In the northern third of the state, the frost-free days often number fewer than 80, not well suited to the growing of such cash crops as corn, wheat, and soybeans. Cranberries, a cold-climate crop, grow well in northern Wisconsin. In the southern third of the state, frost-free days can exceed 130, making corn and soybeans profitable farming enterprises.[10] Lake Superior and Lake Michigan influence the nearby climate, creating relatively cooler summers and milder winters near their shores. On the Door Peninsula, surrounded by the waters of Lake Michigan to the east and the bay of Green Bay to the west, cherries, grapes, and apples thrive.

In addition to suitable soil, sunshine, and frost-free days, farming requires water. Wisconsin is a water-rich state, receiving well more than thirty inches of moisture in

Wisconsin Landscape Facts

- Wisconsin's area is 34.8 million acres (56,153 square miles). Inland lakes comprise 982,000 acres, or 3 percent of the state's surface area.
- Water forms three of the state's boundaries: Lake Superior, Lake Michigan, and the St. Croix and Mississippi Rivers.
- Wisconsin is 295 miles at its widest and 320 miles at its longest.
- Wisconsin boundaries total 1,379 miles.

- The highest elevation in the state is 1,952 feet at Timm's Hill in Price County. The lowest is 579 feet along the Lake Michigan shoreline.

NOTES

Adapted from "Wisconsin—Location, Size, and Extent," www.city-data.com/states/Wisconsin-Location-size-and-extent.html, ed. Lynn Lemanski; and *State of Wisconsin 2011–2012 Blue Book* (Madison: Wisconsin Legislative Reference Bureau, 2011), pp. 675–678.

a typical year, with about two-thirds of that coming during the frost-free months. In some of the dry, sandy parts of the state, particularly the central sands region including parts of Waushara, Adams, Portage, Wood, Waupaca, and Marquette Counties, irrigation from underground sources has made the droughty soils profitable for such crops as potatoes, cucumbers, sweet corn, green beans, and peas.

Door County cherry trees in bloom

PHOTO BY DOOR COUNTY VISITOR BUREAU, COURTESY OF THE WISCONSIN DEPART-MENT OF TOURISM

Although Wisconsin is a northern state with famously long winters, it also has warm summers with ample rainfall, making it ideal for several kinds of agriculture—in particular dairy farming, which requires acres of forage crops, plus corn for silage. Additionally, for much of the state the growing season is long enough that corn, soybeans, and even alfalfa can be grown as cash crops. Especially in the southern half of the state, the soil lends itself to the growing of canning crops such as peas, sweet corn, and snap beans.

But perhaps the most important factor in Wisconsin's diverse agriculture equation are the people who settled here, bringing with them both their farming skills and the values necessary for working long hours, sharing work with neighbors, and creating strong rural communities.

Wisconsin Climate Facts

- The highest temperature recorded is 114°F at Wisconsin Dells on July 13, 1936. The lowest temperature on record is minus 55°F at Couderay on February 2, 1996, and February 4, 1996.
- The average date for the last spring freeze ranges from early May along Lake Michigan and in the southern counties to early June in the northern-most counties.
- The first freeze in fall occurs in late August and early September in northern counties and in the central lowlands; however, July frost is not uncommon in the north and the central Wisconsin lowlands. First freeze occurs in mid-October in areas along Lake Michigan.

- Average annual rainfall ranges from 30 to 34 inches in the western uplands and northern highlands. It drops to about 28 inches in the central plains and Lake Superior coastal area.
- Average annual snowfall varies from about 30 inches at Beloit to more than 100 inches in northern Iron County. The duration of snow cover ranges from 85 days in southernmost Wisconsin to 140 days along Lake Superior.

NOTES

Adapted from "Climate of Wisconsin," www.uwex.edu/sco/stateclimate.html.

2

FIRST PEOPLE

As the great glaciers retreated and sea levels rose, the land warmed and became habitable for humans, and people began arriving in what is now the Upper Midwest. These prehistoric inhabitants were descendants of the Upper Paleolithic hunters who are believed to have crossed a land bridge from Siberia to Alaska.[1] A more recent theory about their arrival suggests that "Pleistocene peoples may have entered the region at an earlier time by water-craft, or along shorelines now inundated by current ocean levels."[2]

Physical evidence of Paleo-Indians in the Upper Midwest dates back some twelve thousand years. According to Jennifer Harvey of the Great Lakes Archaeological Research Center, "The first people to enter Wisconsin appear to have arrived from the south and southwest in very small numbers . . . and tended to occupy the landscapes associated with glacial ice margins as these retreated north into Wisconsin." Evidence of these early inhabitants uncovered in Brown and Door Counties includes "distinctive projectile point styles: Clovis, Folsom, Scottsbluff, Eden, and Agate Basin."[3]

Other physical evidence of the Paleo-Indians includes petroglyphs, stone tools, and pottery shards. According to author Patty Loew, "These fragments of the past suggest that the earliest Native people subsisted mainly on a diet of plants and small mammals—rabbits, raccoons, and squirrels—as well as larger ones such as deer and elk." Nonphysical evidence—songs and stories that have been passed down by oral tradition—tells us much about early inhabitants' lives as well, including their appreciation and reverence for the plants that sustained them. "Whereas non-Indian anthropologists explain the tribes' increasing reliance on agriculture as an evolution

This photograph, taken about 1912 by archaeologist Charles E. Brown, shows cultivated fields untouched by white settlers. A mile from the shore of Lake Winnebago (in Vinland Township, Winnebago County) and now known as the Eulrich Site, it was investigated by archaeologists in the mid-1960s and attributed to the Oneota Culture. WHI IMAGE ID 27951

from hunting and gathering," Loew explained, "some Native elders and historians view their origin stories as proof that they have always had agriculture."[4]

During the Woodland Era (1000 BC–AD 1000), early peoples increased their farming activities. "Subsistence practices remained rooted with cycles of hunting-gathering, but horticulture became progressively more important," noted Harvey. The growing of maize spread to the northern limits of Woodland people's range by AD 1000.[5]

In the Mississippian Period (AD 1000–1500), agricultural crops became permanent and prominent features of early people's diets. The Mississippians, according to Harvey, "were a fully sedentary agricultural people depending on maize, beans, and squash."[6] As Native people's agricultural endeavors expanded, so did their way of life. "With a more reliable food supply," Loew explained, "tribal populations increased and Native Americans began to live in larger, more permanent villages."[7]

Beginning around AD 1000, Oneota communities established farming villages on river terraces and lakes; like the Mississippians, they grew corn, beans, and squash. According to Robert Birmingham and Leslie Eisenberg in their work *Indian Mounds of Wisconsin,* "After 1300, the Oneota in Wisconsin seemed to have consolidated into two principal densely populated centers: a western concentration on the sandy Mississippi River terraces around present day La Crosse, and an eastern concentration along the Middle Fox River, including Lake Winnebago. There are sites as well at nearby Green Bay and on the Door Peninsula."[8]

The land that is now Aztalan State Park in eastern Jefferson County was the site of a Middle-Mississippian village that thrived between AD 1000 and 1300. The people who settled at Aztalan built large, flat-topped mounds and surrounded their village with a wooden stockade. And they were farmers. Indeed, archaeologist Robert Birmingham has referred to Aztalan as "Wisconsin's first farming town."

Well-preserved garden beds like these near the town of Brazeau (Oconto County) can provide clues about early people's farming practices. Native Americans across the Upper Midwest built garden beds—also called ridged fields—to increase yields by enhancing the nutrients available for their crops and providing more growing space. The beds could cover hundreds of acres around a community in any given year and were built over many centuries. By two thousand years ago, Indians were cultivating pepo squash (*Cucurbita pepo*), marshelder (*Iva annua* variety *macrocarpa*), sunflower (*Helianthus annuus*), erect knotweed (*Polygonum erectum*), goosefoot (*Chenopodium berlandieri* subspecies *Jonesianum*), and bottle gourd (*Lagenaria siceraria*). Giant ragweed, may grass (*Phalaris caroliniana*), and little barley (*Hordeum pusillum*) were also grown.
OFFICE OF THE STATE ARCHEOLOGIST OF WISCONSIN

An artist's conception of the ancient fortified village at Aztalan
WHI IMAGE ID 28935

While researchers have estimated that Aztalan included forty-five acres of agricultural land, Birmingham pointed out that "this area may not have been the only place where crops were grown. Archaeological surveys found fragments of stone hoes to the southwest of the town . . . suggesting this area was also cultivated."[9]

By AD 1000, Birmingham and Eisenberg explained, "Virtually all people living in areas of the Midwest where agriculture could be successful were cultivating crops, especially corn, to one extent or another."[10] Other important early crops included

sunflowers, erect knotweed, giant ragweed, maygrass, barley, and bottle gourds. In the northern regions of the state and in some central wetland areas, wild rice was harvested as a food source starting around 1,900 years ago. Beans arrived in the region around 800 years ago, and later corn was often planted alongside squash and beans in the mutually beneficial grouping known as Three Sisters.[11]

By the early 1600s, just before Europeans arrived in the Upper Midwest, Native Americans numbered about one hundred thousand in the region. The prominent

A Replica Native American Garden

At Pope Farm Conservancy in Middleton, archaeologists from the Wisconsin Historical Society work with area fourth-graders to create a replica Native American garden each year. Crops planted have included squash, sunflowers, and gourds, recalling gardens of a thousand years ago in the Upper Midwest. Through hands-on activities that include planting in spring and harvesting in early fall, students develop a new understanding of Native Americans' important contributions to agriculture.

School kids learn about early horticultural practices at Pope Farm Conservancy. OFFICE OF THE STATE ARCHAEOLOGIST OF WISCONSIN

cultures at that time were the Huron and Ottawa east of Lake Huron; the Ojibwe ranging north of Lake Huron and all around Lake Superior; and the Menominee, Ho-Chunk, Sauk, Fox, and Miami.[12]

French explorer Jean Nicolet is generally credited with being the first European to set foot in what is now Wisconsin, arriving in 1634 at Red Banks near the present-day city of Green Bay. It is likely that Nicolet was met by Ho-Chunk, Menominee, and Potawatomi when he arrived on shore "displaying metal objects that the Ho-Chunk later described as 'thunder sticks.'"[13] By the time of Nicolet's arrival, Native American communities, many of them heavily dependent on farming, had been trading with one another for centuries. Soon these Native people would also be trading with the new arrivals. With the introduction of European trade goods such as metal hoes, axes, and tools for clearing the land, Ho-Chunk and Menominee farming practices would evolve as well.[14]

CARVING OUT A LIFE
ON THE FRONTIER

After the arrival of Europeans, French fur traders and Wisconsin Indians quickly began trading goods, a partnership that continued into the eighteenth century. In the early nineteenth century, lead miners would begin immigrating to southwestern Wisconsin, opening up an entirely new economic enterprise. And by the mid-nineteenth century, the timber barons arrived, establishing logging camps and cutting down thousands of acres of northern Wisconsin forests. Although farming was not yet a predominant economic activity, in each of these eras the settlers had to survive and feed their families, and they did so with vegetable gardens and small-scale farming.

As historian Alice Smith explained, "Regardless of the motives that had brought the American and the European to Wisconsin, their immediate concern was to earn a livelihood. . . . Most newcomers began at once to produce their basic items, aiming first at subsistence, but expecting soon to sell a surplus in the local or national market."[1]

THE FUR TRADE

For twenty years after Jean Nicolet landed at the shores of Green Bay, the French—with little interest in colonization and even less in farming—largely ignored his discovery. It wasn't until the fall of 1654 that French explorers Pierre-Esprit Radisson and Medard Chouart, Sieur des Groseilliers, followed Nicolet's route, eventually arriving in present-day Door County. They spent the winter there with the Potawatomi and in spring 1655 paddled up the Fox River, across Lake Winnebago,

FRENCH FUR-TRADERS AT LA BAYE

In this drawing (creation date unknown), French fur traders negotiate with Native people at La Baye. WHI IMAGE ID 60960

and up the upper Fox, stopping at the home of the Mascoutin Indians, near present-day Berlin. Radisson and des Groseilliers lived with the Mascoutin during that summer and from there explored much of Wisconsin. Some historians believe they discovered the upper Mississippi River, although credit for that generally goes to Louis Joliet and Father Jacques Marquette.[2]

Marquette, a Jesuit missionary, and Joliet, a trader and explorer, set forth for Wisconsin on May 17, 1673, representing France's primary interests: religion and the fur trade. They followed the same route as Radisson and des Groseilliers, arriving near present-day Berlin on June 7. They too apparently stayed with the Mascoutin Indians before continuing up the Fox River. With help from Indian guides, they made their way across the marshy one-and-a-half-mile portage at present-day Portage to the broad Wisconsin River. On June 17, they reached the Mississippi.[3]

The discovery of the Fox-Wisconsin route to the Mississippi transformed Wisconsin into an important trade center. Explorers, missionaries, and fur traders could now travel by canoe from one side of Wisconsin to the other with relative ease. With access to this natural waterway, the interstate highway of its day, the fur trade boomed. It would continue for nearly two hundred years. The European demand for beaver furs was enormous, and the French trappers and traders set out to meet it. Working out of outposts at Green Bay, Prairie du Chien on the Mississippi, and La Pointe in the far north, French traders swapped woolen blankets, metal knives, awls, kettles, flints, and porcelain beads for the Indian trappers' beaver hides. The French loaded their canoes with hundreds of pounds of beaver pelts each spring and paddled their way to Montreal.[4]

White settlers at the fur trade villages planted gardens in hopes of stocking their own larders and trading any extra produce. According to Alice Smith, in Green Bay the crops planted "were mostly the common garden vegetables, together with potatoes, some oats, and spring wheat. The residents at Prairie du Chien raised quantities of small grain such as wheat, barley, and oats, as well as potatoes and onions, and sold the surplus to traders for goods or exchanged it with the Indian for venison, ducks, geese, or dressed deerskins."[5]

By the 1830s and 1840s, fur trading in Wisconsin was in decline: "Furbearing animals in the Wisconsin area were thinning out, and, as if to aggravate the situation, new American traders were crowding in."[6]

H.Lewis pinx.   Lith. Inst Amz & Cᵒ Düsseldorf.

PRAIRIE DU CHIEN, WISCONSIN
in 1830

Engraving (dated 1830 but created in 1848) of Fort Crawford at Prairie du Chien

WHI IMAGE ID 22616

THE LEAD MINING ERA

The Indians living in southwestern Wisconsin knew about lead in the region long before any Europeans came to the area; indeed, Native people had been collecting lead there for centuries. Marquette and Joliet heard about the lead mines from Indians as they traveled the Fox-Wisconsin waterway to the Mississippi in 1673, and Indians are believed to have shown Snake Cave (near today's Potosi) to French explorer Nicolas Perrot in 1690. The Native people used lead as decoration and later for bartering with the French and British traders, who used it to make lead shot and other goods. As Ho-Chunk chief Spoon Decorah recalled in 1887, "Our people once owned the lead mines in Southwestern Wisconsin. . . . Some dug lead for their own use, but most of them got it out to trade off to other Indians for supplies of all sorts."[7] As the Indians realized how much the European explorers valued the lead, they began mining it in larger quantities for trade.[8]

After the Indians ceded their lands south of the Wisconsin River to the United States in the series of treaties signed between 1804 and 1832, lead mining became the leading economic activity in Wisconsin.[9] The villages of Mineral Point, Wisconsin; Galena, Illinois; and other prominent mining towns were considered more important than Milwaukee or even Chicago as the lead trade grew.

Early Wisconsin lead miners using a windlass
WHI IMAGE ID 8990

Lead miners at work in Cassville, Grant County, circa 1900

WHI IMAGE ID 2406

Soon lead was in high demand for the manufacture of pewter, pipes, weights, paint, and ammunition, especially for the expanding US military. Lead miners streamed up the Mississippi River into what are now Grant, Crawford, Iowa, and Lafayette Counties. The population of Wisconsin's lead mining region reached 4,253 in June of 1829; those miners extracted more than thirteen million pounds of refined lead.[10] The lead miners spent little time constructing shelters; their main and all-consuming goal was mining, with the hope of accumulating great wealth in the process. Many simply burrowed holes into the hillsides for shelter, earning them the nickname "badgers."[11]

The extraction of the lead, which in the early years was found mainly near the surface, was relatively easy and required little equipment. But the heavy "gray gold" was a challenge to transport. The old fur-trade route along the Fox-Wisconsin waterway was too shallow for heavy lead-laden boats to maneuver, so by 1839 a wagon road was built connecting the mining region with Milwaukee. As historian Reuben Gold Thwaites wrote in 1900, "Great canvas-covered caravans of ore-laden 'prairie schooners' toiled slowly from the mines to the Lake Michigan docks, a distance of about a hundred and fifty miles."[12]

Richard Wearne, Lead Miner and Farmer

Richard Wearne left Cornwall, England, on July 7, 1848, with the intention of mining lead in Wisconsin. Fifty-one years old, Wearne arrived with his wife and eight of their nine children, who ranged in age from very small to young adult.

According to Wearne's journal, the family sailed from England to Canada and then to Milwaukee, where they landed on September 3, 1848. They arrived in Dodgeville on September 12. On September 24, Wearne purchased 160 acres in Linden Township, Iowa County, which he named Wearnes Creek. As he explained, "The reason I bought [this farm] is on account of water to erect a small wheel for an iron foundry and I and my brother have been talking about it for years. The land is not adapted for a good tilling spot, but a good hay bottom and good for rearing cattle. My sons did not like the place but John, my brother, spoke highly of it."

Wearne immediately began digging for lead on his land, but he also took up farming. A year after their arrival in Wisconsin, Wearne wrote:

Sunday April 1, 1849. A fortnight agone we sold 1005 pounds of lead at $18.00 per thousand. The thawing threw water in our diggings [lead mine].

Sunday, June 24, 1849. I bought this week a yoke of oxen steers for $55.00.

September 2, 1849. We saved 16 tons of hay and closed it in and broke about one acre of land to till next year. We sold 2,000 pounds of mineral [lead] at $23.00 per thousand. Weather is cold at times. We made a shed for the cattle and now making a cow house.

March 24, 1850. We sold 2,360 pounds of mineral at $24.00 a thousand. We bought a sow and six piglets.

Wearne's journal entry reflected the mood of many miners of the day: "Weather is cold. All the go is California. My boys is very disaffected. Any place but this." By April 3 of that year, he was writing of

It didn't take long for word of the burgeoning industry to travel throughout the country and even beyond, and in Cornwall, England, miners experiencing economic hardship saw opportunity in Wisconsin. By this time much of the easily obtained lead near the surface had been depleted, and experienced Cornish miners brought with them the know-how for deeper, hard-rock mining.[13] By 1850, not long after the peak of the lead rush, around six thousand Cornish immigrants had settled in Iowa, Grant, and Lafayette Counties, many of them in Mineral Point.[14]

In the 1840s, Wisconsin's lead production represented more than half of the nation's output. But by 1850, lead mining was on the wane. Demand had declined, and exciting opportunities elsewhere—including the California goldfields—lured away many of the miners. Those who stayed behind continued to dig for lead, but

Richard Wearne, Lead Miner and Farmer

family members leaving to seek brighter fortunes: "I was last Sunday taking my farewell of brother Zack. Richard my son left Wednesday. Four in company and another company for California. May God bless them. When shall we meet again?"

Challenging times continued for the Wearne family as lead mining became less and less profitable and the family invested more time and money in their farming endeavors. Those also proved a challenge. Later that spring, Wearne recorded:

> **April 24, 1852.** We sold this week 4,250 pounds mineral at $24.00 a thousand. I paid Mr. Analey $100.00 and Mr. Smith ditto. We commenced plowing this week. No grass yet.
>
> This last year we improved about 9 acres of the southeast corner of the 160 and enclosed in most all of the 160 and built a rock wall shed for cattle 30 feet long by 12 feet within. We bought 1/3 of

a reaper for $50.00. We sold beef, $120.60; hogs $10.00, horses $200.00 for a total of $360.60. Also flour, oats, corn, butter, eggs, potatoes and turnips and yet in need of money. Our crops: wheat, 311 bushels, oats 310 bushels, corn 730 bushels and potatoes 190 bushels. Turnips 400 bushels. Brought in 100 [bushels of turnips] and left 300 out in the field for the cattle. Things at this time look very bad. No money in the country, nothing selling and no one have money to buy. Flour offering for sale at $1.50 per hundred. Credit stopped to most all in all the stores. Last winter a very long hard cold winter.

NOTES

"Richard Wearne's Journal: July 1839 to April 1869." Unpublished, from Ruth Jungbluth, Dodgeville, WI.

they also discovered that the rolling lands of southwestern Wisconsin had considerable agricultural potential.[15] Still, for many the transition to farming was not an easy one.

LOGGING AND LUMBER

After the last glacier retreated, a vast territory comprising the northern two-thirds of the state became nearly completely forested. Hardwoods—sugar maple, hemlock, oak, and birch—grew well on the heaviest soils. In drier areas, stately white pine trees grew to heights over two hundred feet and diameters exceeding fifty inches, while on the driest soils, jack pine flourished. In wet, swampy regions, spruce, tamarack, cedar, and balsam grew.[16]

By the time Wisconsin achieved statehood in 1848, the lead mining era was all but over, and politicians and business leaders recognized the economic potential of the northern forestlands. After the Ojibwe and Menominee ceded their lands to the US government, logging companies and sawmills quickly arrived in the north. The first loggers concentrated on the majestic white pines, which they could float down nearby waterways to be sawn into lumber. After the railroads arrived in the state's northern reaches in the 1870s and 1880s, the lumber companies could transport trees cut farther from waterways and now could also harvest the heavier hardwoods, which would not float.[17] In the period from 1873 to 1895, Wisconsin sawmills cut an estimated sixty billion board feet of Wisconsin timber, with the majority of the lumber shipped out of state. Several millionaire "lumber barons" resulted.[18]

Wisconsin sawmill workers, circa 1899

WHI IMAGE ID 91811

Wisconsin logging camp workers at the turn of the twentieth century
WHI IMAGE ID 94179

Yet while Wisconsin's forests made a few people wealthy, the common lumberjack's life was dangerous and difficult, and the work was mostly a wintertime activity. As was true for the lead miners, most lumberjacks had to supplement their income to provide for their families. For many of them this meant farming, either on their own land or as hired men. "While lumbering flourished," wrote historian Lucile Kane, "farms opened in the woods to sell produce to logging camp and mill town."[19]

And like Wisconsin's lead business, the logging industry could not be sustained. As historian Robert Nesbit observed, "Wisconsin's pine forests were a one-time resource."[20] Many of those once-forested acres would one day become farms, some of them successful, others less so (for more on farming in the cutover, see page 110).

MAKING A HOME
IN WISCONSIN

Following the Indian cessions of 1832–33, US government surveyors entered what would become Wisconsin. In 1832, they established a baseline at the intersection of the fourth principal meridian and the Illinois border, about ten miles east of the Mississippi River. From this location, called "The Point of Beginning," the fourth principal meridian runs straight north to Lake Superior. East-west lines cross the principal meridian every six miles to establish township lines. For legal land descriptions, the township numbers reflect how far north a location is from the baseline (the Illinois border) and how far east or west it is from the fourth principal meridian. (For example, land described as "Section 33, T20 No, Range 10E" is found twenty townships north of the Illinois border and ten townships east of the fourth principal meridian. A typical township is six miles square.)

In 1834, the government established land offices in Green Bay and Mineral Point where surveyed land could be purchased.[1] And by the end of 1836, that part of Wisconsin lying south and east of the Wisconsin–Fox River waterway had been surveyed into neat squares. The surveyors not only mapped the land into sections (640 acres) and quarter sections (160-acre plots), they also estimated and recorded its quality, ranking it as first, second, or third class and noting its physical characteristics: level, rolling, swampy, open prairie, and so on. Thanks to the surveyors' careful notations, potential landowners not only could locate the land on a map but also had a reasonable fix on its quality.

This 1838 survey map of Wisconsin Territory includes townships, counties, prairies, and swamps.
WHI IMAGE ID 92210

The Adsit family was representative of those New Yorkers who made a new home on the Wisconsin frontier. Stephen and Betsey Adsit left New York state and joined their sons Charles and Martin on land acquired in 1845 in the town of Deerfield. The house, constructed in 1859, was possibly a stagecoach stop in its early days, and the two-story addition was used for town meetings chaired by Allen Adsit during his fifteen-year tenure as chairman.

WHI IMAGE ID 26659

YANKEES AND NEW YORKERS

With the government survey completed in 1836 for eastern and southern Wisconsin, speculators, miners, and immigrants began buying up the newly surveyed lands. A wave of settlers arrived from New England and upstate New York, where there was little opportunity for agricultural expansion. People already in Wisconsin called these newcomers Yankees. According to the 1850 census for Wisconsin, the population (excluding American Indians, whom the census takers did not attempt to include) was 305,390; of that number, 103,371 had come from the northeastern states.[2]

Those new arrivals included professional people, pastors, lawyers, and doctors. But farmers were the largest group; indeed, the 1850 census included 40,865 farmers, more than all other occupations combined. Many of them had been dairymen in their home state of New York, a major producer of dairy products at the time. But they saw wheat growing in the Midwest as a more lucrative endeavor. These early settlers constructed homes, barns, schools, and churches that reminded them of what they had left behind in the East. They also brought with them their farming skills and, for many of them, a good business sense.

When Wisconsin became a territory in 1836, its population stood at 11,683. By 1847, a year before statehood, the number had climbed to 210,546; by 1850 it reached 305,390.[3] Even with this surge in population, settlers were scattered mainly across the southeastern third of the state, roughly south of a line drawn from Green Bay to Prairie du Chien.

EUROPEAN IMMIGRANTS

German immigrants soon joined the Yankees in Wisconsin and quickly outnumbered all other ethnic groups arriving in the state. The large influx of German immigrants began about 1839, with Milwaukee and surrounding counties seeing the greatest numbers.[4] By 1885, about one-third of Wisconsin's population would be of German heritage.[5]

Norwegians were the second-largest ethnic group to settle in Wisconsin, and by 1850 two-thirds of all Norwegians in America lived in Wisconsin. The majority settled in the southern and western regions of the state, with Dane County boasting the largest number. By the 1850 census, Irish made up the largest number of English-speaking immigrants in Wisconsin, numbering 21,043.[6] Other ethnic groups settling in Wisconsin before 1900 included Danes, Swiss, Swedes, English, Scotch, Welsh, Icelanders, Finns, French (mainly from Canada), Dutch, Belgians, Italians, Russians, Czechs, and several others.[7]

The Siggelkow family arrived from Mecklenburg, Germany, and settled near Madison. This family picture was taken the day before the family sailed for America.
WHI IMAGE ID 37967

Wisconsin wasn't the only state attracting foreign immigrants, but located as it was far from coastal ports and large commercial centers, the state was at a bit of a disadvantage. To meet the challenge head-on, the Wisconsin legislature created the office of Commissioner of Emigration in 1852, with the aims of recruiting immigrants and protecting them from swindlers and thieves. Upon the founding of the position, Governor Leonard Farwell stated that "Wisconsin had more to offer to emigrants than any other state in the Union, and that foreigners brought with them their love for freedom, their ambition, industriousness and enterprising spirit, which all were needed to make the state flourish." The commissioner, whose office was located in New York City, was charged with "giving to emigrants information regarding soil and climate of Wisconsin, together with information on the state and lines of business . . . which might be pursued with advantage; advising emigrants about the 'cheapest and most expeditious route by which to reach Wisconsin'"; and "giving such further information as will protect emigrants against 'the impositions often practiced upon them.'"[8] The office was open for less than three years, but its closing did not seem to slow down the wave of immigrants pouring into the state.

Settlers themselves encouraged immigration as well, through enticing letters sent to friends and family back home. In January 1854, recent immigrants to Koshkonong (Jefferson County) wrote a glowing account to their siblings still in Norway:

We are firmly convinced that you have waited a long time for a writing and information from us in this, our foreign home. . . . It is almost unbelievable how fortunate it has gone for us the whole time in the new world. There is no one of our ages here who have climbed upward as fast as we. Cattle is now high priced so the first thing each of us did was to sell cattle for 80 dollars each. We own 4 milk cows, 2 that are 2 years old, 2 that are 1 year old and 1 calf. 5 driving oxen, 10 hogs or swine, 20 chickens, 2 geese, and 5 sows. This fall we butchered 4 pretty big hogs.

This fall we cut so much wood that we can sell a hundred dollars' worth. We had a desirable and fruitful year. It is not often that we have this much wood and it also has a high price. There are several here who have cut a thousand bushels of wood. . . . The price per bushel is a dollar, and that is expensive.

I believe that I would advise you to come here to America and that you would find it better here when you shall acquire 100 dollars when you earn only 20 dollars in Norway.[9]

Other correspondents were more cautious in their recommendations. Norwegian immigrant Anders Jensen Stortroen, who settled in Martell Township in the northwestern corner of the state, advised his parents and siblings in September 1857 that "[t]he milk here is just as good as in Norway, and all kinds of foods are as good, there need be no doubt of it. By no means will we advise anyone to come over here, but you must advise yourselves concerning this, since there are many hard paths and many tribulations to endure that one cannot understand before he sets out."[10]

AFRICAN AMERICAN COMMUNITIES

Wisconsin's first African American settlements were in southwestern Wisconsin's lead mining region. Some residents had arrived from southern states as slaves owned by miners; others came to Wisconsin as freed or escaped slaves. In 1840, there were just 185 free blacks and eleven slaves in Wisconsin Territory.

The Emigrant's Hand Book, and Guide to Wisconsin, issued in Milwaukee in 1851
WHI IMAGE ID 54095

THE EMIGRANT'S

HAND BOOK,

AND

GUIDE TO WISCONSIN,

COMPRISING INFORMATION RESPECTING

AGRICULTURAL AND MANUFACTURING

EMPLOYMENT,

WAGES, CLIMATE, POPULATION &C.; SKETCH OF MILWAUKEE, THE QUEEN OF THE LAKES; ITS RISE AND PROGRESS; BUSINESS AND POPULATION; LIST OF PUBLIC OFFICERS; WITH A FULL AND ACCURATE TABLE OF STATISTICAL INFORMATION OF THAT AND OTHER PORTS ON LAKE MICHIGAN; ALSO TABLE OF ROUTES FROM NEW-YORK, BOSTON, &C., TO MILWAUKEE, RACINE, AND KENOSHA; AND OTHER GENERAL INFORMATION TO EMIGRANTS.

Entered according to Act of Congress in the year 1851,
BY SAMUEL FREEMAN,
in the Office of the District Court of the United States, for the District of Wisconsin.

MILWAUKEE:
SENTINEL AND GAZETTE POWER PRESS PRINT.
1851.

Charles Edward Shepard,
early resident of the
Pleasant Ridge community
WHI IMAGE ID 45967

By 1850, no slaves resided in Wisconsin, and the number of free blacks had grown to 635.[11]

Two African American rural communities formed in Wisconsin before 1900. Walden Stewart, a free black, arrived in Cheyenne Valley in 1855. Over the next four years, five other free black families joined him to farm the rich soils of Vernon County. They prospered, and by 1860, according to historian Zachary Cooper, "Two of these farmers were among the four wealthiest out of fifty families in the township in terms of size of farmland and value of livestock."[12]

The Pleasant Ridge community in Beetown (Grant County) traces its origins to 1848, when the William Horner family arrived from Virginia with their former slaves accompanying them. Those former slaves became the nucleus for the community. Charles Shepard and his wife, both former slaves, purchased land from Horner and began raising crops. Other families followed, particularly after the outbreak of the Civil War in 1861.[13]

MAKING A HOME

Wisconsin's early settlers believed that an "ideal farm" was one that included timber, some open prairie land, and marshland—"for fuel and shelter, cultivation, and hay or pasture."[14] Land speculators and the earliest settlers bought up the "ideal" land, leaving many of those who followed to carve a homestead out of the woods. For the settlers, especially those arriving in the late 1840s and 1850s, living conditions were challenging and often dangerous. The winters were long; roads were nearly nonexistent; the distance to a settlement was often considerable; and the land was covered with trees that had to be removed before a crop could be planted. As historian Reuben Gold Thwaites explained, "[S]ometimes a pioneer farmer was fifty or a hundred miles from a gristmill, a store, or a post office, and generally his highway thither was but a blazed bridle path through a tangled forest. Often his only entertainments throughout the year were 'bees' for raising log houses or barns for newcomers and on these occasions all the settlers for scores of miles around would gather in a spirit of helpful comradery."[15]

Two tools served the frontiersman especially well: the rifle and the ax. The "long rifle enabled him to protect his life, overcome his enemies, and feed his body, and the second, the woodsman's ax, to build his home, conquer the forest, and provide for his maintenance of the soil."[16]

Even with ax in hand, a new settler's first shelter was likely to be a hastily erected dwelling, sometimes little more than a hut. Benjamin Heimback and his wife claimed eighty acres in the township of East Troy in 1845, and there they cut timber from the property to build a log cabin and "stopped the crevices with clay. . . . The floor was made of slabs hewn . . . until they would be level and this was kept clean by means of a splint broom. One half of the attic was floored with slabs to which they ascended by means of a ladder and this furnished the sleeping apartments of the cabin."[17]

A bit north, in Outagamie County, frontier conditions were similar. Wellington Sherman and his wife, both from Canada, bought forty-nine acres of land in Cicero in 1876, built a log shanty, and began farming "with one yoke of oxen and a cow." Each year Sherman tried to clear a little more land. In an account of those early years, he recalled, "Spring was the time for making of maple sugar and syrup. We also cut many cords of wood as we cleared new land each year. . . . When harvesting time came, I cradled the grain and Mrs. Sherman raked it by hand and bound the bundles up. Our burdens were made easier when our son, Walter, reached the age of 17 and helped us in the woods and at home."[18]

For many, life on the frontier was hardscrabble at best.
WHI IMAGE ID 25660

A pioneer who settled along the Rock River near Jefferson in the summer of 1837 remembered:

Preceding pages: In this study sketch for a 1948 Wisconsin State Fair mural project, artist Robert Hodgell depicted early subsistence living in the Wisconsin frontier. A pioneer hunts wild game in a small field of cut stumps—an early attempt to tame the wilderness. (For more on the state fair murals, see page 76.)

WHI IMAGE ID 96118; WISCONSIN HISTORICAL MUSEUM 2011.162.3

In December following I took an ax, a ham of pork, and a blanket, walked down to Jefferson, bought a few loaves of bread of E. G. Darling, also borrowed a boat of him—went up to my claim to make the necessary improvements to hold it until spring.

I worked upon my claim for four weeks, chopping trees, building fences, etc. Having made the necessary improvements on my claim, I went back to Rock [R]iver until spring. During the winter I picked enough cat-tails to make me a bed. Also caught and salted a keg of fish, bought a yoke of oxen and prepared to go to my claim in the spring. In April, '38, I borrowed the hind wheels of a wagon, put in a temporary tongue and box, loaded up my shanty outfit, drove to Ft. Atkinson and crossed the river on the ferry, thence to Jefferson; again ferried across, cut my own road through the timber, three miles, and reached my claim. . . . I cleared about two acres, made a harrow with wooden teeth, and planted the land with corn and potatoes. I paid four dollars a bushel for seed corn to plant. . . . Raised a splendid crop of corn and potatoes.[19]

The early settlers arriving in Wisconsin farmed much as people had for hundreds of years. They depended on oxen to do the heavy work, such as breaking the virgin soil, pulling the carts, and transporting people from here to there. "The ox carried the white man's burden . . . they toted them in and did the heavy work around the homestead after they finally got settled. They helped clear the land, did the breaking and plowing, [and] hauled the grain to market. . . . In the spring of the year, the travelers along the highways and byways could hear the familiar cry echoing from every farm place, 'gee,' 'haw'. . . . The ox was a faithful critter, easily trained, docile in demeanor and tough from his horns to his hoofs."[20]

Even with oxen to handle the heaviest jobs, much of the work on the frontier was the backbreaking toil done by settlers themselves:

Corn and potatoes were planted by hand, a boy or girl, or maybe mother dropping the seed while some other member of the family followed covering it with a hoe. When grain was ready for harvest, it was cut with a cradle and some of our Norwegian friends even used old time sickles. . . .

A team of oxen pulled the wagon at a Jackson County farm, circa 1889.
WHI IMAGE ID 25040

The grain was threshed with a flail—a long wooden handle at the end of which a shorter and stouter stick, called a swiple or swingle, was so hung as to swing freely. The bundles of grain were laid in two rows with the heads together and beaten with the flail until the grain was all separated from the straw and hulls. Then on a windy day it was taken out and thrown up in the air with a shovel and the chaff and dust blown out. . . .

Pitch forks and shovels were frequently home made of hardwood. To make a fork, a sapling of convenient size was cut, all of the branches but two which might be nearly opposite each were trimmed off, then these two were bent to a proper angle, cut to the right length, sharpened, and a usable pitch fork was the result.[21]

"Intimate Incidents of Pioneer Life in Richland County"

An anonymous writer from Richland County wrote the following about pioneer life there in the 1860s:

On every farm would be found a flock of chickens, ducks and geese, a cow or two and one or more pigs, and on the farm wheat, corn, oats and potatoes were raised and the gardens produced the usual variety of vegetables. Peachblow and pinkeye potatoes were the leading favorites. . . . The woods and valleys were full of wild fruits—strawberries, raspberries, blackberries, plums, wild grapes and crab apples grew in abundance and were to be had for the taking. Then there was game—rabbits, squirrels, partridges, pheasants and quails and the clear, cold streams were full of brook trout. . . .

The canning of fruit was not practiced in those days but quantities of wild fruit were dried and preserved for winter use. Sweet corn also was cut from the cob, dried and stored in sacks and when needed for use it was baked until soft, then cooked . . . it made very palatable food. . . . There was no near market for perishable products and eggs, butter, milk, surplus poultry and vegetables were consumed at home. When hogs were killed, some roasts were cut up, partly cooked and placed in stone jars [with] hot lard, . . . and surplus fat was poured over them and later on, as the lard was used, the roasts

were taken out as fresh and sweet as when they were first packed. The people lived well, and almost their entire living was produced on the farm.

Nearly all the homes on the farms were constructed of logs. Wood was the plentiful thing there and thousands of great oak, hard maple, black walnut and other fine trees were cut down and burned in order to clear the land. . . . Many of the cabins had but one or two rooms, and if family conditions required more, partitions of rough boards and sometimes spaces for beds were merely curtained off with cheap cloth. Windows were not all glass, but frequently a piece of white muslin was stretched over a frame, oiled and placed in the window frame. They let in light but of course there was no peeking through the window to see who was passing. . . . In most of the cabins, a big fire place was built in one end with a flat stone for a hearth and in our cabin there was a big black bear skin in front of it for a rug. . . .

The fire places were wide and took in a lot of wood. A big log or oak or maple was rolled in and smaller pieces piled in front of it and it surely made a cheerful fire and crackled and snapped at a great rate. . . . Some families did about all of the cooking in the fireplace, having cranes and hooks on which to hang the kettles, and a reflector oven to do the baking.

"Intimate Incidents of Pioneer Life in Richland County"

These irons were made of sheet iron and so arranged that they could be set in front of the fire place and the heat reflected into the oven until it became hot enough to bake the bread.

Matches were not the commonly used articles of the present day and often there would be none in the home for days or even weeks at a time, but always there were live coals in the fire place and if, for any reason, these all died out, some member of the family must go to the nearest neighbors with a shovel or kettle and get some live coals to rekindle the fire. . . .

The mother of a family made all of the clothing, both underwear and outer garments and she knitted the socks and stockings and mittens as well. . . .With cooking, keeping the cabin neat, making and mending clothes, washing, making

soft soap, tallow candles and butter, looking after the babies . . . she had but little time for anything not connected with the needs of the family. . . .

We had a considerable flock of ducks and geese and many times, when I was six or seven years old, I would go a considerable distance up the creek, whither the ducks and geese had wandered . . . and drive them home. . . .

If a family happened to get out of candles a shallow dish was filled with lard or tallow and a rag placed in it and lighted. . . .

NOTES

"Intimate Incidents of Pioneer Life in Richland County: A Personal Reminiscence of Economic Conditions Existing on the Farms of Richland County Sixty to Sixty-Five Years Ago," parts 1–5, *Richland Center Democrat,* March 1924.

WOMEN'S LIVES ON THE FRONTIER

The life of a frontier woman was especially challenging. She dispensed medicines when there was illness, served as a midwife when babies were due, and perhaps most importantly made sure that her family was well fed. She cared for the children; was responsible for the vegetable garden; took care of a small flock of chickens; and sewed, washed, and mended the family's clothes. She milked the family's cow or two and made the cheese and churned the butter.

A pioneer woman who moved to Green Bay in 1824 recalled the following about her early years on the frontier: "The country round about was little trodden by man's footsteps, when we could go anywhere for miles with never a road and never a fence to obstruct our paths, when our neighbors were few, when each

With their variety of tasks keeping them busy from sunup to sundown, pioneer women were even more tied to the farmstead than men.
WHI IMAGE ID 2016

year the entire country would be swept by prairie fires and we had to watch our buildings and stacks to keep from being destroyed, when dangers beset us, but— when life was young."[22]

Many of these women had grown up in New England or Europe "in cozy neighborhoods with relatives and neighbors close at hand."[23] Now they often faced terrible loneliness, as neighbors were far away and husbands were gone for extended periods to earn money. Many Wisconsin farm men left for the logging camps in the north during the winter months, leaving their wives and children to survive the long, cold winters on their own. Pioneer women were hard-pressed to find other females with whom to spend time or commiserate; in 1840, men outnumbered women on the frontier eight to five.[24]

On the other hand, frontier life offered positive experiences for strong or adventurous women. As historian Alice Smith noted, "For the young woman who could travel westward to one of these settled places, preferably with some funds, frontier life had much to offer. In 1842 Racheline Wood urged her sister in Vermont to come to Platteville and take a position as head of a proposed girl's school: 'You can [earn] money three times as fast here as there,' she advised, 'and I believe you will enjoy better health. We have [a] good society better than any other place in the mining sections of the country.'"[25]

THE HOMESTEAD ACT

The US and Wisconsin territorial governments encouraged and assisted settlement and agriculture in Wisconsin in a number of ways. Beginning with the first Census of Agriculture in 1840, the federal government sought to quantify the numbers of farms and farmers as well as record the nature of the various farming enterprises happening across the country.

At the same time, the government was supporting the creation and improvement of basic infrastructure, such as roads and bridges, connecting once nearly inaccessible rural areas to cities. The first telegraph linking Milwaukee and Chicago began operating in January 1848.[26]

The US government gave financial support directly to farmers first in 1839, when Congress appropriated $1,000 for providing farmers information and seeds. This token appropriation and other contributions that followed led to the eventual establishment of the United States Department of Agriculture in 1862.[27]

That same year, Congress passed the Homestead Act, which would have a far-reaching effect on agriculture and rural communities. The act stated that "any person who is the head of a family, or who has arrived at the age of twenty-one years, and is a citizen of the United States, or who shall have filed his intention to become such, as required by the naturalization laws of the United States, and who has never borne arms against the United States Government or given aid and comfort to its enemies, shall from the first of January, eighteen hundred and sixty-three, be entitled to enter one quarter section [160 acres] or a less quantity of unappropriated public lands." Those who met the requirements, paid a filing fee, and lived on the land for a minimum of five years became the owners of the land at no cost. The act gave priority to Union veterans, who could deduct the number of years served in the war from their five-year residency requirement.

With the passage of the Homestead Act, the cry of "free land" echoed across the country and overseas. United States citizens, freed slaves, and hundreds of thousands of European immigrants heeded the call. The act led to a westward expansion that continued for more than a hundred years and resulted in the settling of 270 million acres of formerly federally owned land. And many settlers recognized immediately that the rich soil of eastern and southern Wisconsin had great potential for the production of wheat.

PART II

THE WHEAT ERA

KING WHEAT

By the 1850s, wheat was already a major crop in Indiana and Illinois, and as Joseph Schafer recorded in his 1922 history of Wisconsin agriculture, "The New York farmers, the Pennsylvania farmers, the Ohio farmers who came to Wisconsin in the early rush of settlement were by habit and tradition primarily wheat growers. The New Englanders had been partially weaned from the business, but, like the others, they had a lively appreciation of the ease with which wealth in the form of wheat could be extracted from the limestone rich soils of Wisconsin's prairies and openings."[1]

As historian Alice E. Smith explained, "In view of the expense of getting started and the tight financial situation, it is understandable that the farmer would look for a crop that would grow well on new land in the northern climate, that required little care during the growing season, that would provide food for his family, and, if there were a surplus, that could be hauled to market by ox team over rough roads and would find a ready sale."[2]

Some of the earliest settlers broke and sowed as many as fifty acres of wheat their first year in the state. Once the land was broken, they continued growing wheat on the same ground, year after year; many also expanded their acreage each year. A letter written by F. A. Phoenix on November 19, 1842, proclaimed the virtues of Wisconsin's agricultural lands:

> Our soil and climate are well adapted to the culture of wheat, but the difference in the surface and climate here and in the east, made it necessary to adopt another strategy from that pursued there. We get a first rate

crop, (perhaps the best, quality and quantity considered) from the first breaking of the sward. The sod is turned over in June, from two to four inches deep, and then in the latter part of August or first of September, is dragged and backset, as we term it, or turned over again and the wheat sowed, on 1¼ or 1½ bushels per acre. If sowed early, it covers the ground completely, and withstands the severest winters. It ripens earlier than the crop on old ground, and is generally rather plumper and cleaner, though it should not be cleaner, but it is, as there has been no opportunity for weeds to ripen and fill the ground.[3]

Farming practices were not yet mechanized, and for these early settlers, wheat growing was one arduous task after another, from breaking the ground to sowing the seeds by hand to harvesting and threshing the ripe grain. Prairie grasses, growing six or more feet high and with undisturbed root systems as deep as the plant was tall, proved extremely challenging to break up. With a heavy wooden beam and long moldboard, the breaking plow in common use at the time required as many as ten oxen to pull it; farmers worked together to break the land, as no one farmer owned ten oxen. An early pioneer in southern Wisconsin described the process:

> In wheat raising, the great staple, the country is not surpassed, perhaps in the world. Here, fields yield this crop year after year, and with most slovenly cultivation. . . . [As] to the course of cultivation pursued on the prairies. . . . The land is enclosed with a rail, board, or ditch fence. It is then broken up with from two to six yoke of cattle. The width of the furrow turned over varies from 12 to 30 inches, and is from 1½ to 3 inches thick. The larger the team is, the more economical, as a heavy team will break so much more with the same force of men, as to more than pay for the difference in the number of oxen. The price of breaking is from $1.75 to $2 an acre. The season for breaking is from the 10th of May till the 10th of July. It is not advisable to break earlier or later than these periods. If it is done [later], the sod is a very long time in rotting and does not produce so well. Corn is sometimes planted on the sod—planted when the breaking is being done, at the edges of the furrows. No after culture is given until the corn is cut up at harvest. . . . The first crop [of wheat] is always a certain one, both in quality and quantity—averaging 25 bushels per acre. The land is generally cross plowed immediately after harvest, and sown again to wheat.[4]

Harvesting wheat by hand, as these farmers did with cradle scythes, was arduous work for settlers.
WHI IMAGE ID 53649

Harvesting was hard work as well, as in the early days grain was cut with a cradle, a scythe-like implement, and bound into bundles by hand. On a good day, a strong man with a cradle could harvest two to three acres. One or two bundlers—usually women and children—usually followed the cradler, tying the cut grain into bundles, which then had to be stood up in shocks so the grain could dry. Imagine that a farmer had fifty acres to harvest (which could easily yield as many as two thousand bushels of grain). It would take one man twenty days to accomplish the task—too long, as some of the ripe grain would be lost. But four men could do it in five days. Thus early immigrants could easily find work on the Wisconsin frontier.[5]

Once the shocked grain was sufficiently dry, the farmer hitched his yoke of oxen to a cart and hauled the grain to a storage place to await threshing. These storage buildings were some of Wisconsin's earliest wood-frame barns, called English or three-bay threshing barns. They were built without basements and were usually forty-two to sixty feet long and around thirty feet wide. Storage areas were available on either side of the threshing floor in the middle bay. Floor-to-ceiling doors opened on either side of the threshing floor. During the days before threshing machines became popular, farmers threshed the grain on the threshing floor, either using a flail or having oxen walk over the grain stalks. Once the grain kernels were separated from the straw and chaff, the farmer raked away the straw and tossed the grain kernels and chaff into the air so a breeze could blow away the chaff.[6]

LABOR-SAVING DEVICES

By the 1840s, the mechanical reaper had launched a revolution in agricultural technology. Patented by Virginian Cyrus McCormick in 1834, the reaper was a horse-pulled implement that sliced off the wheat plants using a series of scissorlike cutting knives. The reaper replaced the handheld cradle on most of the larger farms, although many smaller operations continued to use the much less expensive cradle to cut their wheat.

Cyrus McCormick's invention of the reaper changed everything.
WHI IMAGE ID 73880

At the same time, Wisconsin farmers began importing draft horses from Europe, mostly Percherons from France, Belgians from Belgium, and Clydesdales from Scotland, along with less popular breeds such as Shires and Suffolks.[7] Weighing two thousand pounds or more, these draft horses soon took the place of the slow and steady oxen that had done the heavy work and provided transportation on the farm.

With a team of draft horses pulling a reaper, one man could cut as many as ten acres of wheat a day. However, these early reapers merely cut the grain; it still had to be raked from the machine and tied into bundles, requiring additional human power. But sitting on a reaper and driving a team of horses was far easier work than swinging a cradle. McCormick moved his operation to Chicago and began manufacturing reapers in 1847. Yankee George Esterly, who farmed near Janesville, invented his own reaper in 1844, which also became popular in southern Wisconsin.[8]

John Francis Appleby reduced the hand labor associated with the reaper when he invented the knotter. Appleby moved to Wisconsin from New York in 1845. After fighting in the Civil War, he returned home to Mazomanie and began working on a machine that would tie a knot, first with wire. With the addition of a knotter, a reaper became a grain binder, not only cutting the grain but forming it into bundles

An 1887 illustration of McCormick's first reaper
WHI IMAGE ID 39559

Sweep horsepower threshing in Waukesha County, circa 1890
WHI IMAGE ID 31820

as well. By 1874, Appleby's wire tie knotter had become quite successful, but neither farmers nor millers wanted wire—pieces of wire might find their way into milled grain. Appleby continued working on a twine binder and received patents in 1878 and 1879.[9] Farmers quickly replaced their reapers with binders, saving considerable labor and making harvesting grain a bit easier.

To make threshing easier, several inventors worked on developing a mechanical threshing machine. One of the most successful was J. I. Case, another New Yorker. Case developed a threshing machine powered with a ten-horse sweep, which became widely used throughout the grain-growing regions of the country. Using the efforts of five teams of horses walking in a circle while hitched to poles attached to a central hub, the ten-horse sweep transferred horsepower to the machine through a series of gears.[10] Case built a plant in Racine, Wisconsin, and continued to advance the development of mechanical threshing machines.[11]

Planting, too, was soon revolutionized. For thousands of years, wheat kernels had been sown by hand or from a broadcast seeder that hung around the farmer's neck. But in 1860, George and Daniel Van Brunt, brothers from Mayville, Wisconsin, patented a combination grain drill and cultivator pulled by a team. This machine sliced a furrow in the soil for the seeds, placed them on the ground, and then covered them. The Van Brunts moved their operation to Horicon, Wisconsin, where by 1866 they were manufacturing 1,300 grain drills a year.[12]

Now, with a horse-drawn machine to plant the seeds (the grain drill), another horse-drawn machine to cut the grain (the grain binder), and another machine to thresh the grain (the threshing machine), wheat farming required considerably less human labor than when all three of those tasks were done by hand. And it flourished.

WHEAT GROWING SPREADS

Wheat growing expanded across the southern half of Wisconsin, and by the 1850s wheat was the state's major economic enterprise, pushing lead mining to the background. Wisconsin's wheat harvest jumped from 212,116 bushels in 1839 and 1840 to 4,286,131 bushels in 1850. Of the thirty-one states in the country producing wheat in 1850, Wisconsin ranked eighth. That year the leading wheat-producing counties in Wisconsin were Rock, Walworth, Dane, Dodge, and Kenosha.[13] By 1860, Illinois was the leading wheat-producing state in the nation, and Wisconsin was second, with production of 29 million bushels, one-sixth of the wheat produced in the United States.[14]

The 1850 Census of Agriculture revealed interesting statistics about how agriculture had progressed since the first settlers began arriving in the 1820s and 1830s. The state's population had increased from 30,945 in 1840 to 305,391 in 1850. In 1850, Wisconsin's residents lived in thirty-one counties, most of them in the southern half of the state. Milwaukee County had the largest population with 31,077;

Rock was second with 20,750, followed by Washington and Waukesha with more than 19,000 residents each. According to this census, 40,865 people were farmers; the second-most prominent category of employment was laborer, with 11,211.

By the 1860s, Wisconsin was a dominant wheat state.

WHI IMAGE ID 107579

There were 390 flour and gristmill operators, 3,360 carpenters, 1,407 blacksmiths, and 3,001 miners. About three million acres were devoted to farming, about half "improved" (with the land broken and crops being raised) and half "unimproved" (unbroken land plus marshland, steep hillsides, and other land not suitable for cultivation). Farmers owned 30,170 horses, about 64,339 milk cows, and 42,801 "working oxen." In 1850, draft horses were just beginning to replace oxen on Wisconsin farms, but oxen still outnumbered horses.[15]

Wheat was the leading agricultural crop, with more than 4 million bushels produced, followed by oats (3.4 million bushels) and corn (2 million bushels). Other crops included tobacco, 1,208 pounds; wool, 253,963 pounds; peas and beans, 20,657 bushels; barley, 200,692 bushels; buckwheat, 79,878 bushels; flax, 68,393 pounds; flaxseed, 1,191 bushels; maple sugar, 610,976 pounds; and beeswax and honey, 131,605 pounds.[16]

To put the importance of wheat into perspective, during the period 1850–80 wheat was found on more Wisconsin acreage than any other crop. In 1850, wheat acreage nearly equaled that of the acreages of hay, oats, and corn combined.

The Civil War had a considerable influence on Wisconsin's wheat production. During the years 1860–65, Wisconsin produced an incredible 100 million bushels of wheat, two-thirds of which the state exported. According to economist Frederick Merk, "During the war [Wisconsin] produced for exportation larger crops than ever before in her history. Her surplus fed the armies battling at the front, and entered conspicuously into the commerce of the drought-stricken England and France. During the dark days of 1862, when these countries seemed about to intervene on behalf of the Confederacy, this food supply exerted an undoubted influence in holding them to neutrality."[17]

Along with wheat farming, flour milling became a major industry in Wisconsin. Blessed with many rivers and streams, the state was well suited for the construction of flour mills, which required waterpower to operate. This was especially the case in the southern part of the state, where wheat growing flourished in the 1850s and 1860s. In 1860, wheat flour accounted for two-fifths of the value of all the products manufactured in the state; lumber was in second place.[18]

Nevertheless, during the Civil War Wisconsin shipped much of its wheat harvest as raw kernels. One reason was shipping costs—wheat kernels could be shipped as cheaply as milled flour. So Wisconsin's exports increased only from 550,000 barrels in 1860 to 625,000 barrels in 1865. This changed after the Civil War, when many flour mills appeared in small and large towns throughout southern Wisconsin, including Cedarburg, Beloit, Paoli, Lake Mills, Kingston, Prairie du Chien, Berlin, Mazomanie, Iola, Wautoma, and Wild Rose.[19] By 1868, Wisconsin was exporting 875,000 barrels of flour. Milwaukee became a major flour manufacturing center after the war, and in 1868 Milwaukee's flour mills alone produced 625,000 barrels. Another major flour milling center included the twin cities of Neenah and Menasha on the Fox River; in 1870, Neenah boasted eleven flour mills and Menasha had four. These fifteen mills could produce 3,875 barrels of flour every twenty-four hours. Other milling centers emerged in Janesville, Watertown, and Appleton.[20]

The Lemonweir River Flour Mill, built in 1852 in Juneau County
WHI IMAGE ID 36904

WHEAT IN DECLINE

Even though they may have been growing vast acreages of wheat, by the 1870s farmers began to see the end of profitable wheat growing. King wheat's crown had begun to slip. Wisconsin wheat production peaked in 1873, when the state produced 26.25 million bushels. Five years later, the state still had the largest number of acres devoted to wheat of any state, 2.05 million acres. In that year Wisconsin farmers harvested 18.45 million bushels, considerably less than five years earlier; the yield per acre had dropped from 15 bushels per acre to 9 bushels per acre from 1873 to 1878.[21]

Income from growing wheat declined for three major reasons: nitrogen-depleted soils (farmers did not yet know about fertilization and raised few animals to provide natural fertilization); disease and insect infestation (growing the same crop year after year invited disease and insect problems); and the emergence of railroads, which made fertile lands west of Wisconsin ready markets for wheat and new competition for the product.[22]

By 1879, according to historian Joseph Schafer, "So far as southern Wisconsin was concerned, wheat growing was at its last gasp."[23] Farmers stood at a crossroads. Those who knew and loved raising wheat and could not see beyond it picked up and moved west of the Mississippi River. But many Wisconsin farmers chose to stay and began searching for other ways to make a living.

SEEKING ALTERNATIVES TO WHEAT

Many Wisconsin farmers didn't just leave wheat behind; they shifted to a fundamentally different kind of agriculture called diversified farming. Rather than depend on a single crop, farmers had learned to invest in multiple opportunities for income. Other crops, including corn, oats, and hay, began to take the place of wheat. And the numbers of sheep, poultry, hogs, and cows—especially dairy cows—on Wisconsin farms grew to considerable numbers.

CORN, OATS, AND HAY

In 1849, Wisconsin's total production of corn and oats combined amounted to 5.4 million bushels. Thirty years later, corn and oat production combined topped 67 million bushels, more than a twelvefold increase. Production of hay increased sevenfold in the same period.[1] Both crops were grown mainly to feed the increasing number of dairy cows and other animals raised on Wisconsin farms. When a farmer had more of these crops than his animals needed, he sold the excess.

SHEEP

One of the most lucrative of those animals was sheep. During the Civil War, wool brought a premium price, having replaced cotton in homes in the north and found a huge market with the federal government. Coarser wools were woven into soldiers' uniforms, and in Wisconsin, where much of the wool produced was of that grade,

By the time this photo was taken, circa 1874, this Wisconsin farmer had invested in both dairy cows and sheep.
WHI IMAGE ID 26136

the value increased from twenty-five cents a pound in 1861 to $1.05 a pound by 1864. Wisconsin wool production increased from one million pounds in 1861 to four million pounds in 1865, and correspondingly the number of sheep on Wisconsin farms increased from 332,954 in 1860 to 1,260,900 by the end of 1865. When the war ended, the price of wool plummeted to twenty-nine cents a pound as southern cotton fields once more became productive and cotton became available again in the North. Wool growers persisted, especially with wheat fields increasingly being abandoned, but sheep raising did not continue as a major livestock activity.[2]

BARLEY AND HOPS

In addition to planting corn, oats, and hay for dairy and livestock feed, some farmers discovered barley as a valuable cash crop, thanks to the rapidly expanding brewery industry. By 1870, Wisconsin farmers were producing 1.6 million bushels of barley annually.[3] By 1900, barley production increased to almost 15 million bushels.[4]

The burgeoning brewing industry also needed hops. New York was the leading producer of hops by the 1840s, and many Yankees brought their hops-growing knowledge to Wisconsin when they settled in the state.[5] During the Civil War, New York hops production was severely curtailed by an infestation of the hop louse. The door was open for hops production to thrive in Wisconsin, and thrive it did: the state's production of hops increased fivefold from 1860 to 1865. As writer Fred Holmes noted, "Hop growing developed into a veritable craze, gathering renewed force with every new acre planted in the county of Sauk, where it may be said to have originated, and where the crop of 1865 was over half a million pounds, it spread from neighborhood to neighborhood, from county to county, until by 1867 it hopped the whole state over."[6]

In the years immediately following the Civil War, the hops craze reached Adams, Columbia, Jefferson, Juneau, Monroe, Sauk, and Richland Counties, with

Hops pickers near Caledonia (Racine County), 1890s

WHI IMAGE ID 2199

Sauk County the production leader.[7] Bernard Schwartz noted in *History of Hops in America,* "Wisconsin growers enjoyed phenomenal prosperity. The newspapers of the time carried accounts of the building of magnificent residences, of fine carriages, high stepping horses, and trips abroad, all as the result of high prices and bountiful hops crops."[8]

The hops craze also allowed farmers to make improvements to their holdings. In her study of the hops era, Laura Paine wrote, "Buildings were upgraded and equipment was purchased, and although some improvements were subsequently lost, those which were retained contributed to the overall strong agricultural base that Wisconsin enjoys today."[9]

But the hops boom proved short-lived. With farmers jumping on the bandwagon, including many in New York state, oversupply led to a market crash in 1867, as prices plummeted from fifty-five cents a pound to five cents a pound. Hops growers went bankrupt, as did many of the merchants who had supported them.[10]

John Rooney of Baraboo recalled his experience with the hops boom and bust. "In the year 1867, my stepfather asked me to go into the business with him. . . . I soon found I made a mistake. . . . In 1867 we made $1,100 over expenses. In 1868 we lost $3,000. We picked 198 bales of hops and got $172 less than the sacking cost us."[11]

TOBACCO

Pioneer farmers from the East brought skill and interest in growing tobacco to Wisconsin as early as the 1830s, and by 1850 tobacco was grown in Adams, Brown, Columbia, Marquette, Richland, Rock, and Walworth Counties. Richland County produced the most of any county for that year, 740 pounds.[12] By 1870, Wisconsin farmers were producing 960,813 pounds of tobacco annually, most of which was sold locally to be used in cigarmaking.[13]

Many Norwegian immigrants took up growing tobacco, an extremely labor-intensive cash crop. According to historian Frederick Merk, "They [the Norwegians] proved to be well adapted to the industry, for not only were they industrious and painstaking, but they were able to employ in the light work involved in tobacco raising the large families with which immigrants were always blessed."[14]

Two primary tobacco-growing areas emerged, one in southern Wisconsin, including Dane, Columbia, and Rock Counties, and the other in the southwestern part of the state, including the counties of Crawford and Vernon. By 1910, Wisconsin devoted 40,458 acres to tobacco growing.[15]

A tobacco field on a Wisconsin farm, circa 1874

WHI IMAGE ID 26428

Tobacco grown in Wisconsin was used almost exclusively for cigar wrapping. The hot, humid summers and rich soil resulted in quality tobacco leaves that were air-dried in tobacco sheds and when dry were wrapped into cigars. Cigarette tobacco, grown in southern states, was heat cured and was ground up and wrapped in paper to make cigarettes. Edgerton in Rock County emerged as one of the most important cigar-wrapping centers in the country.[16] Viroqua and Westby (Vernon County) became major centers for growing tobacco.[17]

Norwegian immigrant Martin H. Bekkedal arrived in Vernon County in the 1880s. By 1900, he was the largest tobacco wholesaler in the region. He built a two-story brick warehouse in Viroqua in 1906 that was one of the largest and most modern in Wisconsin.[18] According to the October 26, 1922, issue of the journal *Tobacco,* that month Bekkedal sold the warehouse to the Northern Wisconsin Tobacco Pool committee for the use of its members in the Viroqua vicinity.[19]

Tobacco growing never became widely accepted in Wisconsin. It required rich soil—richer than that found in many parts of the state—and a tremendous amount of hand labor. In addition, unlike growing many vegetable crops, tobacco growing was not and probably could not be mechanized because of the fragile nature of the tobacco leaves.

SWEET SORGHUM

Spurred by the difficulty obtaining sugar in the northern states during the Civil War, some Wisconsin farmers turned to growing sweet sorghum, a cornlike plant that grows five to six feet tall and whose juice can be processed into a sweetener similar to molasses. Sorghum acreage increased during each year of the Civil War, as Wisconsin tried to wean itself from depending on outside sources of sugar.[20]

In 1860, Wisconsin produced 19,854 gallons of sorghum syrup, and just three years later the state was producing 600,000 gallons. During the peak year of sorghum production, 1866, Wisconsin farmers produced nearly one million gallons of sorghum syrup. During the war and for some years after, state sorghum conventions were held annually in Madison.[21]

As promising as those figures appear, Wisconsin farmers could not overcome the challenge of a summer growing season that was often too short to properly ripen the plants. Some summers the crop did well, but many summers it did not. After the Civil War, sugar prices fell as cane sugar once more became available, and sorghum largely disappeared from Wisconsin fields.

Jennie and Edgar Krueger perched on a pile of harvested sorghum plants at their grandparents' farm near Watertown, circa 1902.
WHI IMAGE ID 108891

SUGAR BEETS

Sugar beets had been grown successfully in central Europe but did not gain the attention of American farmers until after the Civil War. In the spring of 1868, two German immigrants by the names of Otto and Monnesteel, who had experience growing sugar beets in their home country, rented land near Fond du Lac and planted beets. In 1869, they constructed a "primitive though complete" sugar refinery in Fond du Lac at a cost of $12,000. It was the first sugar beet factory in Wisconsin and perhaps the first successful one in the United States. They manufactured one thousand pounds of beet sugar a day. The *Fond du Lac Journal* reported the following:

> Last week we embraced the invitation of Messrs. Monnesteel, Otto & Company to view and examine their growing crop of sugar beets and the machinery being put up to manufacture sugar. They have a growing crop of eighty acres of beets some two miles east on Division Street, and they have appearance of a large yield, some being already five inches in diameter. From present appearance the yield, as estimated by Mr. Otto, will reach ten tons to the acre. . . . In the cultivation of this ground a large number of boys and girls were employed—some days as high as one hundred—and paid liberal wages. Employment was thus afforded to persons, most of whom would have otherwise been idle. When the crop is ripe it will be gathered into piles and covered with earth until ready to use. The sugar mill is located on the corner of Brook and Cotton Street. . . . [To manufacture beet sugar] the beets are thrown into a revolving washer and thence are carried to other machines where they are ground into pulp, pressed, the juice and the pulp separated, evaporated and dried, coming out a perfect sugar of such grade as may be desired by the operator. . . . The quantity of sugar per ton of beets is 160 pounds, which would give a product of 1600 pounds to an acre. . . . Operations in manufacturing will begin about the first of October when two sets of hands will be employed that the work may go on day and night until the crop is converted into sugar. In this work some twenty-five to thirty persons will find employment. The pulp or refuse is good for feeding cattle and will be sold for that purpose.[22]

Otto and Monnesteel's peak year of production was 1869, and the *Milwaukee Sentinel* was so impressed with the factory that in early 1870 its writers boasted that Wisconsin was producing "more beet sugar than all the other states of the Union combined."[23] But after only one year of operation, Otto and Monnesteel dismantled their factory and moved their entire operation to California, apparently because Otto "found it difficult to induce farmers to grow enough beets to keep the factory going and . . . he became disgusted with this indifference and lack of cooperation." Once the factory became established in California, it became one of the largest sugar beet refineries in the United States.[24]

Between 1869 and 1871, about a dozen beet sugar companies emerged in southern and southeastern Wisconsin. To support the sugar beet industry, the 1870 Wisconsin State Legislature exempted from taxation all property and capital stock related to beet sugar refining. Fifty German farmers in Sauk County quickly formed the "First Sauk County Farmer's Association for the Fabrication of Beet Sugar" and employed a German beet sugar expert to assist them. In 1871, the company produced 134,400 pounds of beet sugar and 72,350 pounds of molasses.[25]

From 1869 to 1920, nine beet sugar factories began operations in Wisconsin, with factories at Chippewa Falls; Janesville; Menominee, Michigan (straddling the boundary between Michigan and Wisconsin); Madison; and Green Bay. By 1935, only the plants in Menominee, Green Bay, and Janesville continued to operate.[26] The Menominee Sugar Company appears to be the last of Wisconsin's sugar beet processing factories; it closed in 1955.

FLAX

Following the failure of wheat, some Wisconsin farmers turned to growing flax. Flax had two primary uses: the fiber was used to make linen, and the seed was a source of linseed oil, a component of some paints. A by-product of the refining process, linseed oil meal, was fed to livestock as a protein supplement. Flax was grown mostly in eastern Wisconsin and especially in Ozaukee and Sheboygan Counties. When the Civil War shut off access to the Southern states' supply of cotton, Wisconsin farmers thought the market for linen would surely rise. The US Congress in 1863 appropriated $20,000 to encourage inexpensive methods for spinning flax fibers on cotton machinery. By 1864, two national flax companies, the New York and De Pere Flax Company and the Northwestern Flax Company of Chicago, distributed free flax seeds to Wisconsin farmers and offered contracts to farmers to grow the crop. Soon a sufficient quantity of flax became available to justify building linen mills. But after the war ended, the flax and linen industry could not compete with cheaper cotton from the South.[27] In 1889, Wisconsin's Bureau of Labor and Industrial Statistics reported two linen mills operating in Wisconsin, employing thirty-eight people; ten years later there was but one linen mill, operating in Albany (Green County).[28]

By 1900, Wisconsin's flax acreage had reached fourteen thousand, but it never took hold as a suitable substitute for wheat.[29] Agricultural economist Benjamin Hibbard wrote in 1904, "There were several reasons why flax could not gain permanently in favor. . . . It would not flourish on impoverished . . . land, yet this was the only place there was to put it except on new broken soil, which usually did well in wheat. . . . [and] it was believed to be peculiarly exhausting on the soil."[30]

POTATOES

On the sandy soils of central Wisconsin, potato farming became an important cash crop during the 1920s and 1930s.
FROM THE AUTHOR'S COLLECTION

From pioneer days on, almost every farmer grew a garden, and potatoes were a main garden crop. Potatoes grew well in much of Wisconsin, they stored well, and they were a nutritious supplement to the farm family's diet. With the collapse of wheat, some farmers began growing potatoes commercially, particularly in central and north-central Wisconsin counties such as Portage, Waushara, Marquette, Waupaca, Marathon, Langlade, and Oneida, where the soil was lighter and naturally acidic

Wisconsin Potato Acreages

- **1850:** 13,231 acres
- **1870:** 64,304 acres
- **1890:** 159,037 acres

- **1910:** 290,185 acres
- **1930:** 215,154 acres
- **1950:** 57,265 acres

- **1997:** 76,500 acres
- **2012:** 64,500 acres

NOTES

Wisconsin Crop and Livestock Reporting Service, *Wisconsin Agriculture in Mid-Century* (Madison: Wisconsin State Department of Agriculture Bulletin no. 325, 1953), p. 67; *1998 Wisconsin Agricultural Statistics* (Madison: Wisconsin Agricultural Statistics Service, 1998); *Wisconsin Crop Production: Potatoes* (Washington, DC: USDA National Agricultural Statistics Service, 2013), p. 2.

(preventing some potato diseases). Potato acreage in Wisconsin peaked in 1922 at 325,000 acres. Then, in the late 1940s and early 1950s, irrigation increased Wisconsin's potato yields by more than six times over those realized in the 1920s.[31] The Wisconsin Potato and Vegetable Growers Association was founded in 1948 to advance research, garner government support, and provide information to consumers.

LEAVING WHEAT BEHIND

By 1880, wheat farming was failing, and failing badly. Wisconsin farmers were in financial free fall, and alternative endeavors such as growing potatoes, flax, tobacco, hops, or sugar beets or raising sheep or beef cattle had not provided the solution they sought. They needed a profitable farming enterprise that would match Wisconsin's climate, its location and landscape, and its mixed ethnic population. Although some farmers would remain committed to a diversified approach, the era of experimenting with wheat alternatives was coming to a close, with dairy having emerged as the best option.

The New Yorkers who had immigrated to Wisconsin knew dairy farming, had experience with making butter and cheese, and understood how to care for cows. As wheat growing faltered, some former New Yorkers once more took up dairy farming. Other former wheat farmers balked at the idea of caring for milk cows, which traditionally was considered women's work.

But necessity often overrides tradition. As historian Conrad Zimmerman wrote in his 1884 history of New Glarus (Green County), "Either cheese or nothing and happily we got cheese. The old wheat fields were seeded with clover and grass. Cows were put out on them. Cheese factories were built. After the fact was proved that there was a ready market for cheese; it took only five or six years until cheesemaking was the main branch of work for the whole farming population. It not only pays better, but the farms are constantly more productive."[32]

Although Zimmerman made the transition to dairy farming and cheese making sound easy, it clearly was not. The gender issue was huge. Milking cows and making cheese was still considered women's work. What's more, the idea of caring for and milking cows year-round did not sit well with former wheat farmers who enjoyed long winters with little work to do. It would take the better part of two decades before milking cows and making cheese would become the primary agricultural pursuits in Wisconsin. Considerable education, support from the University of Wisconsin, and the passing of milk and cheese quality regulations would all contribute to the transition.

Tending to cows was long considered women's work.

WHI IMAGE ID 1806

14. Milking Time, Good Friends in Wisconsin.
(Scenes along the country roads.)

PART III

COWS, CHEESE, AND CHANGE

Life on the frontier was a daily struggle, leaving little time for caring for cows, especially in winter.
WHI IMAGE ID 2382

EARLY DAYS OF MILK AND CHEESE PRODUCTION

Many pioneer farmers who arrived in Wisconsin from the East brought with them (or soon acquired) a milk cow or two to provide milk, butter, and cheese for the family. The cows generally did not produce milk during the winter months, as they huddled behind a straw stack or in a primitive shelter out of the cold winds. Busy planting and harvesting their vast wheat crops, the men left the care of cows to their wives and daughters. And the idea of a creamery or a cheese factory located off the farm had not yet arrived in Wisconsin, except for a few isolated examples.

FIRST CHEESE OPERATIONS

It's difficult to ascribe a "first" to any activity; this is especially true when attempting to identify the first cheese factory in Wisconsin. What constitutes a "factory"? Does the number of cows or the number of farmers involved make a difference? Some researchers have suggested that a cheese-making operation should not be called a factory until it is processing the milk of at least one hundred cows.[1]

On a smaller scale, though, Charles Rockwell of Fort Atkinson is credited with operating the state's first commercial cheese establishment in 1837.[2] A few years later, the Pickett family began a cheese operation near Lake Mills in Jefferson Country. Son J. G. Pickett described the operation this way:

> In the year 1840, my father, Mr. A. Pickett, removed from the state of
> Ohio and settled near Rock Lake, in the town of Lake Mills. . . . But a few

pioneers had preceded him, and civilization in this part of the then terri-tory of Wisconsin was in its infancy. . . . My father saw the opportunity, and so, in the spring of 1841, set about supplying the demand [for dairy]. He had driven from Ohio ten cows, he was satisfied that with that number he could supply the demand of the territory, and I am very confident that he had no competition in the business, but there were no cows to be bought at any price, and had there been any for sale there was no money to buy them. But the idea suggested itself to my mother [Anne], why not cooperate with our neighbors in cheese making? It was a capital and original idea, and was at once adopted by the head of the family. We had four neighbors at the time . . . [and] the four families owned ten cows.[3]

The Picketts' little endeavor is credited with being the first cooperative cheese factory in Wisconsin. Many more would follow. (For more on co-ops, see pages 95–97.)

Another modest cheese-making operation began about a decade later in Sheboygan County. John J. Smith had moved to Sheboygan Falls from New York in 1844 and was joined there three years later by his brothers, J. A. and Hiram. Like many others arriving from the East, the Smiths became wheat farmers. But by 1858 both Hiram and John J. were milking cows. John built a cheese house with plastered interior walls to control temperature and humidity, purchased a cheese vat, and began gathering unsalted curd from neighboring farms to combine with his own to salt, press, and cure into cheese.[4]

Poor quality and lack of uniformity, however, made marketing the cheese a challenge. One writer of Sheboygan County history wrote:

In the autumn of 1858, Mr. Smith barreled fifty-eight cheeses, boxes not obtainable, and took them to Chicago for sale. Leaving his cheese at a warehouse, he called on dealers and endeavored to make a sale. On ask-ing if they would like to purchase, he met with the inquiry, "Where is your cheese made?"

"In Sheboygan."

"Where is that?"

"In Wisconsin."

"We don't want any Wisconsin cheese; can't sell anything but New York cheese, and don't want anything else in our store."

Finally, in desperation, Smith asked another cheese dealer to look

Butter Making Stays at Home

As the factory approach to cheese making began developing in Wisconsin, butter making largely remained in the farm kitchen. Butter had become an important commodity on many Wisconsin farms prior to the Civil War, both consumed at home and sold or traded with storekeepers for goods. By 1860, farmers in Kenosha, Walworth, Rock, Waukesha, Dane, Jefferson, Green, and Fond du Lac Counties were milking a few cows and selling home-churned butter.[1] Nevertheless, the 1870 US census reported no creameries in Wisconsin. In 1880, Wisconsin's creameries produced a total of 140,000 pounds of butter, not a large amount compared to butter making on the farm. Farm kitchen butter production for 1870 was estimated to be more than 33 million pounds.[2]

Wisconsin's emerging dairy industry focused more on making cheese than on butter for several reasons. Butter is a far more fragile product than cheese and is best used shortly after it is churned, while cheese can be stored for extended lengths of time and travels well. In the 1870s and 1880s, when the Wisconsin dairy industry began to expand, the road system was still poor, which meant butter could not be easily moved from creamery to consumer, while cheese could be stored before being transported to market.

Churning butter at a farmstead in Alma (Buffalo County), circa 1905. WHI IMAGE ID 25064

NOTES

1. Joseph Schafer, *A History of Agriculture in Wisconsin* (Madison: State Historical Society of Wisconsin, 1922), pp. 152–153.

2. Eric Lampard, *The Rise of the Dairy Industry in Wisconsin: A Study in Agricultural Change, 1820–1920* (Madison: State Historical Society of Wisconsin, 1963), p. 110.

at his cheese. He paid the dealer one dollar for the half-hour spent examining the fifty-eight barrels. The dealer offered eight cents a pound, emphasizing that he wanted Eastern (New York) not Western cheese.[5]

Mainly because of differences in methods and in sanitary conditions from farm to farm, it was extremely difficult to produce a quality product when curds were collected from several farmers. John Smith abandoned his cheese-making efforts; a year later, in 1859, his brother Hiram joined forces with Ira N. Strong in a new cheese-making operation. Hiram began collecting milk, rather than curd, from his neighbors, giving him more control over the cheese-making process.[6]

Chester Hazen, also from New York state, arrived in Fond du Lac County in 1844 and built a cheese factory near Ladoga, twelve miles from Fond du Lac, in 1864. He is often credited with operating the first true cheese factory in Wisconsin. It certainly was the state's *largest* early factory, and Hazen was soon making cheese with the milk of more than one hundred cows. Hazen shipped a carload of cheese to New York in 1876 and was awarded a gold medal for his cheese exhibit at the Philadelphia Centennial that year.[7]

William Dempster Hoard
WHI IMAGE ID 26649

Wisconsin's shift from wheat-growing state to dairy state can largely be credited to the efforts of relocated New York dairymen such as Chester Hazen and Hiram Smith. And perhaps no one had more influence on the transition to dairy than William Dempster Hoard. Born in 1836 in Stockbridge, New York, Hoard arrived in Wisconsin in 1857 with a love for dairying and dairy cows that he had developed in his home state. But Hoard found that Wisconsin farmers would hear nothing of his ideas about developing a dairy industry—wheat was still king—and so he chopped wood, worked on a farm, taught school, and enlisted for Civil War service. When he returned from the war, the first ravages of the chinch bug and exhausted soil had begun to plague Wisconsin's wheat industry. After trying his hand at selling washing machines and musical instruments and later growing hops, Hoard began writing for the *Watertown Republican.* At last, it seemed farmers were ready to listen to Hoard's preaching about how dairy cows might replace wheat on Wisconsin farms. He soon decided to start his own newspaper, and the first issue of his *Jefferson County Union* rolled off the presses on March 7, 1870.[8]

Hoard took to the road to sell subscriptions, talking with many farmers along the way. He saw the press as a way to educate farmers about dairy farming, and in 1885, he and his son, Arthur, began publishing a newspaper devoted entirely to the dairy farmer. The first issue of *Hoard's Dairyman* was a four-page, six-column supplement to the *Jefferson County Union.*[9]

Hoard's Dairyman Today

In 2014, *Hoard's Dairyman* published twenty issues a year for an average circulation of sixty thousand. Its stated mission was to

> supply dairy farmers and their advisors from North America and around the world with practical, factual information to assist in all facets of their dairy businesses. From growing and storing crops to purchasing feeds, from supplying herd health information to obtaining the most benefit from their veterinary

professionals, from feeding methods to the politics of the farm bill, and from the economics of a new technology to the cost of milk production, all aspects important to the livelihood and lives of dairy farmers and their families are covered in the pages of the magazine.

NOTES

"About Hoard's Dairyman," www.hoards.com/about-Hoards-Dairyman.

Hoard's modest little newspaper quickly became an important voice for dairy farmers, not just in Wisconsin but around the world. *Hoard's Dairyman* became the official publication of the Wisconsin Dairymen's Association, which began in 1872 and in which Hoard was an active member (see page 94).[10]

SELECTING DAIRY CATTLE BREEDS

The New Yorkers' influence over the burgeoning Wisconsin dairy industry extended to the breeds of cattle chosen for the enterprise. Based largely on the easterners' experience and preferences, Durhams and Devons were the first dairy cows in the state.[11] Both were so-called dual-purpose breeds, meaning they could be used both as dairy cattle and for beef. In the mid-1850s, a few pioneer dairy farmers introduced shorthorns, which also were dual-purpose animals but were better at producing milk than meat.

Farmers were skeptical about caring for animals that had the sole purpose of giving milk, but W. D. Hoard advocated for the practice, suggesting that "[j]ust as long as we are with dual purpose notions, just so long will we have no purpose cows. . . . If cows could talk they would be heard all over this country calling for an improved breed of dairymen."[12]

Other single-purpose dairy breeds began emerging. In the 1870s, the Ayrshire became the popular breed, but by 1900 Holstein-Friesian, Jersey, and Guernsey breeds

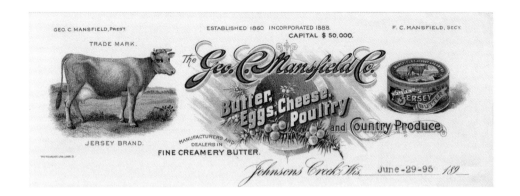

The Geo. C. Mansfield Company of Johnsons Creek (now Johnson Creek) featured the popular Jersey cow on its letterhead.

WHI IMAGE ID 87678

pushed them aside. Farmers slowly moved away from dual-purpose animals but continued debating which breeds of dairy cows were the best milk producers. Jerseys were smaller than Holstein-Friesians and yielded less milk, but Jerseys' milk was of higher butterfat content—and thus their milk was in demand by butter makers. Holsteins did reasonably well on coarse feed and roughage, which made them popular with dairy farmers; though less rich in butterfat, Holstein milk was rich in casein, making it attractive for cheese making.[13] By 1900, the Holstein was becoming the most favored dairy breed in Wisconsin.

EMBRACING THE FACTORY SYSTEM

Thanks to the New Yorkers' experience with a commercial system of cheese making in their home state, small crossroads cheese factories began springing up across southern Wisconsin, some as little as two miles apart. This allowed a farmer with a team and wagon to easily deliver his daily milk production to a factory, which would make the cheese and store it prior to marketing. Between 1864 and 1870, 53 cheese factories were built in the state, and by 1899, 1,500 cheese factories operated in Wisconsin, 1,227 making cheese alone, the others making both cheese and butter. By 1900, more than 300 cheese factories operated in southern and southwestern Wisconsin, 208 of them in Green County.[14]

The factory system was revolutionary in several ways. The quality of the cheese could be more carefully controlled when milk was brought to a central location. Mechanical devices could be used for more efficient production of large batches, and the cheese makers themselves could be the most highly skilled. But perhaps most revolutionary of all, when cheese making left the farm kitchen it was transformed from women's work to men's work.

Women were not at all unhappy with the shift. When Mrs. E. P. Allerton spoke at the third annual meeting of the Wisconsin Dairymen's Association in 1875, she wanted to make sure the audience (mostly men) understood women's viewpoint on cheese making:

> In many farmhouses, the dairy work loomed up every year, a mountain that it took all summer to scale. But the mountain is removed; it has been hauled over to the cheese factory, and let us be thankful time does not hang heavy on the hands of the farmer's wife now that it is done. She did not need the dairy work for recreation.[15]

Like the New Yorkers, many of Wisconsin's European settlers brought dairy farming and cheese-making traditions with them from the old country. As cheese making grew, the Europeans influenced the cheese varieties made in the state. Swiss native Nicholas Gerber first settled in New York state but moved to Green County, Wisconsin, in 1858 and built and equipped a Limburger cheese factory in New Glarus.

Farmers gathered at an early Wisconsin cheese factory—believed to be the Faville Co-op near Lake Mills—circa 1909.
WHI IMAGE ID 76304

Italians brought mozzarella, provolone, and Gorgonzola; the Germans brought Muenster; the French brought Camembert, Brie, and blue cheeses; and the Dutch brought Gouda and Edam.[16]

Thus the stage was set for the establishment of Wisconsin's reign as Dairy State and world-class cheese producer. As writer Ed Janus explained, "The pieces were beginning to fall into place for the ascendancy of the cow and the new type of farmer willing to care for her. By the last quarter of the century, the dairy revolution was well under way."[17] However, before Wisconsin cheese could compete with that of other dairy states, especially New York, quality standards needed improvement. Here is where the education of farmers and cheese makers became crucial. From the production of forage crops for dairy cattle to the building of suitable structures to house the cows, Wisconsin dairy farmers and cheese producers needed instruction so they could produce a high-quality, competitive product.

Workers at Barron Coop Creamery displayed their freshly churned butter, ready to be packed into barrels, circa 1900. In a mere ten years, most butter making had moved from the farm kitchen to the creamery.
WHI IMAGE ID 3238

8

EDUCATING FARMERS

Wisconsin's early settlers learned how to farm from their parents and grand-parents, just as generations before them had done. As long as farming practices didn't change very much, that system worked well. But with the introduction of draft horses and horse-drawn machinery, the availability of Cyrus McCormick's reaper for cutting grain, and the shifts from one-crop farming to diversified farming and ultimately to dairy, farmers thirsted for information and guidance. A new and more formal kind of education to supplement what Grandma and Grandpa had known became a necessity.

AGRICULTURAL SOCIETIES AND FAIRS

Along with the knowledge passed down within families, farmers have always learned from one another. Unlike in other businesses in which "trade secrets" are fiercely protected, farmers traditionally have shared their successes—and failures—with their neighbors. Starting in the mid-nineteenth century, agricultural fairs, at which farmers exchanged tips and techniques (and occasionally did some showing of their crops, animals, or equipment) became popular across the state. Wisconsin's first county fair was held in Waukesha in 1842, six years after Wisconsin became a territory and six years before statehood.

Farmers sought other opportunities to share information as well. Many farmers who moved to Wisconsin from New England and New York when Wisconsin first opened for settlement had been members of agricultural societies in their home

The College of Agriculture at the University of Wisconsin–Madison played a major role in the education of farmers, both on and off campus. In this photo, students learn how to judge beef animals according to the best types for meat production; Agriculture Hall is in the background.

IMAGE COURTESY OF THE UW-MADISON ARCHIVES, #S08196

states. These groups sponsored fairs and conducted meetings where farmers could exchange information and where occasionally outside "experts"—usually farmers from other states—were invited to talk.

In March 1851, farmers and Wisconsin legislators met at the state capitol to discuss organizing a Wisconsin agricultural society.[1] By that time, county ag societies had already formed, in Columbia, Dane, Iowa, Kenosha, Racine, Rock, Sheboygan, Walworth, and Waukesha Counties. Many townships also created smaller societies.[2]

Not long after the Wisconsin State Agricultural Society was created, its executive committee decided to hold an annual cattle show and fair in Janesville. Wisconsin's first state fair was scheduled for October 1 and 2, 1851. Rufus King, editor and owner of the *Milwaukee Sentinel,* wrote a detailed account of opening day:

An area of something over six acres, on the edge of the plateau which looks down upon the rapid and silvery Rock [River], and enclosed by a high board fence, constitutes the fairgrounds. Along two sides of the enclosure are pens for sheep and swine, and stands for cattle. Near the centre is a large and lofty tent for the display of fruits, flowers, fancy articles, paintings, jewelry, etc. In the open space between these centre pieces and the cattle stands on the sides, there is ample room for the exhibition and trial of all sorts of agricultural implements, as well as the display of single and matched horses.[3]

The year before he was elected president, Abraham Lincoln attended the 1859 Wisconsin State Fair in Milwaukee. On that September day, he spoke of the importance of agricultural fairs:

> They are useful in more ways than one. They bring together, and thereby make us better acquainted, and better friends than we otherwise would be. . . . They make more pleasant and strong and more durable the bond of social and political union among us. . . . But the chief use of agricultural fairs is to aid in improving the great calling of agriculture, in all its departments and minute divisions—to make mutual exchange of agricultural discovery, information, and knowledge; so that, at the end, all may know something, which may have been known to but one, to but a few, at the beginning— to bring together especially all which is supposed to not be generally known, because of a recent discovery or invention.[4]

The Wisconsin State Agricultural Society held many of its early state fairs in Madison on grounds that would later become known as Camp Randall.
WHI IMAGE ID 24752

The Wisconsin State Fair continued under the auspices of the Wisconsin Agricultural Society until 1897. In that year the Wisconsin legislature created the

The Wisconsin State Fair

With its roots in early efforts to educate farmers, the Wisconsin State Fair is an enduring institution. Held over ten days at the state fairgrounds in West Allis every August, the fair continues to provide educational opportunities for farmers, especially the young rural people who exhibit their animals and products and compete for prizes. Because the majority of Wisconsin's population now lives in urban or suburban areas, another important mission of the state fair is to educate city people about farming and related activities.

In 1948, the year of Wisconsin's Centennial, the State Fair ran for twenty-three days, August 7–29. For this "Wisconsin Centennial Exposition," fair officials pulled out all the stops to put on a magnificent show commemorating the state's accomplishments in its first one hundred years, with an emphasis on agriculture. They commissioned fourteen massive murals, each one twelve feet high and twenty-eight feet long, depicting a century of agricultural progress. Throughout the exhibition, costumed interpreters stood in front of the display, titled *From Cradle to Combine,* and demonstrated era-appropriate farming practices.[1]

That same year, the State Department of Agriculture also introduced Alice in Dairyland, a program that continues today. Each year in June, a new "Alice" is selected from many applicants. She is

At one section of the Wisconsin Centennial Exposition murals, visitors observed live oxen and a "Prairie Schooner," or covered wagon.

WHI IMAGE ID 87573

The Wisconsin State Fair

The first Alice in Dairyland, Margaret McGuire of Highland, Wisconsin, was crowned in 1948. WHI IMAGE ID 25131

employed by the State Department of Agriculture and Consumer Protection as a marketing ambassador for the state's agricultural products, traveling to schools, county fairs, and festivals; appearing on radio and TV; and generally educating the public about the state's myriad agricultural endeavors.[2]

Fair organizers have continually worked to attract larger crowds, in the 1950s offering such attractions as film stars Roy Rogers and Dale Evans and the Ringling Brothers and Barnum & Bailey Circus.[3] In recent years, the stage show has featured popular musicians in all genres, such as Aretha

Franklin, Peter Frampton, Trevor Jackson, and "Weird Al" Yankovic. An enormous amusement park with more than fifty rides attracts young people, while young and old alike enjoy eating the fair's famous cream puffs, a state fair specialty since 1924. In 2014, fairgoers consumed more than 400,000 cream puffs.[4]

Today the Wisconsin State Fair continues to attract huge crowds; more than one million visitors attended in 2014.[5] As it has since its beginnings, the fair highlights the state's agriculture with the intent of helping consumers understand where the food they eat comes from. The horticulture exhibit, with its array of fruits and vegetables, is a must-see for many; others line up to watch cows being milked. All manner of judging takes place, for young people (4-H and FFA members' projects) as well adults. Entries from cattle to clothing, from canning to kohlrabi are judged and on display for all to see.

NOTES

1. Joe Kapler, "Preserving the Big Picture," *Wisconsin Magazine of History,* Autumn 2011, pp. 26–27.

2. "Wisconsin: History of State Fairs," no date; unpublished material from Robert Williams, Wisconsin Department of Agriculture, Trade and Consumer Protection.

3. Ibid.

4. "2014 Wisconsin State Fair Another One for the Record Books," http://www.wistatefair.com/wp.

5. Ibid.

State Board of Agriculture (later the State Department of Agriculture), which included management of the state fair among its responsibilities. The state fair moved around a great deal during its early years, taking place in Milwaukee, Janesville, Madison, and other cities. By its eighth year, nearly fifty thousand people were in attendance. The fair was suspended during 1861–63 because of the Civil War, and the state converted the fairgrounds in Madison into Camp Randall, a training camp for volunteer troops. In 1886, the fair returned to Milwaukee.[5]

THE FARM PRESS

In Wisconsin's early days, magazines and newspapers were farmers' primary sources of agriculture-related news and information. Wisconsin farmers subscribed to such early national publications as *The Rural New Yorker, Country Gentleman,* and *The Monthly Horticulturist* and later to *Farm Journal, Successful Farming, Capper's Farmer, Prairie Farmer,* and a host of niche trade publications such as *Breeder's Gazette.* With 30 percent of the population in the United States living on farms in the late 1800s and early 1900s, these magazines flourished. *Farm Journal* claimed to have one million subscribers in 1915.[6]

Wisconsin was home to several agricultural publications, the first of which, *Wisconsin Farmer and Northwest Cultivator,* began publication on January 1, 1849, in Racine. Founder and editor Mark Miller also assisted in organizing Wisconsin's first state agricultural society in 1851. *Wisconsin Farmer and Northwest Cultivator* became the official publication of the Wisconsin Agricultural Society, publishing that organization's annual *Transactions.*[7] The publication later changed its name to *The Wisconsin Farmer* and in 1929 combined with the *Wisconsin Agriculturist* (originally the *Racine Agriculturist*). The two editors pledged then that "the endeavor of the consolidated publication will be to extend every possible aid to Wisconsin agriculture and Wisconsin farm folks."[8]

This issue of *The Wisconsin Farmer* from December 23, 1926, featured articles on the Brown Swiss dairy cow breed, potato field experiments, suitable forages for the northern reaches of the state, and "A Merry Christmas to the Whole Household" from the publisher, Dante Pierce.
FROM THE AUTHOR'S COLLECTION

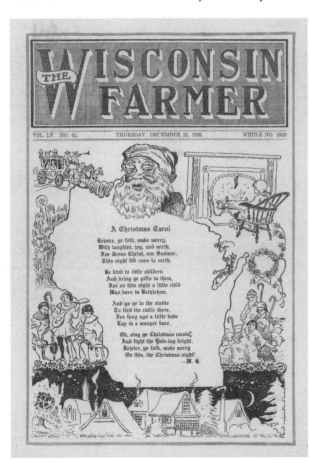

"Why Are People Farming?"

An excerpt from a 1926 issue of *The Wisconsin Farmer:*

Although spellbinders have for years told farmers that they are the "bulwark of the nation" and the "foundation of prosperity," they knew right well that this is not the chief end of their existence. Farmers know that they are engaged in farming to make a living. If they are engaged in farming in order to make a living, what use do they make of their living?

In the pioneer days of Wisconsin and other states, each farm was self-supporting and the returns came largely in terms of family living. That is, a great portion of the wool and flax, the wheat and other products that were produced on the pioneer farm went directly into food and clothing for the family. At the present time farmers think in terms of cash returns from crops and livestock which can be exchanged for family living expenses—and perhaps a margin besides.... Serious problems are arising to face the future civilization of this country and one thing that will help to solve these problems is the kind of education . . . spiritual, physical, and mental, which one receives in the environment of an attractive farm home. . . . The visions and ghosts of yesterday should not haunt us to the extent that they prevent us from stopping the flow of young life to the cities, often overcome by making the farm home modern, by addition of repairs and sensible installations.

NOTES

From *The Wisconsin Farmer* 40, no. 29, July 22, 1926.

One of the best known of the Wisconsin farm publications is *Hoard's Dairyman,* founded by William Dempster Hoard in 1885. Hoard featured in his magazine practical information on all aspects of dairy farming the including care and feeding of cattle, how to build a silo, and proper housing for the dairy cow. He was often criticized, even ridiculed, for his ideas for dairy farming; when he advocated building silos and feeding silage to dairy cows, one wag said, "Didn't that dum fool Hoard know that silage would cause cow's teeth to rot and milk to spoil?"[9] Despite his critics, Hoard continued advocating for the dairy cow and her proper management. He was a giant in the development of Wisconsin's dairy industry, having more influence than most people at the time were even aware. He would go on to serve as Wisconsin's governor (1889–91). (For more on *Hoard's Dairyman,* see pages 68–69.)

THE UNIVERSITY OF WISCONSIN AND FARMER EDUCATION

During the pioneer years, essentially the only formal education available for farm children was the one-room country school. Formal schooling often ended when children were old enough to work on the farm. Few farm kids attended high school, and the possibility of attending college was remote and seldom considered. Yet by the 1860s, with rapid and dramatic changes in farming, most farmers recognized the need for college-level education in agricultural practices.

While the University of Wisconsin had been established at Madison in 1848, its curriculum of geography, Latin, Greek, and English grammar had thus far offered little to support the education needs of Wisconsin's farmers. Few adjustments were made in the university's curriculum until President Lincoln signed the Morrill Act in 1862. Commonly referred to as the Land-Grant Act, the Morrill Act made federally owned lands available to the states—thirty thousand acres for each member of the US Congress. Proceeds from the sale of those lands were to be used for the establishment of an agricultural and mechanics college.

The Wisconsin legislature accepted the land grant on April 2, 1862, and, with eight members in Congress, received 240,000 acres. But legislators couldn't agree on which institution should receive the funds and host the program. Many Wisconsin farmers saw little application of the university's formal curriculum to their needs. The lectures on agricultural chemistry that Chancellor John Lathrop had organized in 1851 were poorly attended and were also generally dismissed as inadequate and inappropriate for helping the state's farm families with their problems and challenges.[10] The state's farmers encouraged the legislature to consider other schools, including Ripon College and Lawrence University.

Finally, in 1866 the Wisconsin legislature awarded the money to the University of Wisconsin. The same year, the Wisconsin legislature bought two hundred acres of land for an experimental farm west of the campus; Dane County contributed $40,000 to develop the farm.[11] With the land-grant money in the offing, it seemed, the rather staid University of Wisconsin leaders were ready to begin listening to farmers.

In 1868, the University of Wisconsin hired William W. Daniells as its first professor of agriculture. Professor Daniells was given the task of developing an agricultural major, but his program differed little from the bachelor of arts major already on campus, and essentially no one enrolled. Meanwhile, Daniells taught chemistry to students in other majors and managed the fledgling campus farm, where he experimented with apples, grapes, and small grains. His superiors at the

An early illustration of
the University of
Wisconsin campus
*THE BLUE BOOK OF THE
STATE OF WISCONSIN*, 1885;
WHI IMAGE ID 23805

university were not impressed with his research efforts, and by the 1870s the
experimental farm had become a source of firewood for the needy students'
woodstoves and a park for Madison residents to visit on Sundays.[12]

Wisconsin farmers were increasingly unhappy with the university's lack of
interest in their struggle to move from wheat growing to other agricultural
enterprises. According to historian Robert Nesbit, "[The dairy pioneers] recognized
the useful role that a more practical agricultural college could play, both in problem-
solving research and in the propagation of dairying skills."[13] In 1878, the Wisconsin
Agricultural Society lobbied the governor to appoint a farmer to the university's
board of regents. Governor Harrison Luddington appointed Hiram Smith, the
pioneer cheese maker from Sheboygan Falls, who immediately became an advocate
for farmer education.[14]

Smith urged university officials to add a second full-time professor of
agriculture, which they did in 1880 when they hired William A. Henry. University
president John Bascom outlined Henry's duties: "1. To give instruction in botany;
2. To superintend farm experiments and improvements; 3. To attend, in the winter
months, local meetings of farmers; and 4. To build an agricultural department."[15]

William A. Henry

During the winter of 1879–80, with Hiram Smith's prodding and with the assistance of Professor Daniells, several local agricultural societies and representatives of the State Agricultural Society met and planned six farmers' institutes. Held in Galesville, Elkhorn, Auroraville, Appleton, Baraboo, and Salem, the institutes were one- and two-day events with Professor Daniells as the main speaker. The institutes continued each year without taxpayer assistance until the 1884–85 legislative session, when a bill was passed appropriating $5,000 to support this farmer education program. The funds were assigned to the Board of Regents of the University of Wisconsin, and administrative control of the farmers' institutes moved to the university.[16] W. H. Morrison, superintendent of the farmers' institutes in 1887, wrote, "[These institutes] were well received by farmers generally, making an advance in the agricultural heart and brain, stimulating animal husbandry and improved methods in various departments of farming. The tendency of these Institutes has been to awaken inquiry, to promote comparisons of methods, to pool their experience, and create a desire for a more extended intelligence that in the end will exalt farming to a profession."[17]

The institutes were held from December through March and were extremely popular with farmers. In the winter of 1885–86, thirty sessions were held all over Wisconsin, covering such topics as "A Plea for Fodder Corn," "Feeding Cows for Profit," "Fish Culture on the Farm," and "Mutton Breeds of Sheep."[18]

Also in 1885, the University of Wisconsin began offering the farm short course, a twelve-week winter program on the Madison campus intended for young farmers (sixteen and older) who had completed a basic education in a one-room country school. Few farm boys could attend the University of Wisconsin's four-year program or enroll in courses offered by the Department of Agriculture (the UW's College of Agriculture would not come into existence for another four years), and thus the farm short course was intended to "allow the young farmer to leave his home for the university after the fall work is done and he can be spared from the farm. He should not pass any severe examinations, and he should return to the farm in the spring, when he again is needed. This course should be intensely practical and helpful to such young farmers."[19]

Professor William Henry turned his research attention to dairy and livestock farming, with an emphasis on practical applications. His research into silage and related experiments impressed Governor Jeremiah M. Rusk, who helped pass legislation in 1883 establishing an agricultural experiment station as a part of the university. The station's first annual report listed the board of regents committee members in charge of it, including Hiram Smith as chairman and officers W. A. Henry, professor of agriculture; Wm. Trelease, professor of botany and horticulture; and H. P. Armsby, professor of agricultural chemistry. Research projects reported for that year included Henry's experiments with new varieties of wheat and oats, cutting seed potatoes, sorghum seed meal as pig feed, sweet skim milk as food for calves and pigs, and studies of corn smut, onion mold, apple scab, and leaf blight.[20]

In 1887, the US Congress passed the Hatch Act, which provided $15,000 annually to each state for the establishment of an agricultural experiment station. With its experiment station already established, Wisconsin could use the federal money to considerably expand the station's activities.[21]

Students attend a UW farm short course lecture by Ransom A. Moore, professor of agronomy and longtime director of the short course program.

WHI IMAGE ID 5584

Early Ag Research at the UW

While the University of Wisconsin was educating a new type of farmer, its researchers were also making important contributions to the development of Wisconsin's agriculture, especially the fledgling dairy industry.

H. L. Russell, the first person in the United States to earn a PhD in bacteriology, joined the UW faculty in 1893. His research contributions included promoting the pasteurization of milk. When raw milk was used in cheese making, the cheese had to be cured a minimum of sixty days for the natural curing process to kill harmful organisms; with pasteurization, cheese could be consumed shortly after it was made. Russell also began a tuberculin testing program for cattle in 1894.[1]

Agricultural physicist Franklin Hiram King arrived at the University of Wisconsin in 1888; his research interests ranged from the water-holding capacities and fertility of soils to groundwater movement, but he is best known for his research on silos. Early silos were underground pits, followed by square upright structures, and in both styles spoilage problems loomed large. Other researchers, including William Henry, had concluded that corn silage fed to dairy cattle in the winter would assure milk production during the cold months of the year, but spoilage was still a major problem, particularly in the corners of square silos, where trapped oxygen contributed to the development of molds. King developed the revolutionary idea of a cylindrical upright silo.[2] As writer Ed Janus noted, "With the silo the land yielded more, cows ate much better, and milk flowed year-round."[3]

Crop breeder R. A. Moore joined the College of Agriculture in 1895 as an assistant to Dean Henry. Moore became chairman of the new Department of Farm Crops (later Department of Agronomy) in 1903 and did some of the earliest research work in the country on the use of alfalfa as dairy cattle feed. The work of later UW researchers R. A. Brink and L. F. Graber would result in the release of high-yielding and winter-hardy vernal alfalfa in 1953.[4]

Emil Truog, a Wisconsin farm boy and a University of Wisconsin graduate, began his teaching and research career in the UW–Madison Soils Department in 1909. His best-known contribution to Wisconsin agriculture was the development of a relatively simple soil test that could be used to determine

In 1889, the University of Wisconsin combined all of its agriculture programs in a new College of Agriculture, with William Henry as its dean. A year later the college began offering a twelve-week short course for cheese and butter makers. In the program's first year of operation, only two students enrolled, but by the second year seventy students were in attendance.[22]

Under Dean Henry's leadership, the UW College of Agriculture would become a national leader in dairy science and its allied fields.[23] The college's first catalog, for the academic year 1888–89, listed departments in agricultural chemistry, veterinary science,

Early Ag Research at the UW

the acidity or alkalinity of soil. "This simple and dramatic test was the first soil test anybody could do without extensive laboratory equipment," wrote Walter E. Scott in his 1954 profile of Truog.[5] Forage crops like alfalfa do not grow well in acidic soil; now farmers could determine if their soil was acidic and reduce the acidity level by adding lime. Thousands of acres of Wisconsin's farmland could now be used to successfully grow these legumes.

Of the many stories about the early research discoveries at the College of Agriculture, perhaps none is stranger than the story of sweet clover. In 1933, a farmer from Deer Park, Wisconsin, suspected that recent cow deaths on his farm had something to do with the sweet clover hay they had been eating. The farmer met with Professor Karl Paul Link, a biochemist in the College of Agriculture, bringing with him samples of the sweet clover hay and a jar of noncoagulated blood from one of his dead cows.[6]

Intrigued, Link began research. In 1941, he isolated an anticoagulant substance in sweet clover hay and also learned that the substance was highly toxic to rodents. The substance, which Link named warfarin after the Wisconsin Alumni Research

Foundation (WARF), became one of the most common rat poisons in the world. Later studies resulted in the development of compounds used in medical practice, in particular Coumadin, which is widely used throughout the world for treating heart patients and preventing blood clotting.[7]

NOTES

1. John W. Jenkins, *A Centennial History: A History of the College of Agricultural and Life Sciences at the University of Wisconsin-Madison* (Madison: University of Wisconsin-Madison College of Agricultural and Life Sciences, 1991), pp. 28–29.

2. Ibid.

3. Ed Janus, *Creating Dairyland* (Madison: Wisconsin Historical Society Press, 2011), p. 35.

4. *University of Wisconsin Agronomy Department: The First 100 Years* (Madison: University of Wisconsin Agronomy Department, 2003), pp. 109–121.

5. Walter E. Scott, ed., "Emil Truog—Soil Scientist," *Wisconsin Academy Review* 1, no. 3 (Summer 1954), pp. 16–17.

6. Jerold A. Last, "The Missing Link: The Story of Karl Paul Link," *Toxicological Sciences,* http://toxsci.oxfordjournals.org/content/66/1/4.long.

7. Ibid.

---

agricultural physics (later soils), and horticulture. Soon other departments were added: animal husbandry (1890), food science (1893), agricultural engineering (1904), agronomy (1904), agriculture education (1907), agricultural journalism (1908), economic entomology (1909), poultry husbandry (1909), agricultural economics (1909), experimental breeding (genetics; 1908), plant pathology (1908), veterinary science (1911), forestry (1913), animal bacteriology (1914), rural sociology (1930), dairy science (1938), and wildlife ecology (1939).[24]

Henry himself continued to devote time to researching and writing about the newest dairying methods, in 1898 publishing his book *Feeds and Feeding,* one of the

The College of Agriculture Barn

In 1897, Dean William Henry hired noted Chicago architect J. T. W. Jennings to draw up plans for a new barn to be built on the west side of the University of Wisconsin campus. Jennings chose an architectural style similar to barns seen in Normandy, France. Designed to house dairy cattle, the wood-frame barn would also serve as a research site and accommodate large numbers of students.[1]

UW agricultural researcher (and silo advocate) F. H. King designed a cylindrical silo that was built near the northeast corner of the barn. The silo was lined inside and outside with brick and was filled from the top. King also developed the barn's ventilation system.

In his June 1898 annual report for the agricultural experiment station, Dean Henry wrote:

> During the past year a barn for dairy cattle furnished with commodious quarters for judging livestock by our students has been completed on the University Farm at a cost of about $16,000, with $2,000 additional for equipment. Our Agricultural College now has a dairy barn which is worthy in some measure of the great dairy industry pursued by our people, and in the room devoted to stock judging we have the comfortable quarters so much needed by the students of the Agricultural College.[2]

In 2002, the UW dairy barn was added to the National Register of Historic Places, and in 2005 the Secretary of the Interior designated it a National Historic Landmark, at the time the only barn in the United States so listed.

The UW's dairy barn, seen here circa 1904, featured an elevated ramp (at right) that allowed teamsters with wagons to haul loads of hay to the upper haylofts.
WHI IMAGE ID 55520

NOTES

1. Jerry Apps, *Barns of Wisconsin,* 3rd ed. (Madison: Wisconsin Historical Society Press, 2010), pp. 118–122.

2. William A. Henry, *Fifteenth Annual Report of the Agricultural Experiment Station of the University of Wisconsin* (Madison: University of Wisconsin, 1898), p. 3.

first guides to the scientific feeding of livestock. Henry was, according to Nesbit, "a man of great energy" and "a keen judge of the talents of his staff," and indeed one of his faculty members, agricultural chemist Stephen Moulton Babcock, in 1890 "gave the world the answer to one of dairymen's most vexing questions."[25] Babcock's invention—

the Babcock test—used centrifugal force and chemical separation to determine the butterfat content of milk. Now creameries and cheese factories had a quantitative standard by which they could determine how much to pay farmers for their product, based on its butterfat content.

By the early 1900s, the UW's winter farm short course had proven highly successful, with attendance remaining high, but an educational need remained for older farmers who wanted more than what was available during the two- and three-day farmers' institutes held around the state. Farmers wanted recent agricultural research results from the experiment station, they wanted to meet the researchers and

In a photograph dated 1917, Stephen Babcock (right) discussed his butterfat tester with Dean William Henry and university president Stephen Chamberlin.

WHI IMAGE ID 104680

ask them questions, they wanted to visit the large and innovative campus dairy barn, and above all they wanted more opportunities to talk and share ideas with farmers from around the state. In 1904, the first weeklong farmers' course in agriculture convened in Madison, with 175 farmers from across the state attending; participants had to be older than twenty-five so the new program would not interfere with the farm short course designed for young men. The farmers' course was free for Wisconsin residents; out-of-state participants paid ten dollars to attend.[26]

The bulletin announcing the course described the program's benefits as follows:

> The farmer pupils are given definite, helpful instruction, often of a nature which cannot be gained by attending Farmers' Institutes or meetings held elsewhere at the University. The equipment of the Agricultural College in the way of apparatus, machinery, tools, livestock, books, etc. has cost far more than a hundred thousand dollars. All of this, so far as possible, is used for instruction purposes and helps immensely in rendering the lectures plain, comprehensive, and interesting to farmer students.[27]

Farm women, too, wanted more opportunities for education, and the farmers' institutes began offering women's programs in 1892 on such topics as "What the Home Nurse Should Know," "Casserole and Caloric Cookstove Cookery," and "Food for the Growing Child." From 1892 to 1907, eleven cooking schools were held each year. Beginning in 1908, the farmers' institutes published an annual cookbook. Upon the publication of the first volume, George McKerrow, superintendent of the farmers' institutes, wrote to UW Board of Regents president William Dempster Hoard:

> I hereby take pleasure in transmitting to you Farmers' Institute Cook Book No. 1. The favor with which the Farmers' Institute Bulletin Report of the Cooking Schools held in conjunction with our Farmers' Institutes for the past 15 years has been received prompted me to advise the publication of a practical cookbook for the farm women of Wisconsin. The art of good cooking is one of the best accomplishments of the housewife; the palatability and digestibility of food has very much to do with the good health of our people.[28]

In 1905, the farmers' course added a housekeepers' conference, also held on the Madison campus and promoted as "entertainment and instruction for the farmer's wife and daughters." Taught by members of the UW's Department of Home Economics,

A cooking class during the women's short course, circa 1915

IMAGE COURTESY OF THE UNIVERSITY OF WISCONSIN DIGITAL COLLECTIONS, #SOHECENT.JEC126.BIB

the week of classes included food preparation, care of children, house furnishing, and skills in purchasing groceries and other items for the home. Participants toured a kindergarten, a hospital, and the dairy department of the College of Agriculture. In Chadbourne Hall they observed "modern machinery for laundry work and cooking." The program was free to Wisconsin residents, and Madison families living near the campus provided room and board for program participants for five dollars for the week.[29]

COUNTY SCHOOLS OF AGRICULTURE

Upon the recommendation of State Superintendent of Schools L. D. Harvey, the Wisconsin legislature in 1901 passed legislation establishing county schools of agriculture. Proponents had argued that the agricultural colleges at the state universities were "too far removed from the masses to ever become universally available."[30] The state would pay one-half of the money needed for the instruction, not to exceed $2,500, while the county where the school was located was responsible for the cost of equipping the school and the other half of the instructional costs. The schools were to be free for those attending.

The first county agriculture school opened in Menomonie, Dunn County, in 1902. "This school is intended for young men and women from the country who have finished or nearly finished the country schools. The short course in the winter term is for the older and busier people who can spare only a few weeks during the winter for school purposes."[31]

Vocational and Technical Education

In 1901, the state of Wisconsin hired Charles McCarthy to head up the state's Legislative Reference Library. McCarthy had recently earned his PhD from the University of Wisconsin–Madison and was hired as a cataloger for this new library in the State Capitol building.[1]

The reference library soon became an invaluable resource for state legislators who wanted information on laws passed in other states as well as background information for pending laws. McCarthy's office began drafting legislation for legislators. McCarthy also quickly became concerned about Wisconsin's educational situation in these early years of the twentieth century—in particular the number of young people who quit school and went to work, often with little preparation.[2]

Through McCarthy's efforts and encouragement, Milwaukee senator Edward Fairchild introduced a bill in 1909 to create the Commission on Industrial and Agricultural Training to study education in Wisconsin and report its recommendations at the next legislative session. In 1911, the Wisconsin legislature passed legislation to create vocational-technical education in the state (chapter 616, Laws of 1911). The first of its kind in the country, the law called for the creation of "continuation schools." In October 1911, Racine became the first Wisconsin city to open a continuation school.[3]

In 1917, the US Congress passed the Smith-Hughes Act, which provided federal dollars to help pay the salaries of administrators and teachers of agriculture, home economics, and the trades. By the 1920s, all agricultural programs administered by the State Board of Industrial and Agricultural training were conducted in rural high schools and the county schools of agriculture. By 1924, the State Board had introduced night classes for adult farmers, usually taught by regular high school and county agriculture school instructors.[4]

During the Depression years of the 1930s, enrollment in vocational agriculture remained high. For instance, for the school year 1939–40, 201 high school vocational agricultural departments enrolled nearly ten thousand full-time students and more than three thousand evening students. World War II

The Dunn County School of Agriculture proved successful, and its fame quickly spread. A Chicago newspaper in 1903 applauded the school's efforts:

> County schools of agriculture are a new feature in the American system of education. . . . In Dunn County, Wisconsin . . . the county school for farmers' sons and daughters had an enrollment of sixty-four students within the first few months of its existence, and the twenty-five farmers' institutes held in the county last fall and winter by the instructors of that school were each attended by hundreds of earnest, interested farm people. . . . In all the instruction, of the school the practical side of the training is

Vocational and Technical Education

created a shortage of agricultural instructors, however, and vocational agriculture enrollment decreased.[5] After the war, with GI Bill funding, many veterans enrolled in the farm training programs, and by 1956 more than sixteen thousand Wisconsin WWII vets had received on-the-farm agricultural training.[6]

Continuing to grow and expand their programs, by the 1970s the vocational-technical schools offered a broad array of courses related to agriculture, including production, supplies/services, mechanics, forestry, and ornamental horticulture. By the early 2000s, several of the technical schools, now called technical colleges, offered programs in sustainable agriculture. These included Blackhawk Technical College, Chippewa Valley Technical College, Madison Area Technical College, and Northeast Wisconsin Technical College.[7]

In 2014, Wisconsin's technical colleges numbered sixteen. Programs in agriculture and natural resources at the technical colleges today include farm business, dairy herd management, veterinary technician, and laboratory science among many others, and schools offer a range of degree options, from associate degree programs to technical diplomas to apprenticeships.

NOTES

1. Kathleen A. Paris, "Education for Employment: 70 Years of Vocational, Technical and Adult Education in Wisconsin," *State of Wisconsin 1981-1982 Blue Book,* ed. T. Rupert and P. Robbins (Madison: Wisconsin Legislative Bureau, 1981), pp. 95–214.

2. Ibid.

3. Ibid.

4. Ibid.

5. Ibid., p. 215.

6. Ibid., p. 130.

7. "Wisconsin College and University Programs and Projects in Sustainable Agriculture," UW–Madison Center for Integrated Agricultural Systems, www.cias.wisc.edu/wisconsin-college-and-university-programs-and-projects-in-sustainable-agriculture.

8. *Wisconsin Agricultural Education & Workforce Development Council 2013 Annual Report,* www.wiaglink.org/documents/about/WAEWDC_2013_Annual_Report-FINALI.pdf.

emphasized. Practical and useful work is the foundation stone upon which the school is built. At every point the school is made to cooperate with the farm, the shop, the dairy, and the home."[32]

In addition to Dunn County, county agricultural schools were established in Winnebago, La Crosse, and Milwaukee Counties. None of them continue to operate today, but in the early 1900s these schools made important contributions to farmers' education, supplementing the efforts of the University of Wisconsin, the farm press, and other educational sources available to farmers in those days.

9

DAIRY EXPANDS AND ORGANIZES

As Wisconsin farmers learned the methods of dairy farming and moved past the idea that milking cows and making cheese was women's work, the industry grew rapidly. Wisconsin boasted 310,000 cows in 1870; by 1900 that number had increased to 965,000.[1]

Milk Cows in Wisconsin[2]

Year	Number	Year	Number	Year	Number
1867	245,000	1920	1,832,000	1980	1,815,000
1870	310,000	1930	2,015,000	1990	1,731,000
1880	471,000	1940	2,165,000	2000	1,344,000
1890	750,000	1950	2,160,000	2010	1,262,000
1900	965,000	1960	2,150,000	2013	1,270,000
1910	1,390,000	1970	1,814,000		

With hard-won lessons acquired during the rise and fall of wheat, improved opportunities for education, and technological advances such as upright silos and Babcock's butterfat test, Wisconsin dairy farmers were in the process, as Ed Janus described it, of "transforming a literal cottage industry into a modern, efficient, and profitable world enterprise."[3] The next challenges would be to overcome the perception that Wisconsin dairy products were of low quality—and to win a market.

Before the Civil War, agriculture was the nation's major industry. After the war, other industrial enterprises began to overtake agriculture, and by 1890 income from

By 1900, many Wisconsin farmers had made the switch from wheat growing to dairy farming.
WHI IMAGE ID 4775

manufacturing exceeded that from agriculture. As an economic class, farmers were steadily falling behind urban businessmen. According to the USDA's 1940 yearbook of agriculture, "Thousands of small producers could not readily combine to fix prices or control output, with the result that in some cases the gross as well as relative returns were reduced."[4]

Manufacturing's economic power soon became political power. Business leaders—either captains of industry or robber barons, depending on one's point of view—"sought to manipulate tariffs, control banking and currency, escape taxation, grab land subsidies for railroad and timber companies, obtain government contracts, and prevent governmental interference with the 'law of supply and demand'—and they succeeded," the USDA reported.[5] Farmers were in dire straits. They were losing money and lacking political clout. Many already belonged to agricultural societies through which they shared farming strategies, participated in fairs, and found a social outlet. But a new type of organization was necessary, one that would give farmers political clout.

THE WISCONSIN DAIRYMEN'S ASSOCIATION

It didn't take long for many of the farmers who had switched from wheat to dairy to begin to question the wisdom of their decision. As the vast majority of their milk was now being made into cheese, they were hoping for better cheese prices. Farmers bet that by organizing, they could improve their situation. In 1867, a convention of Illinois and Wisconsin dairymen met in Rockford, Illinois, and formed the Illinois and Wisconsin Dairymen's Association, which in 1869 became the Northwestern Dairymen's Association. In Wisconsin, Fond du Lac County farmers organized a dairymen's association in 1870, led by Chester Hazen.[6]

Two years later, in 1872, Chester Hazen, Hiram Smith, and William Dempster Hoard, among others, organized dairy farmers into the Wisconsin Dairymen's Association. Fellow founder and early cheese maker Stephen Faville stated that one of the organization's purposes was to secure "some united action with regard to the marketing of dairy products. As the matter now stands, the producers of butter and cheese were at the mercy of a disorganized market, or at least what organization existed was against rather than for them."[7] At the group's first official meeting, on February 15, 1872, Chester Hazen was elected president and W. D. Hoard agreed to serve as secretary.[8]

At that meeting, Chester Hazen urged members to consider the demands of a changing marketplace:

Wisconsin Dairymen's Association letterhead, 1899

WHI IMAGE ID 87908

We've got to think well beyond Wisconsin when we talk about marketing our cheese, and we've got to listen to what out-of-state markets want.

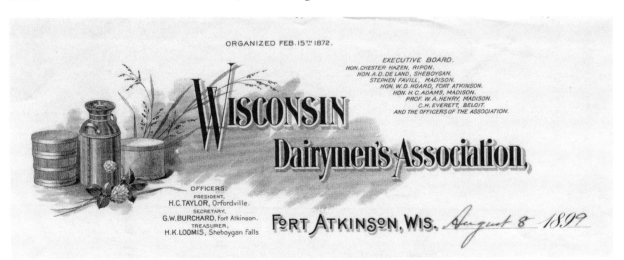

ORGANIZED FEB. 15TH 1872.

EXECUTIVE BOARD.
HON. CHESTER HAZEN, RIPON.
HON. A. D. DE LAND, SHEBOYGAN.
STEPHEN FAVILL, MADISON.
HON. W. D. HOARD, FORT ATKINSON.
HON. H. C. ADAMS, MADISON.
PROF. W. A. HENRY, MADISON.
C. H. EVERETT, BELOIT.
AND THE OFFICERS OF THE ASSOCIATION.

WISCONSIN Dairymen's Association,

OFFICERS:
PRESIDENT,
H. C. TAYLOR, Orfordville.
SECRETARY,
G. W. BURCHARD, Fort Atkinson.
TREASURER,
H. K. LOOMIS, Sheboygan Falls.

FORT ATKINSON, WIS., August 8 1899

St. Louis wants a soft cheese, weighing about sixty pounds. New York wants a harder cheese that is slightly colored. Chicago prefers cheese that is made in a thirteen-inch hoop. And in the Liverpool, England, market, cheese that is made in a fourteen-inch hoop and weighs about fifty pounds will bring a half cent more per pound.[9]

Later that year, the Wisconsin Dairymen's Association formed a board of trade in Watertown where dairy farmers could sell their product at auction; in 1873 the group formed a similar market in Sheboygan Falls.[10] But the newly organized association did more than advocate for better markets; it also pushed for a higher-quality product. At the group's third annual meeting, Hazen said, "The aim of a good dairyman should be to excel or take the first rank in his profession." Hazen went on to explain at length what moving to "first rank" meant. Dairy farmers should select the best cows they could find, provide them with good shelter, feed them regularly in summer and winter, make sure they had plenty of pure water, and milk them at regular times. He concluded, "Dairymen stand in the front rank of agriculturists in America. Let us elevate our standard to where it rightfully belongs, and maintain it by adding influence and dignity to our calling."[11]

DAIRY COOPERATIVES

Almost as soon as cheese making moved off the farm, dairy farmers and cheese makers began to join forces to make and market their products. Anne Pickett became one of the first in Wisconsin to organize a cooperative with her neighboring dairy farmers, in 1841. In 1870, a group of farmers two miles north of Lake Mills organized a cooperative cheese factory. Using their own money, they built a cheese factory and elected one of their group as factory manager. The manager hired a cheese maker and other factory help. "From each one hundred pounds [of cheese] sold, $1.50 was taken from gross receipts to pay off the cost of machinery and buildings as soon as possible. After the original outlays had been met, the price for making cheese was quantity of milk which had been delivered for the year."[12]

In the 1870s, few additional dairy cooperatives began operations. Privately owned factories prevailed at this time as many farmers were content to produce milk and not be involved in its marketing and processing. Additionally, with the passage of the Sherman Antitrust Act of 1890, farmer cooperatives came under the new law's provisions, and some milk marketing cooperatives were charged with restraint of trade. The Capper-Volstead Act of 1922 changed this, giving farmers the right to "bargain, process and market together, [and] provided the necessary protection to farmers to organize marketing and bargaining cooperatives." The number of dairy cooperatives in the United States peaked before World War I, but the amount of milk marketed through cooperatives increased.[13]

OTHER FARMER ORGANIZATIONS

In 1866, President Andrew Johnson asked the US secretary of agriculture to send a clerk to the Southern states to evaluate the region's recovery after the Civil War. What clerk Oliver Hudson Kelly saw in the war-torn South touched him deeply. As a member of the Masonic fraternity, Kelly envisioned the formation of a "farm fraternity," and he worked with other federal government clerks and a fruit grower to organize a secret order that would promote the interests of farmers and provide them educational opportunities. On December 4, 1867, the group formed the National Grange of the Patrons of Husbandry, which became known simply as the Grange.[14]

The Grange insisted it was apolitical, but almost immediately its members began discussing political questions outside of Grange meetings. Soon Grange-inspired groups became involved in government reform, attempting to lower freight charges and enact legislation for state regulation of railroads, which became known as Granger Laws.[15]

Wisconsin's first attempt at organizing a Grange occurred in 1869 when Oliver Kelly stopped in Madison on his way to his Minnesota farm. The attempt failed because Kelly, according to agriculture historian LaVerne Marquart, "attempted to sell the new organization to his 'city friends' instead of 'dirt farmers.'"[16] Nevertheless, local Grange organizations slowly emerged in Wisconsin. At the first state meeting, held in Portage on October 24, 1872, delegates from twenty-six local Grange organizations attended. Eventually Wisconsin would have five hundred Grange groups. By 1875, national Grange membership exceeded 850,000.[17]

The Grange movement's early accomplishments were substantial; along with railroad regulation they included promoting the organization of cooperatives and farmer-owned banks. The Grange fought to make the US commissioner of agriculture part of the president's cabinet, and in February 1889 President Grover Cleveland appointed Norman J. Coleman as the first secretary of agriculture. Coleman served only a few weeks, and then former Wisconsin governor Jeremiah M. Rusk was appointed to the post.[18]

A Cooperative State

Starting in its earliest days, the state of Wisconsin thoroughly embraced the idea of cooperatives, or organizations formed to work for the mutual benefit of all members. Many cooperatives were organized in the state in the years following World War I—80 in 1919, 60 in 1920, and 50 in 1921—with a wide variety of purposes. Some sold agricultural supplies, purchasing them in bulk and then selling them to members. Two hundred farmers' mutual fire cooperatives (farmer-owned and -operated insurance co-ops) reported a combined membership of more than 240,000 in 1936. Many local telephone services—at one time as many as five hundred in the state— were customer-owned cooperatives.

The Wentworth Farmers' Cooperative Association in Douglas County was organized in 1919 by a group of Swedish, Finnish, and Norwegian farmers. WHI IMAGE ID 4476

After the passage of the Rural Electrification Administration Act of 1935, electric cooperatives began springing up, and by June 30, 1940, the REA had made twenty-seven loans to local electric cooperatives in Wisconsin. Other Wisconsin cooperatives included artificial breeding co-ops and production credit associations that provided short-term credit to farmers.[1]

No matter its size, every cooperative operates under the Capper-Volstead Act, and every member has one vote. Many smaller cooperatives merged and became larger as the years passed, often leading to problems of member loyalty. As Professor Robert Cropp explained, "Members don't feel as close to large co-ops as they do to small co-ops. With small co-ops the members pretty much know one another—all come from the same neighborhood—and therefore elect amongst themselves a board of directors with one member, one vote. But with the large co-ops, members are scattered over more than one state. Members still have one member, one vote, but the membership is divided into districts, with members in that district electing a delegate to represent them at the co-op's annual meeting to elect directors and pass resolutions."[2]

NOTES

1. Florence C. Bell, *Farmer Co-ops in Wisconsin.* (St. Paul, MN: St. Paul Bank for Cooperatives, 1941), pp. 2–5.

2. Personal correspondence from Robert Cropp, professor emeritus and dairy economist, University of Wisconsin–Madison, March 29, 2012.

The Grange was instrumental in the creation of rural free delivery (RFD) of mail. Until that time, post offices were located in country stores; when farmers came to town to pick up their mail, they often shopped as well, and storekeepers believed rural free delivery would cut into their business. Despite their protests, experimental rural delivery began in 1896; eight years later the popular service became part of the US Post Office Department.[19]

By the 1880s, the Granger movement was in decline. It had organizational problems; its leaders lacked political experience and made tactical errors. In addition, farm prices had begun to rise and freight rates had been somewhat lowered, removing some of the organization's original purpose. From 1874 to 1880, the national number of Granges fell from twenty thousand to four thousand.[20]

As the Grange faded, the National Farmers' Alliance rose. Forming in 1877 and with a more radical agenda than that of the Grange, the Farmers' Alliance helped form the Populist Party to "restore the government of the Republic to the hands of the 'plain people.'" The organization's rallying cry was, "The farmer feeds them all."[21]

Although always seen as strongly independent, farmers discovered the strength in numbers represented by these early farmer organizations. Both the National Farmers' Alliance and the Populist Party eventually became more potent advocates for agriculture than the Grange, setting the stage for later farm organizations, including the National Farmers Union and the Farm Bureau. (For more about the Farm Bureau, see page 124.)

A rural free delivery truck on its route, circa 1915
WHI IMAGE ID 71650

Cheese Makers Organize

Organized in 1891, the Wisconsin Cheese Makers Association set its mission as keeping an eye on state government, especially those branches that advocated regulations affecting the cheese industry. In the early years, the association's mission was to help individual cheese makers. It provided educational opportunities and sought to improve the quality of Wisconsin cheese. It also served as a social organization for cheese makers and their spouses. The organization continues to this day, conducting educational events, seminars, workshops, and conferences, as well as sponsoring contests to promote excellence in cheese making.

NOTES

Jerry Apps, *Cheese: The Making of a Wisconsin Tradition* (Amherst, WI: Amherst Press, 1998), p. 70.

Winners of the 1958 Wisconsin Cheese Makers Association awards

WHI IMAGE ID 1848

PROBLEMS EMERGE IN THE FLEDGING DAIRY INDUSTRY

By 1900, Wisconsin was clearly on its way to becoming the nation's premier dairy state. With a strong and rapidly expanding market, dairy farmers and cheese makers began making money. But just as things were improving, a few unscrupulous people began to take shortcuts. Some farmers began watering their milk—adding water before delivering the milk to the cheese factory. Some dishonest cheese makers used skim milk and then added lard or stale butter to the product to make up for the lack of butterfat. This product, known as "filled cheese," was difficult to detect when it was first made, but it didn't age well and lost much of its flavor over time. Filled cheese shipped to England was not fit for consumption by the time it arrived. The British market complained loudly.

The Wisconsin Dairymen's Association was well aware of the filled cheese problem and petitioned the Wisconsin legislature to identify the culprits who were giving the industry a bad name. The legislature responded by creating the office of the Dairy and Food Commissioner in 1889. In his first report, Commissioner H. C. Thom wrote: "There is not an article of commerce that requires greater skill in handling in order to secure favorable markets. No industry has been so perverted. No business exists that has been so basely manipulated, and no article of food has been so degraded by counterfeiters. In no time has the honest manufacturer met with such dishonest competition."[22]

Severe action followed. Violators were warned; several were fined fifty dollars. The state and the food commissioner also went after farmers who watered their milk. Commissioner Thom offered detailed suggestions to cheese factories as to how they might nab those who added water to their product: "[A] committee appointed by the Directors [of the cheese factory] shall visit the premises of the patron, see his cows milked morning and evening, and have the quality of such milk compared with the record of the test made of the milk which he was previously furnishing."[23] It is not an overstatement to say that those strict requirements, including new standards for quality and inspections, saved Wisconsin's cheese industry and helped the state build a reputation for high-quality cheese that continues to this day.

In 1910, Wisconsin's cheese production reached 148 million pounds, greater than New York state's had ever been. In 1927, Wisconsin produced 71.5 percent of the nation's cheese. By 1922, Wisconsin had its largest number of crossroads cheese factories, 2,807. More than a thousand new factories had been built between 1900 and 1918.[24]

THE UNIVERSITY MEETS CHANGING NEEDS

Charles Van Hise, who became president of the University of Wisconsin in 1904, was a strong advocate of making the university's resources available to all of the people of the state. His philosophy, which became known as the Wisconsin Idea, cited the motto "The boundaries of the university are the boundaries of the state."

The UW's College of Agriculture continually sought innovative ways to share its research findings and innovations with all state residents. During the winter of 1904–05, the college's agricultural experiment station and the Burlington Railroad began running special agricultural "lecture trains" on the railroad's lines. Experiment station staff presented lectures at each stop.[25]

Most popular were the livestock trains, which operated in cooperation with the state Livestock Breeders' Association. Henry Luman Russell, appointed dean of

Starting in the winter of 1904–05, the University of Wisconsin College of Agriculture and the Burlington Railroad sent lecture trains around the state. Livestock trains, as seen here, were the most popular; others featured agricultural crops, such as potatoes and forage crops.

IMAGE COURTESY OF THE UW-MADISON ARCHIVES, #S06850

the College of Agriculture in 1907, wrote, "These trains were met at almost every scheduled stop by hundreds of farmers who were greatly interested in the exhibition of improved livestock and appliances on display in the exhibition car. Special efforts were made to demonstrate the waste and actual loss which follows the growing of poor quality livestock of a scrub character in contradistinction to the returns secured from animals of selected breeding."[26]

But even with the well-established short courses and women's programs held on campus, the popular farmers' institutes, and now the equally popular education trains traversing the state, farmers wanted more. The shift to dairy farming and cheese making, along with other significant changes in Wisconsin's agriculture, increased farmers' demand for the most up-to-date information. New dairy farmers had myriad questions, from "What breeds of cattle will work on my farm?" to "What crops should I grow to ensure high milk production?" Many Wisconsin farms remained diversified, and farmers also had questions about raising hogs, poultry, sheep, and beef cattle. In eastern and southern Wisconsin, some farmers had begun growing vegetable crops for the developing canning industry; in the north and northeast, others were experimenting with apples, cherries, and cranberries. The demands on the College of Agriculture had become overwhelming.

By 1908, administrators at the College of Agriculture and the agricultural research station were concerned that their staff members were spending too much time on answering letters, meeting with farmers, and preparing user-friendly research reports, at the expense of new research. That year, Dean Russell reported that his administrative staff's workload had become staggering. "Some 12 stenographers have been required for the work last year [1908]. Nearly 45,000 letters were written, 23,000 manuscripts, and 102,000 mimeography sheets of matter were prepared and sent out in compliance with requests."[27]

After considerable lobbying on the part of Dean Russell and others, the 1908 Wisconsin legislature appropriated $30,000 for the Agricultural Extension Service. Dean Russell insisted that the new extension service be connected as much as possible to existing departments in the College of Agriculture. Initially two sections of this new program were organized: one would be devoted to carrying the results of the various agricultural research studies directly to the farmers, and the second to teaching practical courses in general agriculture for those unable to attend the university in Madison.[28] The new Agricultural Extension Service developed alongside a General Extension Division that provided non-agriculture-related educational opportunities off campus (the General Extension and Agricultural Extension would be combined to form the University of Wisconsin–Extension in 1965).

Home economics courses, previously in the College of Letters of Science and transferred to the College of Agriculture in 1908, became a part of agricultural extension, and programs for boys and girls not yet of college age began. Initially called boys' and girls' clubs, by 1911 they were called 4-H clubs, with the four-leaf clover as their symbol.

To lessen the experiment station staff's outreach tasks, the College of Agriculture established an agricultural press service in 1909. Its weekly report distributed news of experimental and demonstration work to more than a hundred agricultural journals and some 350 weekly newspapers. In 1912, the Agricultural Extension Service added county agricultural representatives, so that those based in Madison would not have to travel to the far corners of the state. These university representatives lived in the communities where they worked and could often quickly recognize the problems and needs of people living there. Dean Russell explained the new position as follows: "[The county agricultural representative] will be of direct aid to the farmer, enabling him to establish a more productive and permanent system of agriculture. As such, he should become an economic factor in the county, but it should also be his chosen mission to awaken and develop the community spirit and help guide the social forces along the pathway of progress."[29]

E. L. Luther became Wisconsin's first county agricultural representative, with headquarters in Rhinelander, Oneida County, in 1912. The county provided Luther

A clothing demonstration for women by the UW's Agricultural Extension at the 1921 state fair

WHI IMAGE ID 54770

College of Ag Branch Research Stations[1]

The College of Agriculture opened its first research station outside of Madison in Spooner in 1909. Others soon followed. These branch stations provided sites across the state where the college's researchers could develop new crop varieties, explore farm management strategies, conduct feeding trials, and engage in a host of other research activities designed to improve the state's agricultural efforts. Field days at the branch stations invited farmers to see the new research firsthand and discuss their concerns and problems with the researchers. These research stations represented another dimension of the Wisconsin Idea, extending the resources of the university to the far corners of the state.

• **Arlington** (Dane County): Located about twenty miles north of Madison, this two-thousand-plus-acre station is the site of extensive research projects involving both crops and livestock. It includes livestock housing, greenhouses, and laboratories. This station was developed between 1955 and 1963 to replace Madison Hill Farms, which was sold for development.

• **Hancock** (Waushara County): At this station research features irrigation strategies, with a focus on cucumbers, potatoes, snap beans, field corn, sweet corn, and alfalfa. Considerable attention is given to ground water quality, environmental quality, and wind erosion.

• **Kemp** (Oneida County): In the heart of Wisconsin's North Woods, this station is dedicated to natural resources research and education. It is located on the shores of Lake Tomahawk and opened in 1960.

• **Lancaster** (Grant County): Research projects examine farming the unglaciated soils typical of southwestern Wisconsin, including soil and water conservation, field crops, beef cattle feeding, and rotational grazing. It opened in 1963.

• **Marshfield** (Wood County): Located in north-central Wisconsin in dairy cow country, this station features dairy research with an emphasis on heifer rearing and management. Other projects focus on land drainage, soil fertility, waste management, and crop storage. In the early 2000s, the station shifted both its location and its mission. The university turned part of the original acreage back to the city of Marshfield for use as a research park and purchased 620 acres north of the city. On this new land, the university launched a sophisticated dairy research program that focuses on dairy herd replacements and nutrient management. The station is a cooperative effort involving the USDA's Institute for Environmentally Integrated Dairy Management. Partners include USDA Agricultural Research Service; US Dairy Forage Research Center; USDA Natural Resources Conservation Service; the University of Wisconsin–Madison College of Agricultural and Life Sciences; and the National Farm Medicine Center/Marshfield Clinic Research Foundation.[2]

• **O. J. Noer** (Dane County): Located southwest of Madison, this station features a multidisciplinary focus on turf grass species including strategies for fertilization, irrigation, pest management, and other topics. It opened in 1992.

• **Peninsular** (Door County): Established in 1922, this station, located north of Sturgeon Bay, focuses on the production, management, and processing of fruit crops such as apples, cherries, strawberries,

College of Ag Branch Research Stations[1]

raspberries, and grapes. This station is the repository of the world's largest collection of wild and cultivated potato species—a potato gene bank.[3]

• **Rhinelander** (Oneida County): For over sixty years, this station has conducted potato breeding research. The station is home to the Wisconsin Potato Varietal Breeding Project, which has produced several new varieties of commercial potatoes now grown around the world.

• **Spooner** (Washburn County): Major research projects at this northern station feature field and horticultural crop production and management, irrigation, and forestry. Since 1936, this station has been a center for UW–Madison sheep research, including dairy sheep research.

• **West Madison** (Dane County): On the western edge of Madison, this 570-acre station features research on urban agriculture. The station also grows high-quality forages for the campus livestock research programs.

• **US Dairy Forage Research Center** (Sauk County): Located near Prairie du Sac, this research facility opened in 1980 and is a cooperative effort between the US Department of Agriculture and the University of Wisconsin–Madison.

NOTES

1. Personal correspondence from Phil Dunigan, associate director, Agricultural Research Stations, March 16, 2012; and www.ars.wisc.edu.

2. "Marshfield Research Station Turns 100 in March," *Wisconsin State Farmer,* March 16, 2012; and personal correspondence from Phil Dunigan, September 18, 2012.

3. "Spud bank stores world's varieties," JSOnline, www.jsonline.com/news/wisconsin/potato-genebank-stores-worlds-varieties-3a69qhv-165181546.html.

The Spooner research station runs the country's only dairy sheep research program.
SEVIE KENYON/ UW–MADISON CALS

with an Indian motorcycle on which he made his rounds. The county representative system spread widely, and soon all the state's northern counties had one in place, with the central and southern counties close behind. Similar programs were launched throughout the United States.[30]

At this time the federal government provided limited funds to support county extension activities through its Office of Farm Management, a unit of the United States Department of Agriculture. That amount for 1912–13 was just $165,000 for the entire nation. As a member of the National Association of Agricultural Colleges and Experiment Stations in 1911, Dean Russell was instrumental in lobbying Congress for more federal assistance, and on May 8, 1914, after considerable debate in both houses, Congress passed the Smith-Lever Act, calling for counties, states, and the USDA to work in cooperation to pay for agricultural and home economics education to the farmers of the nation. The university agricultural extension now was formally known as Cooperative Extension.[31]

Eventually the county representatives would become known as county agents. As Wisconsin's Cooperative Extension service expanded, it added extension specialists at the state level to assist the county staffs. These specialists served as intermediaries between the agricultural researchers and the county agents by helping to translate complicated research findings into simplified information the agents could use in their educational programs. Trained in specific subject areas such as agronomy, agricultural economics, rural sociology, land use, and particular animals and crops, extension specialists wrote bulletins, gave talks at county meetings, and worked individually with agents.

As officials had hoped, the Cooperative Extension, with its county-based cadre of agents supported by state-based specialists, allowed the college's researchers to devote more time to their research. In 1907, the university hired Elmer Verner McCollum in the agricultural chemistry (later biochemistry) department. McCollum began work on an animal nutritional project involving heifers and was the first researcher in the country to work with rats. The results of his research efforts led to the discovery of vitamin A.[32]

College of Agriculture researchers began looking at broader topics related to farming and rural communities. Courses were offered in the economics of agriculture, and agricultural economists researched such topics as agricultural marketing, cooperatives, farm management, and pricing. The Department of Agricultural Economics was organized in 1909 with Henry Charles Taylor as the first chair.[33] Taylor wrote, "It is highly necessary that the farmer, as well as any other businessman, should know at all times just how his business stands, what parts are profitable,

A Jefferson County extension agent visited with 4-H members working on a rabbit project, 1922.
IMAGE COURTESY OF THE UW-MADISON ARCHIVES, #S07547

what unprofitable, and how he should re-direct his activities to assure success. For this purpose the farm must of necessity be looked upon as a whole."[34] In 1919, Taylor moved to Washington, where he became the first chief of the Bureau of Agricultural Economics.

The university created the Department of Agricultural Education in 1907 to prepare teachers of agriculture for high schools, county agricultural schools, and normal schools. Research, often conducted in cooperation with the UW School of Education, focused on such topics as country school consolidation, agricultural curriculum for high schools, and career choices for rural youth.

In 1908, the UW formed an agricultural journalism department—the first in the country—with the purpose of making the college's research bulletin service more efficient. Its efforts soon broadened.[35]

Not only was the university interested in improving the economic aspects of agriculture in the state, it was also interested in understanding and improving rural life. In 1911, the College of Agriculture hired rural sociologist Charles J. Galpin in the

Ag-Related Education at UW–Platteville and UW–River Falls

Agricultural colleges at the University of Wisconsin–Platteville and the University of Wisconsin–River Falls made notable contributions to the education of Wisconsin farmers and to the state's agricultural industry.

The Smith-Hughes Act of 1917 made federal money available to the states to advance vocational education in agriculture, trades, and home economics in secondary schools. Today both UW–Platteville and UW–River Falls train vocational agriculture teachers for high schools in Wisconsin.

UW–Platteville began in 1866 as Wisconsin's first "normal school" for the preparation of one-room country schoolteachers. In 1959, the Wisconsin

The 1910 agriculture class at Platteville Normal School
UW–PLATTEVILLE SW WISCONSIN ROOM

Department of Agricultural Economics. One of Galpin's early research projects, titled "The Social Anatomy of an Agricultural Community," was conducted in Walworth County. In 1918, Galpin published his book *Rural Life,* one of the first textbooks in the fledgling field of rural sociology. In it he discussed "Psychology of Farm Life," "The Structure of Rural Society," "The Social Role of the Housewife," "Farmer's Churches," and other topics.[36] He was the first to attempt to describe in detail the nature of rural life based on carefully conducted research studies.

Starting in the earliest days of settlement, farmers understood that to succeed they must keep learning. Long before lifelong learning became a trend, farmers—

Ag-Related Education at UW–Platteville and UW–River Falls

Institute of Technology, originally the Wisconsin Mining Trade School, merged with Platteville State Teacher's College to form the Wisconsin State College and Institute of Technology at Platteville. The name was changed to Wisconsin State University–Platteville in 1966. In 1971, when all state universities were merged to form the University of Wisconsin System, the name became University of Wisconsin–Platteville.[1]

The preparation of high school agriculture teachers was an important part of UW–Platteville's curriculum and remains a feature of the university's School of Agriculture today. Majors offered include agribusiness; animal science; ornamental horticulture; reclamation, environment, and conservation; soil and crop science; and a preprofessional program in veterinary medicine. The college's Pioneer Farm, a 450-acre demonstration, teaching, and research facility five miles southeast of Platteville, includes dairy, swine, and beef herds plus corn, soybean, and alfalfa cropping.[2]

In 1875, the University of Wisconsin–River Falls began as a state normal school. The school established a Department of Agriculture in 1912; in 1951 the school added liberal arts courses and changed its name to Wisconsin State College at River Falls. Graduate course offerings were added in 1964, and the institution's name was changed to Wisconsin State University–River Falls. With the merger of the state universities into the University of Wisconsin System in 1971, the institution became the University of Wisconsin–River Falls.[3]

UW–River Falls Dairy Learning Center, located at the Mann Valley Farm just northwest of River Falls, offers hands-on opportunities for students to learn about the latest in dairy management and dairy science technology. The farm is also the site of various dairy cattle research projects, especially those featuring nutrition and composted bedding systems.[4]

NOTES

1. "School of Agriculture," University of Wisconsin–Platteville, http://www.uwplatt.edu/agriculture.

2. Ibid.

3. "Majors and Minors," University of Wisconsin–River Falls, www.uwrf.edu/Majors.

4. Ibid.

men and women, young and old—continued their education throughout their lives. In response to their thirst for knowledge, both formal and informal educational opportunities emerged, ranging from the farm press and agricultural organizations to such formal institutions as the University of Wisconsin's College of Agriculture.

AGRICULTURAL
PRACTICES AND
COMMUNITIES CHANGE

By the early 1900s, Wisconsin had been transformed. Fur trading and lead mining were in the distant past, and wheat farming, too, had essentially disappeared. Dairy barns were appearing in the southern and central Wisconsin countryside, huge buildings that dwarfed the other structures on the farmstead.

The shift to dairy farming resulted in changed agricultural practices that few former wheat farmers had envisioned. More than being just a new way to earn a living, dairy farming had vast implications for the land, for farm families, and for rural communities.

TAKING FARMING TO THE CUTOVER

By the end of the nineteenth century, most of the state's southern farmland was already settled, while in the north, as historian Lucile Kane noted, "[t]he large scale lumber business which had supported the region's economy was gradually closing out and moving on to the fresh forests of the West and the South."[1] Lumber companies were eager to sell. Many agricultural leaders, looking to the north and seeing thousands of acres of stumps, brush, berry bushes, and soil that appeared to have potential for farming, saw opportunity.

In 1895, Dean William Henry of the UW College of Agriculture, using funds approved by the Wisconsin legislature, produced a publication titled *Northern WI: A*

The *Hand-Book for the Homeseeker* was filled with photos like this one, promising bountiful crops of everything from cabbage to potatoes, sweet corn, pumpkins, grapevines, and grains of all sorts.
WHI IMAGE ID 1791

Hand-Book for the Homeseeker. Widely circulated in this country and beyond, the booklet proclaimed the economic promise of farming in northern Wisconsin. In the introduction, Dean Henry wrote:

> If this Hand Book shall be an instrument in removing the great ignorance and even prejudice which prevails in the southern half of our own state concerning the agricultural possibilities of northern Wisconsin, and if it shall convey to our people and those of other states and countries a true knowledge of this region, much good will have been accomplished. There is already a goodly tide of settlers flowing into northern Wisconsin; if it accomplishes its designed purpose, this book will swell the number materially, bringing to us an intelligent, worthy class of people who are posted in advance on the kind of country they are coming to and who, knowing this, are not likely to leave us disappointed after a few years' stay. Furthermore, these people, if guided by our Hand Book, will embark in agricultural industries, which are remunerative to themselves and tend to the best interest of our commonwealth.
>
> With farms supplanting the forest, northern Wisconsin will not revert to a wilderness with the passing of the lumber industry, but will be occupied by a thrifty class of farmers whose well directed, intelligent efforts bring substantial, satisfactory returns from fields, flocks and herds.[2]

Other boosters set about luring pioneers to the north as well. In fact, Kane wrote, "It seemed that everyone wanted to get in on the boom. Land departments of railroads, lumber companies, banks, grocers, druggists, ministers, lawyers, judges, doctors, real estate companies, and professional speculators became dealers in cutover land."[3] The Wisconsin Colonization Company purchased fifty thousand acres in Sawyer County and set about building a model town for settlers to inhabit.

In response to these solicitations, several thousand settlers came to the cutover region.[4] These new arrivals faced many challenges—and stump removal topped the list. It was estimated that an average acre of cutover land in Oneida County held as many as 117 stumps, most of them pine, which had a wide-spreading root system that resisted decay and defied removal.[5] As journalist Ray Stannard Baker wrote in 1902, there was "no desert more pitifully forlorn, more deserted, more irreclaimable, and more worthless than the man-made deserts of northern Wisconsin. . . . [They] are hideous, grotesque, pitiful, a reminder of the reckless wastefulness of man."[6]

To help farmers remove the remnants of the logging era and move on to cultivating their newly acquired farms, the University of Wisconsin's College of Agriculture sent county agents into northern counties starting in 1912. In 1916, the college and railroad companies began a program that sent "Land Clearing Special" trains across the north. At each stop, college representatives offered instruction on everything from blasting stumps to effective use of mechanical stump pullers and sold dynamite to farmers. In 1917, six hundred people attended the stump removal demonstrations, purchasing ten tons of dynamite and using it to clear some nine thousand acres of cutover lands. But their efforts made only a dent in the clearing of the northern lands for farming. By 1920, about thirty-eight thousand acres had been cleared, less than 3 percent of the stump-studded northern county acreage. By the end of 1928, farmers had exploded 600,000 pounds of dynamite and had cleared but sixty-five thousand acres, about 5 percent of the 1.1 million acres that was supposed to become farmland.[7]

Tales of dynamite accidents fill the pages of northern Wisconsin history. Nancy Maier, of Birnamwood, recalled this tragic story: "My grandfather, Fred Machmueller, was killed on May 22, 1935, while blasting tree stumps. He was sixty-five years old. He went to check on a stick of dynamite that didn't go off and it exploded as he

Removing stumps with a horse-powered winch, as seen on this farm in Sawyer County, was slow and onerous work.
WHI IMAGE ID 92803

This UW College of Agriculture truck carried workers to the cutover—and advocated the safe use of explosives. WHI IMAGE ID 7147

neared the stump, a chunk hitting him. My dad, Andy, was seventeen at the time and had to go home and tell his mother the sad news."[8]

Even with the stumps removed, much of the northern region was still strewn with stones left by glaciers. Andy Machmueller recalled how they removed stones on his home farm:

Around 1930 my dad decided it was time to clear our night cow pasture of stones so we could plant it with a crop. Nearly all hardware stores had dynamite, so he went to town for a box of dynamite. He would take a crowbar and made a hole under a large rock. Then he would shove two sticks of dynamite in the hole with twelve inches or more of fuse. The fuse came on a roll and you could cut the length you needed and put it into the end of the dynamite stick. The fuse had a cap smaller than a .22 rifle casing, which had been pressed onto the end of the fuse before it was placed into the dynamite. The cap ignited the dynamite after the lit fuse had burned to reach the dynamite. The blast would go off and throw the stone out of the hole. Sometimes it would split the rock, making it easier to remove. The rocks were removed with a team of horses. . . . We hauled sixty-six stone boatloads of rocks from the four acres. After the large rocks were blasted out, large holes were left. We hauled loads of dirt to fill them.

Whenever the blasting was done, we left some windows in the house open so they would not be broken.[9]

Some farmers stuck it out and managed to make a living in the challenging cutover territory despite the stumps and stones, cold winters, and short growing seasons. But many left, their dreams unfulfilled.

THE FARMSTEAD EVOLVES

A wheat farmer's farmstead generally consisted of a farmhouse, perhaps a small three-bay threshing barn, a horse barn, a granary, a smokehouse, and a pump house. But for dairy cows to become good producers of milk, especially during Wisconsin's bitterly cold winter months, they required a large, substantial barn. New Englanders and New Yorkers brought their ideas for barns with them—at first small, three-bay threshing barns for the storage and threshing of wheat. The Europeans brought the barn styles they knew from their home countries—Norway, Germany, Poland, Finland, Sweden, Switzerland—most of them of log construction and reflecting their ethnic roots.

But with the demand for more housing space for dairy cows and more storage space for hay, larger barns emerged. The most prominent in Wisconsin was the bank barn, so called because it was built against the side of a hill, or bank, so the farmer could haul hay directly to the second-story storage mow. The livestock were housed in the first floor stable area, usually located partially underground and beneath the haymow. The walls of the basement level were typically built of fieldstone in the glaciated areas of the state and of quarried rock in the nonglaciated areas.[10]

Several variations of the bank barn appeared. The traditional Pennsylvania bank barn, found in southern and eastern Wisconsin and in particular in Green and Sheboygan Counties, had hewn beams formed with a broadax. The beams were as large as twelve inches by twelve inches and were connected using wooden pegs. The outside of the barn was usually covered with vertical boards, often twelve inches wide and sixteen feet long. These earliest bank barns usually had gable roofs; after 1900, gambrel-roof bank barns began appearing in large numbers.[11]

Bank barns became the most popular style of dairy barns in Wisconsin. Cattle were housed in the basement and hay stored above. Pictured above is a bank barn under construction around 1900.
WHI IMAGE ID 37271

Vernon County, Wisconsin, claims to have more round barns than any other county in the United States.
WHI IMAGE ID 10446

Round, octagonal, and other polygonal barns were built as well. African American barn builder Alga Shivers built at least fifteen round barns in Vernon and Monroe Counties. Ernest Clausing, a German carpenter, built octagonal barns along Lake Michigan from Milwaukee to Port Washington; one was moved to Old World Wisconsin, a historic site near Eagle, where today it serves as a restaurant.[12]

Farmers soon learned that for dairy cows to maintain high milk production during the winter months, additional feed sources were necessary beyond dry hay stored in the barn. By the 1870s, European farmers, especially French and German, had begun to experiment with storing green corn fodder in a pit and allowing it to ferment, creating silage. The *Report of the Commissioner of Agriculture for the Year 1875* described early French and German silage-making efforts, and August Goffart's book *The Ensilage of Maize and Other Green Forage Crops* was translated into English in 1879. Both publications caught the attention of farmers seeking sources of winter feed for their cattle.[13]

The first silos were trench or pit silos, many of them built inside a barn. Levi P. Gilbert of Fort Atkinson is credited with building the first silo in Wisconsin, in 1877. Gilbert's straw-lined pit silo was thirty-two feet long, twelve feet wide, and six feet deep. Dr. L. W. Weeks of Oconomowoc built a silo in 1880, and John Steele, a Dodge County farmer, constructed one that same year and filled it with twenty-five tons of corn fodder. But using silos and silage was not without controversy, and at first there was no rush on Wisconsin farms to construct them. Some farmers claimed that when cows ate silage they would lose their teeth or it would eat out their stomachs or cause trouble at calving time. Some even claimed that cows eating silage would become drunk and stagger about. The biggest fear was that silage would affect the quality of milk. The editor of *Farm Journal* wrote in April 1881: "We shall not proclaim silage a humbug, because that may not be the right word to describe it. But it is only a nine day's wonder. Practical farmers won't adopt it, except here and there, and in 10 years from now the silos being built will be used for storing potatoes, turnips, beets or ice."[14]

The editor was wrong, of course. By 1889, Wisconsin was estimated to have two thousand silos.[15] By 1915, assessors reported 55,991 silos in the state, and by 1923, the number of silos in the state soared to more than 100,000.[16] Wisconsin was on its way to having the most silos of any state in the nation.[17]

The shape, size, and materials used for silos began changing by the late 1890s. Pit silos allowed considerable spoilage, especially in the corners, where mold could develop. Upright wooden silos reduced the problem, but they were still square—that

A silo under construction, circa 1900

WHI IMAGE ID 37268

is, with corners—and spoilage continued to plague farmers. Franklin H. King, a UW researcher, developed an early cylindrical silo that would revolutionize the storage of silage and the feeding of cows (see sidebar on page 84).

The earliest tower silos were of wood stave construction, followed by poured concrete and then concrete stave. Wood stave silos required metal hoops to keep the wood from shifting, and they were subject to rot; concrete silos did not have these problems. Some silos were made of glazed tile or of bricks. By the late 1940s, metal silos, especially those manufactured by the A. O. Smith Company of Milwaukee, gained considerable popularity in the state. The company had developed a system for fusing glass to steel, which made the resulting material both strong and resistant to rust.

CROPPING APPROACHES CHANGE

In wheat farming, the same crop was grown in the same field year after year. With the emergence of dairy farming, cropping strategies changed. Dairy cattle needed pasture for grazing during the warmer months of the year, and they needed hay for winter feed.

While the wheat crop had been sold off the farm as a cash crop, the crops grown on a dairy farm were for the most part consumed on the farm by the dairy cattle and, for many farmers, by hogs and poultry as well. Dairy farmers learned that to earn a reasonable income from milk sales, they had to feed their cattle well. This meant high-quality pasture grasses and legumes and high-quality hay.

Having learned their lesson from the depleted soils of the wheat era, farmers implemented the principles of crop rotation. A rotation generally began with a crop of corn, some harvested for silage and some for the grain and corn stover (cornstalks minus the corn kernels). The following year, the farmer plowed down the corn ground and planted it with oats, which would serve not only to provide grain and straw but also as a nurse crop for alfalfa, clover, and grass seed. In year three, the field would become a hayfield, the hay to be harvested and stored in the farmer's barn. In years four and five the field would continue as a hayfield if it was yielding reasonable crops. In years six and seven the field became a cow pasture. In year eight, the hayfield was plowed down to become a cornfield, and the sequence began again.

Dairy farmers quickly discovered that manure has a way of accumulating. They learned that by spreading the manure accumulated during the winter months on the cornfield before plowing, it would maintain, and even enhance, the soil's fertility. They also learned that by planting legumes, they could enhance the nitrogen level of their fields. And most important, they learned that including hay and then several years of pasture in their crop rotation allowed far less erosion of their soils due to the effects of wind and water.

The 1870 agricultural census reported that Wisconsin farmers grew 462,000 acres of corn, 547,000 acres of oats, and 953,000 acres of hay. By 1910, corn acreage reached 1.5 million acres, oats 2.1 million acres, and hay 3.1 million acres.[18]

As evidenced by the increase in corn, oats, and hay acreages over that forty-year span, Wisconsin farmers clearly were practicing crop rotation—a dramatic change from the days when they grew wheat year after year on the same fields. Of course, these statistics also reveal the expansion of the dairy industry in the state, and its attendant need to provide pasture for cows during the summer months as well as ample feed (corn, oats, silage, and hay) during the long winter months.

A farmer spread manure on his fields, circa 1912
WHI IMAGE ID 47807

NEW TOOLS FOR FARMERS

Wheat farming required relatively little specialized equipment. For growing wheat, a farmer needed a team of horses, a plow, a disc and a smoothing drag for preparing the soil, a grain drill for planting seed, a grain binder for cutting the grain, and a threshing machine for separating wheat kernels from straw, plus a wagon to haul the grain.

A 1900 dairy farmer needed all of those implements (especially if he grew oats). In addition, to handle the corn crop the farmer needed a corn planter, a cultivator for weed control, a corn binder to cut the stalks, a corn husker-shredder, and a silo filler for cutting the corn and blowing it into the silo. For the hay crop, he needed a mower for cutting the hay, a rake for gathering the cut hay, a specially made hay wagon for hauling it, and a rope and pulley hay carrier for pulling the hay into the barn's haymow. During the winter months, when the cows were kept inside the barn, a farmer needed a manure spreader to haul the manure from the barn to the fields.

Farmers needed additional storage space for this collection of farm implements, resulting in the building of machine sheds, expanding the number of farm buildings in the farmstead. Additionally, these new machines needed maintenance and often repair. During the off-season when the farmer wasn't using a particular implement, he was tinkering with it, adjusting it, lubricating it, and making it ready for the upcoming season. It seemed a dairy farmer's work was never done.

RURAL COMMUNITIES ADJUST

With the arrival of the dairy cow, farm family operations and rural communities changed as well. It's doubtful that former wheat farmers, who enjoyed extended time off in the winter from the rigors of farmwork, anticipated how tied down they would be once they began caring for a dairy herd. Cows had to be milked twice a day, every day, 365 days a year. No vacations. No days off. In the winter months, not only did the cows have to be milked and fed, they had to be bedded (usually with oat straw) and the barns cleaned of manure—every day. A farm family's life, including its social life, was dictated by its cows.

Being a successful dairy farmer required substantially more skills than those needed for wheat farming. As Charles J. Galpin, the University of Wisconsin's first rural sociologist, explained, "The American farmer is soilsman, horticulturist, animal husbandman, dairyman, orchardist, teamster, engineer, marketer, economist."[19]

Farmers near Waupaca used a horse-powered treadmill to power a silo filler on the farm of F. D. Parish, circa 1895.
WHI IMAGE ID 93309

Because farmers were geographically separated from their neighbors, they relied on their own skills and ingenuity to keep a farm operation going. At the same time, however, they depended on their neighbors, both for their assistance and for the social contact. Former wheat farmers were well acquainted with community threshing bees after the wheat harvest. Threshing bees continued, but now the crop threshed was oats, and sometimes wheat and rye as well. Other opportunities to gather and share both the workload and camaraderie were silo-filling bees, during which farmers filled their silos with cut green corn, and corn-shredding bees during the ripe corn harvest in late fall.

As rural sociologist Paul Landis pointed out, "In rural society much association demands a more complete participation than in the city; thus rural life is conducive to the development of close friendships. . . . True, neighbors may be few and far apart, but contacts with them are usually intimate and meaningful."[20]

While farmwork itself created sufficient opportunities for social interaction among the men, who hauled milk to the crossroads cheese factories each day and regularly visited the local gristmill that ground their cow feed, similar opportunities for women were few and far between. Women played an essential, though often underappreciated, role in the work of the farm. In addition to tending to farm chores, such as feeding the dairy calves, managing the vegetable garden, and tending the chicken flock, women bore the children and looked after them; did the cooking and baking and preserving; looked after the health of the family; sewed, washed, ironed, and repaired the family's clothing; and made sure the children did their schoolwork. Farm women were usually stuck at home, especially during the long winter months. They had little contact with other women in the neighborhood, except perhaps the occasional quilting bee, card party, or neighborhood dance. Sunday morning church services provided a social outlet for all family members, but church services were often missed during bad weather in winter.

Luckily, by this time telephones were found on many Wisconsin farms; some of the first were installed as early as the 1890s. Not long after, small, independent telephone companies, many of them cooperatives, spread across the state, bringing telephone service to rural communities.[21] Some households used a party line, in which as many as a dozen families shared a single line. One knew when to answer the phone by listening for a distinctive ring pattern—one long and three short rings, for example. Phones quickly became not only a way to do business or call for help in an emergency, but also a social tie among often isolated farm people.[22]

Radio provided another vital link between farmers and the rest of the world. Not long after commercial and public radio became available in the 1920s, farmers came to rely on the new medium both as a source of news and entertainment and as a supplier of information essential to their farming operations. They depended on the broadcasts of up-to-date weather and market reports. Many commercial radio stations also employed farm directors, who shared stories of successful farming operations, featured interviews with farm experts such as county extension agents, and reported on the meetings of farm organizations and other agricultural activities.

Like the mills and general stores that came before them, the cheese factories popping up across much of southern and central Wisconsin quickly became social centers. As farmers waited each morning to unload their milk, they visited and swapped stories. In some places a country school, a tavern, or a church was erected nearby.

The villages and small cities, often located on streams or rivers where grain mills and saw mills had been constructed, adjusted to accommodate the expanding

WHA Radio

As early as 1900, the US Department of Agriculture's Weather Bureau was experimenting with using wireless broadcasts for both collecting and disseminating weather information. On December 1, 1916, 9XM Radio, broadcasting from Science Hall on the UW–Madison campus, began regular broadcasts of weather information. Those southern Wisconsin farmers able to receive WHA's programs soon came to depend on the weather and market information to help them with their everyday farming operations.[1]

Radio station WHA's exhibit at a 1922 radio show in Milwaukee included a map suggesting the station's statewide reach. WHI IMAGE ID 23505

In January 1922, the University of Wisconsin changed the station's call letters to WHA; the same month, WHA covered the UW's farmers' course in agriculture, the annual educational program that attracted thousands of farmers from around the state interested in new agricultural ideas. Farmers who were unable to attend but who had radios and could receive the radio programs in their communities could benefit from the opportunity as well.[2]

Regular farm programs were an important part of WHA's broadcast mission by 1922, often featuring UW College of Agriculture professors and researchers along with topics related to home economics. In 1930, graduate student Kenneth Gapen became responsible for the noon farm show; he left for the USDA in 1935 and was replaced by Milton Bliss. In 1941, station officials conducted a survey and learned that regular listeners to the station's noon farm program, which also aired on affiliate stations, resided in sixty-five of the state's seventy-one counties. By this time state FM stations carried the noon program, which providing the expanded coverage. Maury White followed Bliss in the early 1950s and continued until 1968. Today the noontime show, now called Midday Report and hosted by Larry Meiller, has listeners in nearly all parts of Wisconsin plus Illinois, Iowa, Minnesota, and Michigan.[3]

NOTES

1. Randall Davidson, *9XM Talking: WHA Radio and the Wisconsin Idea* (Madison: University of Wisconsin Press, 2006), p. 16.

2. Ibid., p. 61.

3. Ibid., pp. 242–250.

The Wisconsin Farm Bureau Federation

As farming and rural life changed, farmers continued to seek ways to organize for their mutual benefit. By 1919, Wisconsin farmers were forming local farm bureaus based on a model begun in Broome County, New York, in 1911. In May 1920, several farmers from mainly southern Wisconsin counties met to discuss organizing a state farm bureau.[1] The same year, the American Farm Bureau Federation (AFBF) was formed, with some twenty-eight state farm bureau organizations as affiliates; Wisconsin affiliated with the national organization later that year.[2] As described in a history of the WFBF, the national organization "was unique in its makeup. It developed not in a mood of violent rebellion, as so many organizations had in the past, but in the spirit of self-help and mutual cooperation. . . . One of the first public pronouncements of the Wisconsin Farm Bureau showed its concern for better marketing systems, and at the same time, its dislike for radical methods."[3] For instance, when farmers considered a wheat strike to improve prices in 1920, the WFBF executive board on stated:

The Wisconsin Farm Bureau Federation does not endorse "strikes" as a means of controlling the price of farm products; however, we do insist that if our farmers are to continue producing farm products they must receive a margin over the cost of production. Also we believe that every farmer has and should have the right to sell his products at such time as market demands insure a reasonable price. . . . It would be good business policy for farmers to discontinue heavy marketing and allow the market to adjust itself.[4]

Along with efforts to improve agricultural markets and pricing, the WFBF worked to improve rural living conditions through such initiatives as advocating for electricity on the farm. The organization also held social events to bring farmers together. For instance, in 1926, the WFBF's annual meeting featured a horse-pulling contest and a farm family banquet.[5]

dairy industry. Flour mills became gristmills, modified to grind oats and corn for dairy cattle feed. Entrepreneurs opened feed and seed stores where farmers could purchase oats, corn, alfalfa, clover, timothy, and other seeds. They also sold the supplemental feeds, such as linseed oil meal, peanut oil meal, and soybean oil meal, that some farmers used to increase the protein content of their cattle feed.

Implement dealerships opened, selling farmers everything from manure spreaders to hay loaders, hay mowers to corn cultivators—all of them at first pulled by horses, and all necessary to provide the feed that dairy cattle required. Blacksmith shops, initially busy with shoeing horses, now added the business of sharpening sickle bars for mowers and grain binders and pounding out plowshares.

The Wisconsin Farm Bureau Federation

From the WFBF's earliest days, women played an important role in its activities. At the Wisconsin Farm Bureau's 1938 annual meeting, women members achieved a goal they had worked for since the early days of organization: the creation of the Associated Farm Bureau Women. In 1946, the Associated Farm Bureau Women gained a seat on the parent organization's resolutions committee, earning an even stronger voice in the WFBF.[6]

In 1948, the WFBF created the Farm Bureau Young People Program, "dedicated to teaching rural youth better farming methods, citizenship and leadership."[7] The Wisconsin Farm Bureau Federation also spawned other affiliate organizations, including the Farm Bureau Mutual Casualty Insurance Company, Wisconsin Cooperative Farm Supply, Badger Livestock Sales, Inc., and Midwest Livestock Producers.

The Wisconsin Farm Bureau has long supported educational activities. An extremely popular program is Ag in the Classroom, launched in 1985. This program provides educational tool kits to teachers with the intent of helping young people understand farm life and where their food originates.

Today the Wisconsin Farm Bureau Federation comprises sixty-one county farm bureaus and calls forty-two thousand farmers members, making it "Wisconsin's largest general farm organization representing farms of all sizes, commodities and management styles."[8]

NOTES

1. "Wisconsin Farm Bureau Turns 90," Wisconsin Farm Bureau Federation, news release, May 27, 2010.

2. *Seventy-Five Years of Farm Bureau in Wisconsin* (Madison: Wisconsin Farm Bureau Federation, 1994), p. 74.

3. "Wisconsin Farm Bureau Turns 90."

4. *Seventy-Five Years of Farm Bureau in Wisconsin*, p. 14.

5. Ibid., p. 17.

6. Ibid., pp. 25–26.

7. Ibid., p. 34.

8. "About WFBF," Wisconsin Farm Bureau Federation, http://wfbf.com/aboutwfbf.

Where horse dealers had been common for many years, now cow dealers appeared, buying and selling dairy cattle. More veterinarians opened offices, and those already in rural communities and previously known as horse doctors now had to expand their expertise to treating dairy cattle. Lumberyards added products as farmers built dairy barns or enlarged their horse and wheat barns to accommodate dairy cattle.

Rural communities emerged, connecting the farms with the nearby villages. Each depended on the other. The farmers needed the supplies and the marketplace found in the villages, and the village businesses relied on the farmers for much of their business. This would continue to be the structure of most of Wisconsin's rural communities until after World War II, when dramatic changes would again occur.

Farmers delivered milk to a cheese factory near Boaz, Richland County.

WHI IMAGE ID 84114

DIVERSIFICATION ENDURES

Even though dairy farming had become the major economic endeavor for the majority of Wisconsin's farmers by the early 1900s, most of them also continued diversified farming. This meant that many farmers, in addition to their dairy cows, raised hogs—sometimes as many as a hundred—to take to market. They had a poultry flock, selling eggs and broilers off the farm. Some raised a few head of beef cattle. In addition to the crops grown to feed their dairy herd, many farmers continued to grow cash crops—potatoes, strawberries, cucumbers, green beans, and tobacco—in small acreages and in areas of the state where these crops grew well. A few farmers whose hay crop yielded more than they needed for their dairy animals sold the excess off the farm.

Most dairy herds were small at this time, some fewer than twenty milk cows. Farmers had little or no control over the prices they received for their product, so they kept another enterprise or two from which they could earn money when milk prices were low, illness struck the herd, or some other unforeseen problem reduced their dairy business income. Some of these ventures provided supplemental income to dairy farming; others became major agricultural pursuits in their own right.

PART IV

BEYOND THE
MILK PAIL

A butcher shop in Palmyra (Jefferson County), photographed around 1910, offered its customers a variety of fresh meats.

WHI IMAGE ID 9351

11

LIVESTOCK AND MEAT PROCESSING

Many of Wisconsin's early settlers processed their own meat from animals that they raised. Most farmers, even those who concentrated on growing wheat, raised a few hogs for home consumption, butchering a hog or two in the fall, smoking the hams and bacon, and salting other cuts. In addition, some made sausage and canned some of the meat. Town and city dwellers, meanwhile, depended on local butcher shops to provide them with fresh and processed meats.[1]

As diversified farming took hold, farmers began looking to livestock as a potential source of income. In Milwaukee—largely settled by Germans, who brought with them a heritage of sausage making and buying—a commercial meatpacking industry emerged as early as the mid-1840s. John Plankinton came to Milwaukee from Delaware in 1844; in 1850, he began packing hog and beef products at a company he formed with partner Frederick Layton.[2] Up to that time, for the most part farmers had delivered live animals to local butchers who processed the meat and sold it fresh to customers.[3]

With Milwaukee's population growing rapidly from 1840 (population 1,712) to 1860 (45,246), the demand for meat products increased dramatically. Plankinton and Layton recognized the needs for centralized meat processing and a centralized shipping area where hogs, calves, cattle, and sheep could be gathered and then moved to packing plants in the city. Their encouragement and the support of the city of Milwaukee resulted in the construction of the first Milwaukee stockyards in 1869. Layton and Plankinton's partnership dissolved in 1861; in 1864 Plankinton went into business with Philip D. Armour, who had arrived in Milwaukee in 1859.[4]

Cattle pens and water tanks at the stockyards in Milwaukee, date unknown
WHI IMAGE ID 47526

The Civil War had a considerable influence on meatpacking, especially for pork products. Pork was a staple for the Union Army, and John Plankinton was ready to meet the army's needs. (He also refused to sell pork to the seceded states of the South.) In 1860, 51,000 hogs were butchered and packed in Milwaukee. In 1862, that number soared to 182,465.[5]

The refrigerated railcar, introduced in 1879, had a dramatic influence on the expansion of the meatpacking industry as well. Now fresh meat could be shipped long distances and processing could take place all year long rather than during only the winter months. By 1880, meatpacking in Milwaukee had become a major industry. Together the city's seven packing plants packed enough pork to make Milwaukee the country's fourth-largest meatpacker. In 1881, Plankinton and Armour employed seven hundred people and were slaughtering hogs at the rate of four thousand a day.[6] In its advertisements, the Plankinton Company claimed to use everything from the hog except the squeal. The intestines were used for sausage casings, the blood and bone for fertilizer, the fat for lard, the bristles for paintbrushes, the feet for glue, and the skin for leather.[7]

Patrick Cudahy was another giant in the Milwaukee meatpacking industry. Cudahy immigrated there with his family from Ireland in 1849, and by 1874, at the age of twenty-five, he was a superintendent at Plankinton and Armour. When Armour left the company in 1884, Cudahy became a junior partner; and Plankinton, upon his retirement in 1888, passed the business on to Patrick and John Cudahy. The Cudahys, calling the new business Cudahy Brothers, moved their operation to a fifteen-acre site two miles south of the Milwaukee city limits in 1893. Their new facility allowed them to handle up to seven thousand hogs and five hundred cattle a day.[8]

The number of hogs on Wisconsin farms increased from 512,778 in 1870 to 1.8 million in 1910.[9] The number of beef cattle and calves in the state rose from about 770,000 in 1870 to 1.85 million in 1900 and 3.0 million in 1925.[10]

The Milwaukee meat processing industry continued to grow at the turn of the twentieth century. During the winter of 1897–98, more than one million hogs were butchered at Milwaukee plants. As the dairy industry expanded, so did the market for veal calves. And when dairy cattle outlived their usefulness to produce milk, they were processed into meat for sausage and hamburger. The calf market expanded from 34,022 head in 1891 to 77,993 in 1907.[11]

In 1893, William Plankinton, son of John Plankinton, organized the Plankinton Packing Company on the site the Cudahy brothers vacated when they moved south of Milwaukee.[12] The new Plankinton firm became a major meat processor.

In 1918–19, meatpacking was the second most important industry in Milwaukee's economy (bringing in $68.2 million), after the top-ranking iron, steel, and heavy machinery sector ($155.7 million). (Leather products were number three,

Plankinton Packing Company's letterhead boasted of the company's Globe brand of hams, bacon, and lard.
WHI IMAGE ID 87755

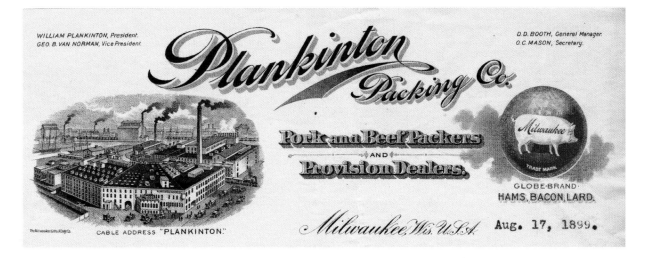

Wisconsin's Favorite Packers

Wisconsin's beloved Green Bay Packers football team has its roots in the meatpacking industry. In 1919, Earl "Curly" Lambeau became ill with tonsillitis while back home in Green Bay during his winter break from Notre Dame University. When he had recovered, he had missed too much of the semester to return to Notre Dame, and he began working for the Indian Packing Company in Green Bay. Lambeau had played high school football in Green Bay and spent a season in the Fighting Irish's backfield under Coach Knute Rockne, and he wanted to get back on the field. He contacted his old friend George Calhoun, sports editor of the *Green Bay Press Gazette,* to help put together a group of local boys interested in playing football.

Lambeau estimated he needed five hundred dollars to equip the team with football jerseys, shoulder pads, and a dozen footballs, and he went to his employer to ask for the money. His boss, George Peck, agreed; his only request was that the company name appear on the uniforms.

Writer Calhoun referred to the new team by the name "Packers" in a *Press Gazette* article on August 14, 1919. In 1920, the Acme Packing Company bought the Indian Packing Company, but the team sponsorship continued. Green Bay's National Football League team has remained the Packers ever since.

NOTES

William Povletich, *Green Bay Packers: Trials, Triumphs, and Tradition* (Madison: Wisconsin Historical Society Press, 2012), pp. 4–7.

at $45 million, and the brewing industry was number four, at $35 million.) Between 1895 and 1905, five large packing plants were located on Milwaukee's Muskego Avenue: Bodden Packing Company, Fred Gross and Brothers Company, R. Gumz and Company, Plankinton Packing Company, and the Layton Company.[13]

The Peck Packing Company in Milwaukee was primarily a beef slaughterer. Milton Peck was born in Milwaukee in 1904; his family had come from Czechoslovakia in the 1800s. During World War II, Peck leased his plant to the National Tea Company and worked for them as an employee. In 1951, he purchased the Ideal Packing Company and became one of the first meatpackers to specialize in the slaughter and boning of cows and bulls, most of which came from Wisconsin's dairy farms. The Peck Packing Company grew to eight hundred employees.[14]

Meat processors existed outside Milwaukee. One of the largest of those was Oscar Mayer. Oscar F. Mayer immigrated to Chicago from Bavaria in 1873 at age fourteen. He worked for a time in the stockyards of Armour & Company and for retail meat operations in Chicago. By 1880, Oscar F. knew the meat industry well

Oscar Mayer employees making sausage during World War II
WHI IMAGE ID 34557

Oscar Mayer's Weinermobile, circa 1950
WHI IMAGE ID 84447

Storied Sausage Makers

In addition to its long history as a leading meat processor, Wisconsin has from its earliest days been in the sausage-making business. This can be attributed in part to the state's large German population, many of whom brought with them a love of bratwurst and other sausages. Three of the best-known names in sausage are still going strong today.

USINGER'S

As legend has it, Fred Usinger came to Milwaukee from Germany with four hundred dollars in one pocket and the other pocket full of his favorite sausage recipes, which he had accumulated while working as an apprentice to a sausage maker in Frankfurt. In Milwaukee he worked for a widow who operated a small butcher shop on Third Street. Eventually Usinger bought out the widow's business, married her niece, and established a worldwide reputation for his sausages. In the early days, Usinger's biggest business was Milwaukee saloonkeepers, whose customers looked forward to the shop's quality free lunches.[1]

Fred Usinger died in 1930, but his legacy lives on, and the fourth generation of Usingers operate the company, still on its original Third Street site and with additional production and distribution facilities.[2]

JONES DAIRY FARM

The Jones family moved to Wisconsin from Vermont in 1838 and settled in Fort Atkinson, where they grew grain, milked dairy cows, and raised some livestock. In 1889, at age thirty-five, Milo Jones was crippled by rheumatoid arthritis, thereafter spending his days in a wheelchair. It was

Jones Dairy Farm's letterhead depicted the iconic farmhouse where family members still live. WHI IMAGE ID 91602

and wanted to start his own business. He wrote to his brother, Gottfried, in Bavaria and asked him to join him. Gottfried had been learning the sausage-making business in his home country. A third brother, Max, also joined in the venture. By the turn of the century, the Mayer brothers had forty employees, with salesmen delivering their products to every part of Chicago, and by 1918 the company's annual sales had grown to $11 million.[15]

Oscar G. Mayer, son of Oscar F., graduated from Harvard in 1909 and joined the business. While visiting relatives in Madison in 1919, Oscar G. learned of a bankrupt farmer's cooperative meatpacking plant that was for sale. He suggested his father purchase the plant as a source of slaughtered animals that they could process. In 1919,

Storied Sausage Makers

then, according to family lore, that Milo decided to use his mother's recipe to make pork sausage. Instead of using the typical pork trimmings, he used choice cuts of pork such as hams, loins, and shoulders. Milo quickly learned the power of advertising and began placing ads for his sausage in national magazines. Jones Dairy Farm celebrated its 125th anniversary in 2014.[3]

KLEMENT'S

Klement's was founded by John, George, and Ronald Klement in 1956. The brothers purchased Badger Sausage on the south side of Milwaukee and in 1961 changed the name to Klement's. At first they made primarily bratwurst, Italian sausage, and Polish sausage. By 2012, Klement's was making one hundred varieties of sausage for delicatessens, food service, and snacks.[4]

One of the company's most popular marketing strategies involves "live" sausages racing along the warning track before the seventh inning at Brewers baseball games in Milwaukee. The races began as

virtual races in the early 1990s, taking place on the Brewers' scoreboard. In 2000, actual sausages—that is, people dressed as sausages—began running the race. Today the racing sausages include bratwurst, Polish sausage, Italian sausage, hot dog, and chorizo.[5]

NOTES

1. "About Usinger's," Usinger's Sausage, www.usinger.com/about-usinger.

2. Ibid.

3. "Our History," Jones Dairy Farm, www.jonesdairyfarm.com/aboutus/story.aspx; and "Milo C. Jones," Wisconsin Meat Industry Hall of Fame, www.ansci.wisc.edu/Meat_HOF/index.htm.

4. "John, George, and Ronald Klement," Wisconsin Meat Industry Hall of Fame, www.ansci.wisc.edu/Meat_HOF/index.htm.

5. "Famous Racing Sausages," Klement's, www.klements.com/racing-sausages.

the company's name became Oscar Mayer & Company. Oscar G. Mayer was named company president in 1928, by which time company headquarters were in Madison.[16]

Adept at marketing, the Oscar Mayer company would introduce packaged sliced bacon in 1924 and the Weinermobile—a wiener-shaped vehicle that toured the country promoting Oscar Mayer products—in 1936.[17]

THE UW'S CONTRIBUTIONS TO MEATPACKING

A meat science and muscle biology program, a part of the College of Agricultural and Life Sciences at the University of Wisconsin–Madison, began in 1927. Gustav Bohstedt,

Wisconsin Association of Meat Processors (WAMP)

The American Association of Meat Processors has its roots in a number of earlier food-packing trade groups. The Wisconsin affiliate, the WAMP, formed in 1939. Today the WAMP works "for the benefit and protection of small and medium sized meat firms" throughout the state.[1]

The WAMP is one of the largest associations of its type in the United Sates. At its annual convention, meat processors from around the state enter their products for judging. This annual meeting has become the largest state-processed meat competition in the United States.[2]

NOTES

1. Wisconsin Association of Meat Processors, www.wi-amp.com/; www.aamp.com/about-aamp/aamp-history.

2. Personal correspondence from Robert Kauffman, September 20, 2012.

chairman of the animal and dairy husbandry department in 1930, saw the need for a meats laboratory on campus where experimental livestock could be slaughtered. The laboratory was built near the Stock Pavilion on the agriculture campus. Robert Bray joined the Department of Animal Husbandry in 1941 and developed three meats courses. After military service, Bray completed a PhD in 1949, the first meat-related doctorate awarded at the UW–Madison.[18]

Bray's and his colleagues' research involved solving the problem of PSE (pale, soft exudative) in pork. Bray's research team became international leaders for their work on meat quality problems, making notable contributions to the meat-processing industry.[19]

12

CRANBERRIES

Cranberries are native to Wisconsin and were well known to Indians long before the first Europeans arrived in the state. They grew abundantly in marshy areas, especially in what would later be Wood and Waushara Counties. Native American people ate cranberries fresh; they ground them, mixed them with cornmeal, and baked the mixture into bread; and they mixed dried cranberries with wild game to create pemmican. They sometimes softened the berries' tart bite with maple sugar or honey.[1]

Cranberries grow in sandy bogs and marshes. Wisconsin growers flood the marshes to assist with harvest.

ANDY MANIS/WISCONSIN STATE CRANBERRY GROWERS ASSOCIATION

Wisconsin's first people also discovered cranberries' medicinal qualities. Some believed eating cranberries calmed the nerves or used cranberry poultices to draw poison from wounds. They also used the juice of cranberries to dye blankets and rugs an attractive red. Indians traded or sold the wild berries to white settlers, and it is thought that the early Dutch or German settlers called the fruit "craneberries" because the cranberry stem and blossom resemble the neck, head, and beak of a crane. It's also possible the name reflected the birds' appetite for the bright red berries.[2]

The first commercial cranberry production in the United States is attributed to Henry Hall, a Revolutionary War veteran who lived on Cape Cod in Massachusetts. In 1816, Hall transplanted cranberry vines to land behind his home that had been drained and sanded. He fenced the area to protect it from his cows. By 1820, Hall was shipping cranberries to Boston and New York City. Soon, others, seeing the success of Hall's operation, also planted cranberry beds. By 1835, New Jersey recorded commercial cranberry growers, followed by Wisconsin in the 1860s and Oregon and Washington in the late 1800s.[3]

Cranberry growing expanded rapidly after Benjamin Eastwood published *A Complete Manual for the Cultivation of the Cranberry, With a Description of the Best Varieties* in 1857.[4] During the Civil War, demand for cranberries boosted prices and further encouraged commercial production.

Early settlers in Wisconsin who lived within easy traveling distance of a wild cranberry bog picked cranberries for their own use long before anyone grew them commercially in the region. What is believed to be the first sale of cranberries in Wisconsin took place in 1829, seven years before Wisconsin Territory was formed, when Green Bay trader Daniel Whitney recorded in his journal that he bought three canoe loads of cranberries harvested by Indians near Cranmoor (near present-day Wisconsin Rapids).[5]

But it is cranberry grower Edward Sacket of Sackets Harbor, New York, and later Chicago, who is credited with starting the first commercial cranberry operation in Wisconsin. Around 1860, Sacket purchased seven hundred acres of bog land covered with cranberry vines north of Berlin, Waushara County. Sacket cleared away brush and debris, dug ditches, built dams and a warehouse, and created a substantial operation. By 1865, he was producing 938 barrels and selling them for around $15 a barrel. Just four years later, a Sacket son earned $70,000 from the family's cranberry crop.[6]

Noting the Sackets' success, the nearby Carey brothers ditched and diked their land near Auroraville, north of Berlin, and sold a thousand barrels of cranberries in their first year of operation. In 1872, their peak production year, they sold ten thousand barrels.[7]

The cranberry boom led to urgent pleas for pickers.
WHI IMAGE ID 45749

WANTED! WANTED!

200 Cranberry Pickers. 200
75cts. per bushel, 75cts.

25 MEN to work by the day.—Besides 35 first class Rakers,
For whom we are building a Hall for their special purpose,

At HITCHCOCK on SEPTEMBER 1st, 1884.
We will pay as much as others do for the same kind of work. We will try to make our patrons as comfortable as we can

A special train will leave Tomah on Sept. 1st at 10 a. m., for Hitchcock.—Fare Reduced to 40cts.

Free Ball in the evening.—Day laborers had better bring blankets.—Boarding house accommodations for all who may desire board. Respectfully,
Wisconsin Cranberry Co.

Others quickly got into the business, creating a cranberry boom in Waushara County. Land once thought worthless had become extremely valuable. By 1875, the Careys and Sackets each grew three hundred acres of cranberries. Other growers in the Berlin area included J. D. Waters, Ruddock Mason and Company, and J. D. Williams. That year, cultivated cranberry acreage in the state totaled about one thousand, with a harvest of about a hundred bushels per acre.[8]

Wild cranberries grew in abundance in Jackson, Juneau, Monroe, and Wood Counties and were extensively harvested there by the middle 1860s—but not cultivated, as they were in Waushara County, until the 1870s. The first cultivated cranberries in the Wisconsin River valley were planted in 1871 on a marsh near present-day Cranmoor in Wood County.[9]

Cranberry growing was well established in the Cranmoor area by 1875. With the arrival of the Wisconsin Valley Railroad to the region in 1873, transportation in that part of the state improved greatly. Marsh owners dug miles of drainage ditches and constructed dams that allowed them to control water levels in the cranberry marshes. Workers constructed the dams, sometimes miles in length, of sand and peat.[10] Before this, some growers staved off the effects of frost—not at all uncommon in the north in early autumn, before the cranberries were ready for harvest—by burning smudge pots to create clouds of black smoke that drifted across the bogs,

Wisconsin State Cranberry Growers Association (WSCGA)

First organized on February 8, 1887, in Tomah, Monroe County, the twenty-member WSCGA voted at its first annual convention that year to adopt "the scale of prices for rakers at $1 per day." New members paid fifty cents to join.[1]

In 2012, the WSCGA had 250 members, many of them fourth- and fifth-generation cranberry growers. One of the organization's goals is to "implement farming techniques that optimize cranberry production while reducing environmental impact at the same time. Across the industry growers are developing new, more efficient tech-

nology, implementing conservation strategies on marshes such as alternative energy production, and working with academic research leaders to produce the best berry possible."[2]

NOTES

1. "Wisconsin State Cranberry Growers Association History," Wisconsin Cranberry Discovery Center, http://content.wisconsinhistory.org/cdm/ref/collection/cran/id/5280.

2. "WSCGA Celebrates 125th Anniversary at Annual Ag Day in Madison," Wisconsin State Cranberry Growers Association, news release, February 8, 2012.

keeping air temperatures above freezing. Now, with the ability to control water levels, the growers could flood their bogs when there was danger of frost.

The area around the town now called Cranmoor, in Wood County, was especially well suited to cranberry growing, with its combination of marshes and uplands and abundance of water and sandy soil. The soil was also naturally acidic, which cranberry plants prefer.

By the early 1900s, the Berlin area was producing cranberries on a limited basis. However, a few miles to the west, Wood, Portage, Adams, and Juneau Counties had become major cranberry centers. Soon other counties, including Monroe, Jackson, Clark, and Eau Claire, developed cranberry bogs; a few years later, with cranberry production flourishing in the central and western counties, several northern Wisconsin counties got on the cranberry-growing bandwagon, including Vilas, Oneida, Lincoln, Price, and Sawyer.

THE HARVEST

Cranberry harvesting began in late August and continued into October. Cranberry growers hired local young people, and in some cases Native American families, to do the picking. In the early days, workers picked cranberries by hand in six-quart pails, which had become the standard picking container by the 1870s. Handpicking was slow and tedious, although when large numbers of young men and women were involved, it sometimes became a social affair, with pickers holding parties and other evening events.

Handpicking was expensive for the grower as well. A good cranberry picker could pick up to two bushels per day and received seventy-five cents a bushel, or $1.50 a day, for his or her efforts. In 1872, one Berlin cranberry marsh employed three thousand pickers. The same year, W. T. Cosgrain, chief engineer of the Sturgeon Bay and Lake Michigan Ship Canal, offered this advice to cranberry growers: "[W]hen the berries are ripe for gathering, flood the marsh until all the berries are floated and then loosen them from the vines with rakes."[11]

Cosgrain had given good advice, but few paid any attention to it, and handpicking continued until the turn of the century. Slowly the idea of raking took hold. At first growers raked the ripe berries from dry cranberry vines; later they flooded the bog before raking. Hand raking involved rakers lined up across a bog, each raker taking his swath as he followed the raker in front of him. By the early 1900s, the cranberry

Ho-Chunk and white townspeople picked cranberries by hand near Black River Falls, circa 1905.
WHI IMAGE ID 25044

Vernon Goldsworthy, Cranberry Grower in the North

Commercial cranberry growing in Wisconsin's northern counties followed the successes in central Wisconsin. Vernon Goldsworthy, who managed the Wisconsin Cranberry Sales company from 1933 to 1944 and did a brief stint managing a cherry cooperative, began to explore cranberry growing in the northern part of the state, especially in Oneida and Vilas Counties. Goldsworthy studied maps of northern Wisconsin, looking for land with the sandy soil, water supply, and access roads suitable for a cranberry operation. He had an eye for what was known then as wasteland, and he was able to purchase suitable property for $1.00 to $2.50 per acre. His example caught on. By 1958, twenty-seven growers operated in the Manitowish Waters area of Vilas County, and five more in Oneida County. That year, Goldsworthy had eighty-five acres of cranberry vines at Thunder Lake in the township of Three Lakes.[1]

In a 1959 interview with the *Milwaukee Sentinel,* Goldsworthy claimed the production per acre of cranberries in the Vilas-Oneida County area was the highest in the United States due to "ideal soil, water and weather conditions."[2]

Goldsworthy was also instrumental in starting Cranberry Products, Inc., a processing plant in Eagle River. The business produced canned fruits and fruit products; frozen fruit, juices, and vegetables; fresh and shelf-stable fruit; tropical fruit and melon purees; prepared soups and stews; snack foods; and desserts. The plant closed in 1990, and the business dissolved in 2012.[3]

In 2011, the Goldsworthy family operated marshes in Three Lakes, Clearwater Lake, and Tomahawk, with approximately two hundred acres of vines and about a thousand support acres. The company employed five year-round workers and hired twenty more employees during harvest time. In a good year the family harvests about two hundred barrels per acre (a barrel equals 100 pounds).[4]

NOTES

1. Clarence J. Hall, "From a Study of Inventory Maps There Came Wisconsin Cranberry Developments," *Cranberries: The National Cranberry Magazine,* May 1958, pp. 7–10.

2. "Jaunts with Jamie: Cranberries the Year Around," *Milwaukee Sentinel,* April 23, 1959.

3. "Cranberry Products, Inc.," Macrae's Blue Book, www.macraesbluebook.com/search/company.cfm ?company=552211.

4. Personal correspondence from Linda Goldsworthy, August 19, 2011, September 20, 2012, and October 28, 2014.

rakes, sometimes called scoops, had evolved from basketlike affairs to boxes with bow handles and metal tines.

Raking cranberries required a certain amount of skill. With one motion, the raker, who wore hip boots because the water in the flooded marsh was often knee-deep or deeper, swung his rake through the floating—but still attached—cranberries, lifting the rake at the end of the sweep so the berries gathered in back of the rake's scoop. Of course, all of this had to be done in concert with the man in front and the man in back of the raker. It was clearly a sign of a novice raker if someone couldn't keep up with the man raking alongside him or, worse, if he snagged his hip boot with his rake, allowing cold water to enter and provide a chilled, wet foot for the rest of the day. One could usually spot first-time rakers by the number of patches on their boots.[12]

FROM BOOM TO BUST TO BOOM

By the early 1880s, the Berlin-area cranberry boom was severely challenged. In 1881, heavy rains and flooding of the cranberry marshes resulted in reduced yields. More flooding in 1882 resulted in only half a crop. The flooding continued in 1883, resulting in the marshes being covered with water, causing the partially ripened berries to spoil. Add to the flooding an early September frost, and the crop was doomed, in many cases not worth harvesting at all.

Harvesting cranberries with a rake, circa 1884
WHI IMAGE ID 1874

Warrens Cranberry Festival

First held in 1973, the Warrens Cranberry Festival has become an international event, with attendance near 120,000. Warrens, population 359, is located north of Tomah in Monroe County, in the heart of cranberry country. Held each year in late September, the festival is both a cultural celebration and an educational event. Those in attendance can visit cranberry marshes and learn how cranberries are grown and harvested; watch a cranberry-themed parade; sample foods made with cranberries, from cranberry brats to chocolate-covered Craisins (dried cranberries); and compete in all sorts of contests, including a cranberry recipe competition.

The festival is a registered nonprofit organization. Since 1973 it has given more than $2 million in donations to communities in the area.

NOTES

Warrens Cranberry Festival, http://www.cranfest.com.

The bad times continued, and by 1894 cranberry production in the Berlin area dipped to three thousand barrels. In 1895, production picked up some, but by then the center of commercial cranberry growing was shifting west to Wood County.[13]

so smart to give...

so pleasant to receive

fresh

5 lb. CRANBERRY **GIFT BOX**

Luscious Indian Trail Cranberries . . . so easy to prepare . . . so bright and cheery on the table. A special treat with all meats, poultry, fish. Your hostess will appreciate this beautifully packaged gift.

Delivered Anywhere In the U. S.

$2⁹⁸

Wisconsin cranberry growers have marketed their product successfully for more than a hundred years. This gift box design is from about 1950.

WHI IMAGE ID 87037

After cranberry growing became established in Wood and several other central and northern Wisconsin counties, production entered a boom period, boosted when consumers discovered that cranberries and cranberry products could be enjoyed at times other than Thanksgiving and Christmas. The industry developed new products, including cranberry juice and dried cranberries. New marketing strategies cited the health benefits associated with eating cranberries, eventually creating an international market for the product.

Of the many crops tried after the demise of wheat in the late nineteenth century, most eventually failed to become an economic substitute for wheat. Cranberries are an exception. Production has continued to expand since the crop was first cultivated following the Civil War. And starting in 1994, Wisconsin has led the nation in cranberry production, outproducing longtime leader Massachusetts.[14]

According to the Wisconsin State Cranberry Growers Association, establishing a cranberry marsh costs between $25,000 and $30,000 per acre; additional costs to support a cranberry operation include equipment, buildings, and employees.
© ANDY MANIS/WISCONSIN STATE CRANBERRY GROWERS ASSOCIATION

Mrs. H. H. Wooledge's garden near Antigo in northern Wisconsin, circa 1895, boasted neat rows of strawberries and abundant pie plants (rhubarb).

WHI IMAGE ID 93425

VEGETABLE GROWING, CANNING, AND TRUCK FARMING

From the earliest settlement days, Wisconsin farmers grew home vegetable gardens, which provided families with fresh vegetables to eat throughout the growing season and more to be preserved for use during the winter months. When wheat farming began to fail, many farmers began growing vegetables commercially, either as a primary endeavor or for supplemental income. By 1920, Wisconsin's primary commercial vegetable crops were green peas and sweet corn, both of which were primarily sold to canning companies.[1]

VEGETABLE CANNING

Peas were a good fit for Wisconsin, as historian Fred Stare explained: "The early settlements from Milwaukee to Sturgeon Bay were largely colonized by people from Germany, Belgium, Holland, Luxemburg, Bohemia, Poland and a few other countries. . . . [and] most of these people were pea eating people, so it was quite natural that, as they cleared the land and planted crops, peas were included."[2] Excess peas during the pioneer days were sold as dry peas, as the methods for commercially growing and canning vegetables did not reach Wisconsin until after the Civil War.

A few decades earlier, in 1810, Englishman Peter Durand patented a container made of tin-coated metal, which became known as a can (the name coming from the word *canister*). The technology for processing and storing vegetables and other food

Migrant Workers

At one time Wisconsin's fruit and vegetable crops, from cucumbers to cherries to cranberries, required labor-intensive handpicking. At harvest time, there was never enough local labor available, so migrant workers were hired to help get the job done.

Some Native Americans relied on seasonal farm and orchard work, in particular harvesting cherries in Door County and cranberries in the north, for their incomes. In his memoir *Little Hawk and the Lone Wolf*, Menominee Indian Raymond Kaquatosh, who grew up in Keshena, recalled, "The people who owned the farms in the area would send out trucks to transport workers back and forth from the cherry orchards. When the trucks arrived in our town, we were ready. Off we'd go, headed for Sturgeon Bay. . . . We were given cards to be punched every time we turned in a full bucket of cherries. We earned three cents a bucket."[1]

Many of Wisconsin's migrant workers were of Hispanic origin, spending winters in south Texas and then following the harvest north. Some of the earliest migrants to Wisconsin arrived in the early 1900s to help harvest sugar beets. The number of migrant farmworkers in Wisconsin peaked at fifteen thousand in the 1950s. Some helped harvest cherries in Door County before moving to central Wisconsin to harvest cucumbers, many of them in the Wautoma area. The entire family, even the smallest children, worked in fields from dawn to dusk during the cucumber- and bean-picking season. Some of the migrants arrived as early as late June to help with the weeding of those crops, but the majority arrived in July and remained until September, when they returned to Texas.

Hispanic workers filled buckets with cherries in a Door County orchard, date unknown. WHI IMAGE ID 48938

In the 1940s and 1950s, the housing provided for migrants was often deplorable, usually former sheds and other farm buildings. They had neither electricity nor running water. For those who picked cucumbers, the income a family earned was one-half the value of the cucumbers they picked in a day; the other half went to the farmer who grew the cucumbers. From the 1950s through the 1970s, Wisconsin passed a series of laws to protect migrant workers from exploitation. A 1977 law regulated migrant housing, job contracts, and minimum wages. It also created the Governor's Migrant Labor Council, which made sure that the provisions of the 1977 law were followed.[2]

With mechanization such as mechanical bean and cucumber pickers and mechanized cherry harvesting, plus herbicides that eliminated the need for hand weeding, the number of migrant workers

Migrant Workers

in Wisconsin began declining. By the late 1960s, much migrant work shifted from working in the fields to working in vegetable-processing plants.

By the year 2000, the number of migrant fieldworkers in Wisconsin had declined to fewer than five thousand.[3] Although the number of migrant farmworkers has decreased dramatically and represents a small part of Wisconsin's economy, their contributions continue to be important, especially for those cucumber growers who continue to handpick their crops.

NOTES

1. Raymond C. Kaquatosh, *Little Hawk and the Lone Wolf: A Memoir* (Madison: Wisconsin Historical Society Press, 2014); p. 70.

2. Wisconsin Statutes, 1977, 103.90 to 103.97, http://docs .legis.wisconsin.gov/statutes/statutes/103/97.

3. "Wisconsin Land Use Megatrends," University of Wisconsin–Stevens Point, www.uwsp.edu/cnr-ap/clue/ Pages/publications-resources/LandUseMegatrends.aspx.

On September 15, 1966, thirty members of the independent labor union Obreros Unidos (United Workers), led by Jesus Salas, marched from Wautoma to Madison to petition lawmakers for better working conditions for migrant workers. These and other such efforts led to legislation that immeasurably improved conditions for migrant workers. WHI IMAGE ID 93386

Peas grew well even in the northern cutover region of the state, as seen at the Joseph Seipold farm three miles northeast of Antigo, 1895.
WHI IMAGE ID 93245

products in metal containers instead of glass developed quickly after that, and nine years later, William Underwood brought the innovation to the Americas and started the William Underwood Company in Boston.[3]

The owners of the Landreth Seed Company of Philadelphia were well aware of the pea-producing areas of eastern and northeastern Wisconsin, and they were also aware of the continuing failure of the wheat crop in the state in the years following the Civil War. The company sent young Albert Landreth to Manitowoc in the 1870s to supervise the growing of pea seeds there for shipment back East for use by its customers. Landreth believed that the rich soils of Manitowoc, Sheboygan, Door, and Kewaunee Counties would be well suited to growing peas. He also noted that peas grown in Wisconsin were of higher quality than those grown in the East and suggested they could be grown more economically on Wisconsin's relatively cheap land.[4]

In 1883, Landreth began experimenting with the canning of green peas in his mother-in-law's kitchen in a small hotel in Manitowoc. By 1887, he believed he'd learned enough to open a small commercial canning company; three years later he opened a second plant in Sheboygan. He printed "Lakeside" on his labels, and later the company became known as Lakeside Packing Company (today the corporation is known as Lakeside Foods, Inc.).[5]

In 1909, Lakeside Packing Company began contracting with farmers to grow crops for the cannery; before this the company had rented or leased land. Contracting with farmers gave the company better control over quality, as it paid a bonus to its farmers growing top-quality crops. By 1923, Lakeside was canning not only peas but green beans, tomatoes, cabbage, pumpkin, pickles, sauerkraut, and sweet corn.[6]

In 1890, grocer William Larsen of Green Bay opened a pea cannery.[7] In 1926, the Larsen Company introduced a mixed-vegetable variety. Its popular Veg-All product contained celery, string beans, peas, corn, lima beans, potatoes, carrots, okra, onion, and pimento, all in a single can.[8]

By 1900, twenty small canning plants operated in Wisconsin, many of them starting out as tomato and sweet corn canneries, with peas added later—if the company survived. In 1905, the Wisconsin Canners Association was formed to educate and advocate for its members. (Today the group has members in Minnesota and Illinois as well as Wisconsin and is called the Midwest Food Processors Association.)[9] By 1915, Wisconsin had ninety vegetable-processing plants, and by 1920 the state was packing half of the nation's crop of vegetables, with green peas first and most dominant.[10]

Governor Phil La Follette promoted Wisconsin peas at this display in 1938.

WHI IMAGE ID 45229

Cucumber Salting Stations

During the 1950s, cucumber salting stations sprang up around Wisconsin, particularly in the sandy soil regions where cucumbers thrive. A number of them were located in Waushara County, in Wautoma, Redgranite, and Wild Rose, but they were also established in other cucumber-growing regions of the state such as Waupaca and Oconto Counties.

Major food processing companies, such as H. J. Heinz, owned and operated these little salting stations. The station consisted of a small office, a large open area with a mechanical sorter, and ten or more wooden silolike tanks where the cucumbers were stored in salt and water. The sorting machine sorted the cucumbers by size—one through five, with grade one (gherkins) being the smallest and grade five the largest.

These salting stations took in fresh cucumbers every day and did not shut down until all the cucumbers received that day were sorted and dumped into the brine tanks. In midwinter, the company shipped the cucumbers to their processing plant (in the case of H. J. Heinz, they went to Pittsburgh), where they became slicers, dill pickles, relish, and whatever other cucumber products the company produced.

Fresh produce available for purchase from farm trucks at the Municipal Market on Madison's Capitol Square in 1918

WHI IMAGE ID 105946

TRUCK FARMING

Truck farming was an important part of the vegetable farming industry starting in the late 1800s and continuing to the mid–1940s. In truck farming, the vegetable farmer delivered fresh vegetables directly to customers, which usually meant grocery stores. A cluster of truck farms operated in southeastern Wisconsin, particularly in and around Racine and Kenosha Counties, from the early 1900s to the 1950s.

Urban dwellers, especially those living in the densely populated cities of Milwaukee, Kenosha, and Racine, were a ready market for fresh fruits and vegetables. The rich soils of southeastern Wisconsin, and a climate moderated somewhat by the waters of Lake Michigan, provided ideal growing conditions for vegetable crops such as potatoes, onions, carrots, tomatoes, sweet corn, peas, peppers, and lettuce and for the production of strawberries, raspberries, and apples. The truck farms operating in this area were also within easy driving distance of their market, which made the situation ideal for both producer and consumer.

Kramer Truck Farm

Vegetable farmer Jacob Kramer immigrated to Kenosha County from Germany in 1883, when he was twenty-two. He found work as a farmhand and soon became acquainted with the Frederick Bose family, who arrived in Wisconsin in the 1840s. The Boses were vegetable farmers as well. Jacob married Frederick's daughter Minnie, and the couple continued to grow vegetables on the Bose farm near the city of Racine, eventually becoming the owners.

By today's standards, the Kramer farm was small, only forty-two acres. The family grew three to four acres of fruits and vegetables, including strawberries, red and black raspberries, tomatoes, peas, peppers, green beans, potatoes, and sweet corn, all of which by the 1930s and 1940s they delivered to grocery stores in a 1932 International panel truck. They also grew a few acres of cabbage, which they delivered to the Halt-N-Buy Sauerkraut factory on Lathrop Avenue in Racine. They started the cabbage from seeds, set the little plants in the field with a horse-drawn mechanical cabbage planter, hoed the field by hand, cut the crop by hand, and filled mesh bags with cabbage heads for shipping.

Jacob Kramer discovered early that to keep his grocery store customers happy, he needed to provide vegetables that were fresh, but not too fresh. If the vegetables were fully ripe, they would not keep long in the store. So Kramer picked tomatoes when they were just beginning to turn red, which meant they would travel well and would remain fresh for several days in the stores.

(continued on next page)

The Kramer brothers loaded their wagon with tomatoes to be sold in Racine, circa 1915.

COURTESY OF ROBERT KRAMER

Kramer Truck Farm

(continued from page 155)

Vegetable sales provided about half of the family's income. Robert Kramer, grandson of the first Jacob Kramer, recalled, "We also milked three or four cows, had laying hens, ducks, geese, and a couple of pigs. My mother sold eggs and also sold butter that she made from our own cream." To provide feed for their livestock and poultry, the Kramers grew a few acres of corn and oats, as well as some hay and pasture crops. To earn extra money, young Bob Kramer worked for their neighbors, the Sylvester Piper family, who grew many acres of onions as a cash crop. He received twenty-five cents an hour for the backbreaking job of weeding onions.

According to Robert Kramer, the family did not use the "U-pick" approach popular today, even for their berry crops. "We did all the picking—we picked the rows of berries clean as they ripened and didn't only select the big berries," he remembered. The family also grew sugar beets on a contract basis. "We grew as many as three acres of sugar beets," Robert said. "At harvest time, the beets were dug, the tops removed, and the beets gathered into small piles throughout the field. Using big forks, we pitched the sugar beets onto a high-wheeled wagon, which we pulled to the nearby rail yard, where we loaded the beets onto open railroad gondola cars for shipment to a sugar beet factory in Illinois."

NOTES

Interview with Robert Kramer, December 21, 2011.

Beginning in the 1920s, Racine and Kenosha County farmers grew large amounts of cabbage for both the sauerkraut and the fresh vegetable markets. Growers also stored harvested cabbage and sold it during the winter months when other fresh vegetables were scarce. During the 1930s, a disease called cabbage yellows nearly wiped out the industry, but UW–Madison plant pathology researchers L. R. Jones and J. C. Walker saved the industry by developing yellows-resistant cabbage varieties.[11]

Not all truck farming took place in southeastern Wisconsin. John Williams and his family operated a truck farm in rural Montello, Marquette County, starting in 1925, and many others operated in locations around the state from the 1920s to after World War II. (For more on John Williams's farming operation, see page 172.) Truck farming allowed urbanites to purchase fresh foods and vegetables, especially during times when those were plentiful. It seems that people have always preferred fresh food to its processed counterpart.

14

IRRIGATION AND THE CENTRAL SANDS

W hile agriculture was progressing in much of southern and eastern Wisconsin, the sand counties of central Wisconsin—Portage, Waushara, Marquette, Adams, and Wood—were considered marginal at best (and declared worthless by some) for growing crops. Many of these sandy, flat soils of central Wisconsin were once covered by an enormous lake, formed when the last glacier receded ten thousand years ago. Jokes about the agricultural prospects of those counties abounded, such as, "Even the crows carry their lunches when they fly over."

When the last glacier receded, it created a large glacial lake that covered all of present-day Adams County and parts of surrounding counties (the blue area west of Waushara County on this map). When the glacier lake water drained, it left behind a vast flat, sandy plain. With irrigation, today this area is one of Wisconsin's important vegetable growing regions.

UW–MADISON DEPARTMENT OF GEOGRAPHY, CARTOGRAPHY LAB

Family members and hired help picked and ate potatoes in a sandy field in Waushara County, 1918.
WHI IMAGE ID 58415

(Cranberry growing in the region is an exception, but its cultivation has always been associated with a ready source of water, such as the Wisconsin River and other rivers in the region.)

Despite this, starting in the 1850s many farmers tried to make a living on the sand counties' poor and droughty soil. During years of ample rainfall, these pioneer farmers managed to eke out a living. Many discovered that potatoes grew well in sandy, acidic soils, especially when the rains came on time, and the sand counties were leading potato producers from World War I until the 1930s. During those years, potatoes were grown without irrigation, yet with ample rainfall the yields were more than respectable. Potatoes provided a good cash crop for the small dairy farms sprinkled throughout the area.

But as UW–Madison professor emeritus John Schoenemann, a noted vegetable crop researcher, explained, disaster struck central Wisconsin in the 1930s "with the three 'D's—potato diseases (mainly viruses), persistent drought, and the economic depression. Some veteran growers hung on, and some began experimenting with small-scale irrigation using methods available at the time."[1]

In the early 1930s, John Williams, a truck farmer near Montello, Marquette County, became one of the first vegetable growers to use irrigation extensively, watering his crops with water from nearby Buffalo Lake. Williams used the Skinner System, which consisted of a one-inch wrought-iron pipe fastened to wooden posts three or four feet high with nozzles every three feet apart. This irrigation pipe was permanently located in the fields for the entire growing season. During the 1930s and 1940s, University of Wisconsin horticulture professors grew experimental plots of vegetables and fruits on the Williams farm, because irrigation systems had not yet been developed on the College of Agriculture's farm.[2] (For more on John Williams's farming operation, see page 172.)

Hancock Experiment Station

The Hancock Agricultural Experiment Station of the University of Wisconsin–Madison's College of Agricultural and Life Sciences was an early leader in irrigation research studies. The station began operations in 1916, working primarily with dairy, pasture, and soil fertility studies and shelter belt plantings for wind erosion control. By 1934, the research station had expanded to 223 acres.

In the 1940s, under the direction of superintendent A. R. Alberts, researchers discovered that irrigation could increase vegetable yields by two, three, and even four times over what could be expected from nonirrigated crops.

Researchers at the Hancock Experiment Station study potatoes and potato storage. SEVIE KENYON/UW–MADISON CALS

Some of the earliest irrigation research at the Hancock station involved Russet Burbank potatoes. Led by John Schoenemann in the 1950s, this research resulted in successful growing of the Burbank potato, which commanded a higher price in the market compared to other potato varieties. The successful production of Burbank potatoes was a main reason that the area attracted several large-scale potato-processing plants in the late 1960s and 1970s, including American Potato Company (Potato Buds) and Ore-Ida (frozen products).

NOTES

Personal correspondence from John Schoenemann, April 4, 2012; and interview with John Schoenemann, October 1, 2012.

During World War II, the demand for aluminum in the manufacture of warplanes spurred enormous growth in the aluminum industry. After the war, new aluminum products came on the market, including lightweight portable irrigation piping. Farmers in the central sand counties knew that a huge supply of water rested but a few feet below the surface of old Glacial Lake Wisconsin, and potato growers—including Okray and Firkus of Stevens Point, Krogwald and Pavelski of Amherst, Wysocki of Custer, Perzinski of Arnott, and Burns of Almond—were some of the first to use irrigation with movable aluminum pipes.[3]

This early irrigation work required considerable manual labor, as irrigation pipes had to be carried from field to field. The task provided summer work for many students in the area. In the early years, growers used lakes, streams, rivers, pits, and a few well points punched into the ground as their water sources. By 1959, with government regulation and even prohibition of using these water sources, growers turned to using wells.[4] In the 1960s, a new system of well digging called reverse hydraulic, developed in Nebraska, was introduced to central Wisconsin. These wells, some sixty to a hundred feet deep, included a twelve-inch pipe casing and were capable of producing one thousand gallons of water per minute. The wells were also relatively easy to install,

Big irrigation systems are a common sight in the central sands region of Wisconsin.

SEVIE KENYON/UW–MADISON CALS

usually taking but a day to put in place. Gasoline and diesel engines powered the early irrigation pumps. Soon electric motors ran the pumps; today many of those are as large as 100 horsepower or larger.

Snap beans joined potatoes as an important irrigated crop in the central sands. Up until the mid-1960s, snap beans had to be handpicked, but in 1964 the development of a mechanical harvester for snap beans by the Chisholm-Ryder Company of New York state made large-scale production of snap beans possible.[5] Professor Warren Gabelman of the UW–Madison Horticulture Department researched how to create the largest concentration of bean pods at one time so the crop could be harvested with a machine that passed over the field just once. Gabelman's research involved manipulating irrigation levels and nitrogen fertilization patterns to accomplish this with existing snap bean varieties.[6] Later, peas and sweet corn were added to the list of large-scale irrigated crops grown in the area.

In the late 1950s, the Valley Irrigation Company of Gering, Nebraska, introduced the "center pivot" or circle system of irrigation, with a well in the center of 40 acres

Irrigation Controversies

From 1963 to 1983, the amount of irrigated land in Wisconsin's central sands counties increased sevenfold to about 133,000 acres. The corresponding vegetable yield increases were dramatic. For example, Russet Burbank potatoes grown without irrigation might yield 100–200 hundredweight per acre, but with irrigation the yield could be bumped up to 500 hundredweight per acre.[1]

By 2012, irrigation systems were computer controlled to the extent that an operator could turn off, turn on, and control the application of water from a central location. Vegetable processors, especially those growing snap beans, peas, and sweet corn, welcomed the advantage of scheduling planting and harvesting times so the processing plants could have a constant flow of product at harvest time.

With ever-more advanced irrigation techniques, new vegetable varieties, and modern-day cropping practices, Wisconsin became the leading state for snap beans grown for processing. Today the state competes with Oregon for third place in the production of potatoes.[2]

Yet the increased use of irrigation in the central sands is not without controversy. The effect of drawing ever more water from the aquifer and the ultimate effect on groundwater levels is a topic of continued research. It remains an open question whether and at what point irrigation will cause permanent injury to the aquifer, and whether further development of well drilling should be curtailed.

NOTES

1. Donald Last, "Potential versus Actual Development of Irrigated Agriculture in Central Wisconsin," *Transactions of the Wisconsin Academy of Sciences, Arts and Letters* 71, pt. 2 (1983): 51.

2. Personal correspondence from John Schoenemann, April 4, 2012.

(later 160 acres). A water-powered drive system propelled the irrigation unit in a circle in the early years; later, electric motors located at each tower moved the system around the field.[7]

With ongoing innovation and experimentation in irrigation, Wisconsin farmers continued to believe that that the central sands could become a major crop producing region. And they were right. In 1922, Wisconsin had its highest-ever potato acreage, at 325,000, much of that coming from the central counties. Yields were about 50 hundredweight per acre, so the total state production that year was approximately 26.3 million hundredweight. By 2012, thanks to irrigation, improved varieties, and excellent management, potato yields soared to 455 hundredweight per acre, for a total production of 28.67 million hundredweight that year, enough to place Wisconsin at number three in the nation, behind Idaho and Washington.[8]

The University of Wisconsin–Extension calls its Peninsular Research Station in Door County "a field laboratory for fruit specialists." Researchers there focus on the production and management of a variety of fruit crops, including cherries.

SEVIE KENYON/UW-MADISON CALS

15

FRUITS FROM FIELDS AND ORCHARDS

W hen the early pioneers arrived in Wisconsin, they found a variety of fruits growing wild and available for the picking. Famed naturalist John Muir arrived from Scotland with his family in 1849, when Muir was eleven years old. In his memoir, Muir wrote about the land around their Marquette County farm: "Early in summer we feasted on strawberries that grew in rich beds beneath the meadow grasses and sedges as well as in the dry sunny woods. And in the different bogs and marshes, and around their borders on our own farm and along the Fox River, we found dew berries and cranberries and a glorious profusion of huckleberries."[1]

Wisconsin's climate, with its warm summers and cold winters, and the influences of Lakes Michigan and Superior on adjacent counties encouraged the growing of fruit, first for personal consumption and later for sale.

APPLES

Apples are native to Wisconsin. And over time some of these native apple trees became favorites among settlers, such as the Wolf River variety that was discovered growing as a seedling along the Wolf River near Fremont in 1875.[2]

But many early settlers in Wisconsin, especially those who came from New York and New England, brought with them apple seeds and seedlings of varieties that they had grown in their home states. Many of them became wheat farmers but at the same time tended small orchards, mainly for their own use. Eventually some of those apple growers tried to develop commercial operations, but they did not yet

The Joseph Zettel family grew an apple variety known as Duchess of Oldenburg at their orchard near Sturgeon Bay, circa 1895.
WHI IMAGE ID 93352

realize that their eastern apple varieties would not survive Wisconsin's harsh winters. Discouraged with the results of their efforts, some decided that by organizing they might be able to share what they were learning about hardy varieties that did better in the Midwestern climate.

On October 27, 1851, area horticulturists were invited to a meeting at the Merchants' Insurance Company in Milwaukee to discuss organizing the Wisconsin State Horticultural Society. The group's stated purpose was to "encourage the growth and culture of fruit and ornamental trees, flowers, and vegetables, and to disseminate useful information in reference thereto."[3] Besides planning exhibitions, the WHS collected periodicals about fruits, trees, and vegetables from nursery catalogs and shared excerpts from them with members. Two years later, the Wisconsin Fruit

Growers organization formed, with the specific goal of developing hardier apple varieties that could flourish in Wisconsin.[4]

By the 1870s, commercial apple production in Wisconsin had not improved as growers had hoped. Many gave up, declaring that Wisconsin could not become a commercial apple-producing state because of its long, cold winters. This conclusion proved premature, however. Farm orchards continued to expand during the 1890s, and in 1900 Wisconsin farmers grew 40,905 acres of apple orchards with 1.3 million bearing trees. By that time, specific apple-growing areas could be identified in the state: the Gays Mills district in Crawford County, the Bayfield area in Bayfield County, and southern Door County.[5]

As Wisconsin State Horticultural Society secretary Frederick Cranefield said in 1910, "Except among the comparatively few who are engaged in raising fruit for market, the erroneous notion prevails that conditions in Wisconsin are not well suited to this business."[6] Cranefield explained that many apple orchards failed because growers were continuing to rely on varieties from their home states that simply were not suited to Wisconsin's conditions. He concluded, "Dairying and stock raising have been the dominant industries in Wisconsin, but fruit raising will soon rank with these in importance if not in extent."[7]

Others agreed with Cranefield's assessment. At the 1909 annual convention of the Wisconsin Horticultural Society, University of Wisconsin horticultural professor E. P. Sandsten said, "I am convinced not only from our own experience at the Experiment Station, but from actual observations all over the state, that commercial orcharding can be made as profitable and safe an occupation in Wisconsin as anywhere in the United States."[8]

Professor Sandsten suggested Wisconsin apple growers grow varieties more suited to Wisconsin's growing conditions, such as Duchess, Wealthy, Yellow Transparent, Patten's Greening, and McMahan. He also suggested "localities best adapted to the raising of apples on a commercial scale," including the counties of Sauk, Richland, Lafayette, Grant, Crawford, and Vernon; the lakeshore counties north of Milwaukee and all of Door County; Waupaca and Wood Counties in the center of the state; western Wisconsin counties Dunn, St. Croix, Pierce, and Pepin; the rolling hill country of Monroe, La Crosse, Trempealeau, Eau Claire, and Chippewa Counties; Bayfield County and Madeleine Island; Marathon, Shawano, Langlade, and Oconto Counties; and a strip three to five miles wide along the southern shore of Lake Superior from Superior to Ashland.[9] Looking at Professor Sandsten's list, it's easy to conclude that nearly all of Wisconsin appeared suited to

Apple Entrepreneur

Born in 1842, William Knight began his career by buying cutover land in the north and selling it to settlers intent on farming. Knight recognized the unique climate of the Bayfield Peninsula, insulated by the waters of Lake Superior, as a great place to grow apples. He began planting apple trees of various varieties, and by 1910 he owned and operated the largest orchard in Wisconsin. In the 1920s, Knight built an apple storage cellar from fieldstones picked from his own orchards.

Knight's early work as an apple grower provided the foundation for an apple industry that continues to strive in the Bayfield Peninsula today. A historical marker in Ashland commemorates his contributions to Wisconsin's apple-producing history.

Organic apples at Blue Vista Farm, Bayfield
TRAVELWISCONSIN.COM, COURTESY OF THE WISCONSIN DEPARTMENT OF TOURISM

NOTES

"Bayfield and Apples . . . a Fruitful Combination," Wisconsin Historical Markers, http://wisconsinhistoricalmarkers .blogspot.com/2013/06/bayfield-and-applesa-fruitful.html.

commercial apple growing. Yet Gays Mills, Door County, and Bayfield remained the primary producers.

By about 1910, Wisconsin's apple industry had become a thriving commercial enterprise, and the years 1910–16 saw the peak of commercial apple tree planting. But by the early 1920s, market prices were sagging, and during the Great Depression they reached an all-time low, forcing some growers to shut down.[10] Following the Depression and with the advent of World War II, the apple business rebounded from 492,000 bushels marketed in 1934 to 1,008,000 bushels in 1953.[11]

And yet, consumers continued to expect more from apple growers. Not only did they demand shiny apples that were attractively displayed and conveniently packaged, they also wanted new varieties.[12] Thus Wisconsin apple growers continued their efforts not only to produce high-quality apples of many varieties, but also to develop new marketing strategies, including roadside stands, farm markets, new packaging, and associated products such as apple cider and apple baked goods. In 2010, Wisconsin produced 37 million pounds of apples, ranking fifteenth in the nation in apple production.[13]

CHERRIES

While apples grow almost everywhere in Wisconsin, commercial cherry growing is centered in Door County, where the waters of Green Bay on the west and Lake Michigan on the east moderate the climate. As Hjalmar Holand wrote in his 1917 *History of Door County,* "Further south there is too little steady cold [in spring]; fruit trees burst quickly into bloom with the advent of warm days, and the tender growth succumbs to subsequent frost. In Door County, the buds come on very slowly. . . . During that time they strengthen and become hardy." Then, in the fall, "we have another effect of the waters which so modify the temperature that there is a long time when frosts are not severe enough to destroy the leaves, but allows them to do their work to the fullest extent, ripening the twigs, storing surplus food for spring use, hardening and perfecting the buds. Thus our climate helps at both ends of the season."[14] In addition, the peninsula's alkaline soil (with a pH from 6 to 7) is most conducive to cherry trees.

Arthur L. Hatch, a member of the state's board of agriculture (today known as the Department of Agriculture, Trade and Consumer Protection), and Emmet S. Goff, a University of Wisconsin horticulturist, saw the potential in 1896 for growing cherry trees in Door County. Hatch and Goff planted cherry trees north of the city

A family picked cherries in the town of Gibraltar on the Door Peninsula, 1919.

WHI IMAGE ID 93442

Seaquist Orchards

Jim Seaquist, co-owner and general manager of Seaquist Orchards, follows a long line of Seaquists growing cherries in Door County. It all began in the late 1800s, when Jim Seaquist's great-great-grandfather planted some seven hundred cherry trees north of Sturgeon Bay. In 1912, Jim's grandfather planted more cherry trees.

Jim's father, Dale, followed the path of his father and grandfather, getting his start in the cherry business in 1949, when his father told him he could have a piece of stony land to plant some cherry trees. Seaquist said, "I used my dad's tractor to pick stones with a heavy trailer; you could stop in one place and pick a load of stones. I must have picked a hundred loads of stones from this patch before I could plant trees. This is the third generation of trees on this ground. Topsoil is very thin in places."

The Door County cherry harvest season usually runs from the middle of July to the middle of August. The Seaquists grow several varieties of cherries, so they have fresh cherries available for an extended time. The majority are the Montmorency variety, mainly used in the baking industry; they also grow several varieties of sweet cherries, which they sell in their retail market, along with apples, apricots, and pears.

Dale Seaquist said, "In 2014, our orchards produced about 65 percent of the cherries in the state, and we process about 85 percent of all the cherries processed in Wisconsin."

In the early days cherries were picked by hand, often by migrant workers. Today the Seaquists' orchards are highly mechanized. Dale Seaquist described the harvest procedure:

About ten days ahead of harvest we spray the trees with a natural compound that ripens the juncture between the stem and the fruit. This helps the cherries shake loose more easily. Two machines work down a row of trees, one on each side. Each machine is an inclined plane. The one on the right is the catcher; the one on the left is the shaker. The shaker grabs the tree trunk and shakes off the fruit. An air blast blows some of the leaves away. The cherries are conveyed into a tank of water, which is on the

of Sturgeon Bay; by 1909, several large corporations, including the Sturgeon Bay Orchard and Nursery Company, were following their lead and planting hundreds of acres of cherries in the area. By 1917, over 3,200 acres of cherry trees had been planted. With an eye on expanding beyond the fresh market, in 1918 a group of growers organized the Fruit Growers and Canning Company.[15]

In 1919, Wisconsin produced 4,500 tons of cherries. The University of Wisconsin Peninsular Experiment Station north of Sturgeon Bay began operations in 1922 to help cherry growers solve disease and insect problems and develop new cultivars. By

Seaquist Orchards

second "catcher" machine. These machines do about three trees per minute. They are made in California and cost $180,000 for a pair. We have three pairs of these machines working in our orchards.

When the tank of harvested cherries is full, it is transported to other cold-water tanks on a truck. We have several trucks that are continually hauling cherries to the plant, where we flush cold water through them for four hours. This causes them to get real firm so the pits can be extracted. A tank holds about 1,100 pounds of cherries, and we put twelve tanks on a truck.

Cherries sold at our farm market are picked by hand. Cherries that are machine harvested eventually go into thirty-pound containers and are frozen.

Yields vary from orchard to orchard. One of the determinants of yield is how active bees are during pollination time. "We bring in a semi-load of bees for pollination," explained Seaquist. "We have

the bees here for about a month when the trees are in blossom."

Seaquist Orchards is a family operation run by Dale and his son Jim. Dale's wife, Kristin, manages the farm market, and Jim's wife, Robin, oversees the business office. Dale and son Zack manage equipment maintenance and fruit harvesting. Jim and his son Justin manage the processing plant. At Seaquist Orchards Farm Market near Sister Bay, the family sells everything from cherry jelly to cherry pies, along with apple products. The store is a popular tourist attraction and has received honors as one of the most outstanding farm markets in North America.

In 2012, the family built a new production facility, where Jim's son Cole and his wife, Lisa, manage the making of jellies and jams and other fruit products. This facility also houses a large press used for making cherry juice and apple cider.

NOTES

Author interviews with Dale Seaquist, August 11, 2011, and November 2, 2012; personal correspondence from Dale Seaquist, November 19, 2012; and www.seaquistorchards.com.

the 1920s, the cherry industry had expanded to over ten thousand acres. Finding labor to do the necessary harvesting became a challenge, and migrant workers helped solve this problem.[16] (For more on migrant workers, see page 150.)

Cherry production varies considerably from year to year, depending on weather conditions—a late frost can decimate the crop. As the *Ludington (Michigan) Daily News* reported on May 27, 1930, two days earlier a severe frost had destroyed an estimated 10 to 20 percent of Door County's cherry crop: "Veteran orchard men declared that this was the only dangerous frost at this time of year in their memory."[17]

A pick-your-own cherry operation in Door County, 1967

WHI IMAGE ID 83767

In 1941, Wisconsin cherry production reached 15,600 tons, but in 1943 it plummeted to 2,600 tons. In 1948, Wisconsin produced 25,000 tons of cherries, mainly tart varieties, the most popular being the Montmorency.[18]

For a variety of reasons, mostly economic but also involving disease and aging orchards, many commercial cherry growers quit growing cherries. In 2010, Wisconsin produced 5.7 million pounds of cherries (down from 10.9 million pounds in 2009—a decline due mainly to bad weather conditions). Wisconsin ranked fifth among the states in cherry production, with Michigan leading the way.[19]

Even though the success of cherry production, as with other farming enterprises, depends on the weather, cherries have a rich cultural history in Door County no matter the season's crop. Cherry blossoms and pick-your-own orchards draw thousands of tourists to the peninsula each year.

STRAWBERRIES

From the earliest settlement days to the present, strawberries have been a popular crop for Wisconsin home gardeners. Strawberry production, not as popular or successful as that for apples or cherries, continues with mostly "U-pick" operations in many parts of the state.

For many Wisconsinites, a U-pick strawberry adventure brings the entire family out to the patch. The Apps family had a small U-pick strawberry operation beginning in the late 1940s and continuing into the 1960s. The patch was only an acre, but on some days as many as ten or fifteen people arrived to pick the lush red berries. The patch was under the control of my mother, Eleanor, although she enlisted the help of my father and my brothers with weeding and with picking. We sold the berries to the Wild Rose Mercantile, and that money, along with the sales to the U-pick pickers, provided a bit of additional income for my mother.

A strawberry nursery near Black River Falls around the turn of the twentieth century
WHI IMAGE ID 94907

Williams Lake View Fruit Farms

John Williams graduated from the University of Wisconsin's farm short course in 1903. He worked for a time in California and Florida before returning to the home farm in Marquette County in 1909. At first he operated the place as a dairy farm, milking Guernsey cattle. Then, in 1925, he sold his cows and began growing strawberries, raspberries, and vegetables to sell to A&P grocery stores throughout northern Wisconsin and the Upper Peninsula of Michigan, along with some stores in Milwaukee and Chicago.

By the late 1940s, Williams Lake View Fruit Farms grew more than 350 acres of fruit and vegetable crops. Williams was one of the first fruit and vegetable growers in the state to rely on irrigation (for more on Williams's irrigation practices, see page 158).

In any given year, Williams planted and harvested green peppers, hot and sweet banana peppers, red raspberries, cantaloupe, watermelons, onions, strawberries, cabbage, red potatoes (a variety that looked like new spring potatoes even when harvested in late season), slicing cucumbers, and cucumbers for pickles (grown at one time but not every year), and sweet corn. Williams used the "hydro-cooling" system, widely used by truck farmers, to keep harvested sweet corn fresh. Immediately after harvesting the ears, he immersed them in an eight-by-eight-by-ten-foot container filled with ice-cold water. This stopped the natural aging process, keeping the corn sweet. When it was time to transport the corn, workers packed four dozen ears in a bag, along with a bag of ice.

Almost all of the harvesting was done by hand. During the peak of the strawberry season, in June and early July, as many as 125 workers, mostly young people from nearby Montello and Packwaukee, picked strawberries for the Williams farm operation. The family sold the farm in 1970.

NOTES

Interview with Robert Williams, January 17, 2012.

Wisconsin strawberries packaging, circa 1940
WHI IMAGE ID 91269

Commercial strawberry operations ranged from 1,300 acres in 1918 to 5,500 acres in 1939 and 1940. In 1953, acreage had declined to 1,400. Production ranged from 1.88 million quarts in 1940 to 960,000 quarts produced in 1925.[20]

In 2012, Wisconsin farmers harvested 610 acres of strawberries, down from 700 acres in 2011. The total amount of strawberries harvested in 2012 equaled 31,000 hundredweight, down from 40,000 hundredweight in 2011. Almost the entire crop was sold U-pick.[21]

GRAPES AND WINE

When settlers arrived in Wisconsin, among a plethora of other fruits they found wild grapes. Depending on the growing year, wild grapevines can produce generous amounts of tasty, albeit quite small, grapes. Growing in the wild, often in a woodlot, grapevines will grow to the tops of trees, sometimes as high as thirty feet. Harvesting the fruit before the birds and wild animals did could be a challenge, however.

It was of course possible to make wine from wild grapes, and some settlers did. The oldest winery in Wisconsin began operations in the 1840s, when a Hungarian immigrant, Count Agoston Haraszthy, selected a site on a historic hillside overlooking the Wisconsin River, across from Prairie du Sac, and planted grapevine cuttings he had brought with him from Europe. His experiment failed because of winter damage, and the count pulled up stakes and moved to California's milder climate in 1849.[22]

A few years later, German immigrant Peter Kehl acquired the Prairie du Sac property. Upon Peter's death, his son, Jacob, took over the winemaking operation. But after Jacob died in 1899, there was no commercial wine production in the state until much more recent times. (For more on Wisconsin's winemaking industry, see page 253.)

Studio portrait of Agoston Haraszthy, date unknown

WHI IMAGE ID 6276

Wollersheim Winery

In 1972, entrepreneurs Robert and JoAnn Wollersheim purchased the Peter Kehl property near Prairie du Sac and moved there from Madison. They planted grapes on the rolling hillsides, restored the winery, and experimented with grape varieties to develop ones that could withstand Wisconsin's winters. They hired Philippe Coquard, a Frenchman with experience and degrees in winemaking, in 1984; Coquard later married the Wollersheims' daughter, Julie.

Julie and Philippe operate the winery today, along with Cedar Creek Winery in Cedarburg. The two wineries produce over 240,000 gallons of wine a year.

Wollersheim Winery is partially housed in an 1858 stone building. WOLLERSHEIM WINERY, COURTESY OF THE WISCONSIN DEPARTMENT OF TOURISM

NOTES

Wollersheim Winery, www.wollersheim.com.

16

SPECIALTY CROPS

Following the demise of wheat, Wisconsin farmers looked far and wide for new moneymakers; many looked to capitalize on unique growing conditions or unlikely crops. For some farmers, growing hemp, a relative of marijuana, seemed to provide an answer. The cultivation of ginseng would be another. And those farmers who owned low ground discovered that growing mint and harvesting sphagnum moss that grew wild in some lowlands in west central Wisconsin could be profitable.

HEMP

Researchers in the University of Wisconsin's agronomy department grew the first hemp in the state in 1908. Interested in learning about hemp as a source of fiber, they planted six acres of cannabis plants on the grounds of Mendota Hospital (at the time the hospital was named the Wisconsin Hospital for the Insane, and the hemp acreage became known as "the asylum farm"). The results were so promising that the university planted more experimental plots in 1909, 1910, and 1911 at Mendota, Waupun, and Viroqua. The researchers discovered that not only was hemp an excellent source of fiber, it also killed any weeds that shared its plot of soil. In 1911 at the Waupun site, which was severely infested with quack grass, researcher A. H. Wright reported, "A yield of 2,100 pounds of fiber to the acre was obtained, and the quack grass was practically destroyed."[1]

Observing the success of the university's experiments with hemp, nearby farmers began planting the crop, and by 1915 Wisconsin farmers were growing

Breaking hemp at the Brigham farm near Blue Mounds (Dane County), 1911

four hundred acres of hemp. By 1917, hemp acreage in Wisconsin soared to seven thousand acres.[2]

The demand for hemp fiber, especially in the Midwest, can be traced back to the wheat-growing industry, and more specifically to John F. Appleby's invention of the knotter, which in turn led to the production of twine binders, or "self-binders," as they were sometimes called.[3] The first twine binders used imported Manila jute and sisal to tie the grain bundles. University researchers discovered that domestically grown hemp fiber was superior to the imported fibers. The navies of the world had long used ropes made of hemp fiber for their rigging because the hemp fiber was strong and rot resistant. In the southern states, hemp fiber was used for making not only rope but also clothing and sailcloth.[4]

When former Wisconsin governor Jeremiah Rusk, a Viroqua native, became the first US secretary of agriculture in 1890, the country was experiencing a fiber shortage because of the great demand from the grain binder manufacturers. Rusk established the USDA Office of Fiber Investigations, charged with developing flax and hemp fiber production in the United States, and he appointed Charles Dodge to head up this new office. In that year, Dodge received this message from a binder manufacturer: "There is no fiber in the world better suited to this use than American hemp. It is our judgment, based on nearly ten years' experience with large quantities of binder twine each year, that the entire supply of this twine should be made from American hemp. . . . There are 50,000 tons of this binding twine used annually, every pound of which could and should be made from this home product."[5]

Hemp was not a difficult crop to grow; once planted it required no care until harvest. But turning the hemp plant into fiber was a tedious multistep process requiring considerable hand labor. First the crop was cut and shocked (piled) to dry. Then it was spread out on the ground for several weeks to ret—the natural process by which the plant releases its fiber from the woody core of the stem. Following the retting stage, the material was gathered and carried to a device consisting of slats. The retted stems were placed across the slats and the stems broken to release the hemp fiber. The next step was hand-combing the fiber through blocks of long needles.[6]

Bundles of shocked hemp and the J. Leroy Farmer hemp mill in the background, Beaver Dam (Dodge County), 1943

WHI IMAGE ID 23989

With the Office of Fiber Investigation's encouragement, Wisconsin hemp researchers began experimenting with machines for harvesting and capturing hemp fiber. Andrew Wright, a UW–Madison agronomist, led the way toward mechanization of the hemp industry. As he explained in a 1918 report, "In 1917 a machine especially devised for harvesting hemp was placed on the market. The machine not only cuts hemp, but spreads it at the same time, leaving the stalks in an even swath. The work is done much better than by hand as the butts are more even and there is less crossing and tangling of the stalks."[7]

Whereas previously the hemp stems had been broken by hand with a crude machine, new mechanized breaking machines were developed, and hemp mills emerged. As Wright reported, "The modern hemp mill . . . consists of a receiving room, dry kilns, breaking room with brakes . . . balers, boiler room, engine and fan room."[8]

With the combined effects of mechanization and increased demand for rope and other hemp products brought on by World War I, by 1917 Wisconsin was the number-two producer of hemp in the country, with some seven thousand acres. Kentucky remained number one with eighteen thousand acres. California and North Dakota were tied for third place.[9]

Wisconsin soil and climate were conducive to high yields of the product, and even though the state does not have enough frost-free days to mature hemp seed, the overall production per acre of hemp exceeded that of Kentucky. Wisconsin land produced on average 1,200 pounds of hemp fiber per acre compared to Kentucky's 1,000 pounds per acre.[10]

By World War II, hemp fiber was once again in high demand, particularly for rope for marine and parachute rigging and thread for soldiers' shoes. A battleship required thirty-four thousand feet of rope.[11] At one time during the war, Wisconsin had forty-two hemp mills scattered across the southern region, from Cuba City to Union Grove and from Ripon to DeForest. Many farmers grew hemp, but the government also rented land to grow the crop because there was such high demand.

James G. Neu recalled visiting a relative's family farm in Washington County during World War II. He was a ten-year-old city boy and was interested in learning something about farm life. "I visited the Wedimeyer family farm . . . several times with my parents. . . . While on tour it was pointed out to me that many acres of farm land had been rented by the US government to raise hemp for the war effort. The government planted the crop in the spring and harvested it in the fall. The farm family had nothing to do with this crop and were told not to enter the field."[12]

With the war's end, the demand for hemp rapidly declined and the hemp mills closed. Later, the association of hemp with marijuana led to legislation that made it difficult to grow and market hemp in the United States. Today no hemp is grown in Wisconsin, although in the ditches and odd corners of fields where hemp once stood seven feet tall, a few odd remnants can be found.

Workers processed hemp fibers at a Deforest mill during World War II.

WHI IMAGE ID 34471

GINSENG

Of all the crops harvested in Wisconsin, ginseng is perhaps the most exotic and mysterious. It grows wild in deep woods, as the plant requires heavy shade to do well; in cultivation it is grown in shady plots or artificially shaded beds. The plant is harvested for its root, which has long been claimed to have powerful medicinal qualities. Ginseng once grew wild from Maine to Alabama and west to Michigan, Wisconsin, and Minnesota. It also grows in the cooler regions of Korea, northeast China, and eastern Siberia.[13]

White people learned about ginseng in western New England around 1750. One of the earliest sales of ginseng involved John Jacob Astor, the wealthy North American fur trader. It is claimed he started his fortune by an arrangement he made with the East India Company to purchase ginseng. Astor agreed to split the profits on a shipment of wild American ginseng shipped to China in the late 1700s. The money he received for the exotic root was in the thousands of dollars.[14]

Most cultivated ginseng is grown in shaded beds like these.
BAUMANN FARMS, COURTESY OF THE GINSENG BOARD OF WISCONSIN

Some of Wisconsin's earliest pioneers harvested wild ginseng as a way of supplementing the family's income. An early settler in Richland County recalled his experience with wild ginseng in 1864, when he was seven years old:

> Another industry that added to the family income was the digging of ginseng, for the side hills among the trees were full of this now valuable root and thousands of pounds of it . . . were marketed from Richland County. The price was very low compared to what it now is. I think we got about a dollar a pound for the dried root, but every little bit helped a lot when dollars were as scarce as they were then. Often when passing a farm one would see only some of the smaller children about the place, and on inquiring where the folks were would be informed that "they're out digging" sang.[15]

Between 1858 and 1901, ginseng exports from the United States averaged 278,000 pounds a year, with prices ranging from 52 cents a pound in 1858 to $2.50 in 1901. Almost all of it was harvested from the wild.[16]

Once the value of ginseng roots became widely known, the wild plant became harder and harder to find. Some people began growing it in their gardens but soon discovered it was difficult to cultivate domestically. Ginseng seeds require an eighteen-month dormant period in the soil before they sprout. Nevertheless, by the early 1900s, cultivated ginseng gardens could be found in many regions of the country. Some of the earliest plots were planted in New York state, led by grower George Stanton of Onondaga. Stanton started a small magazine titled *Special Crops* in 1903, and he is often described as the father of cultivated American ginseng. In 1904, Liberty Hyde Bailey, director of New York's Agricultural Experiment Station, wrote, "New York is one of the leading states in the growing of ginseng. Considering the value of the New York product and the attention given to the plant, it is not improbable that New York leads the states."[17]

The year of Bailey's declaration about New York's dominance, ten-year-old Henry Fromm and his older brothers were roaming the woods of their farm in Marathon County, Wisconsin, trapping such animals as fox, mink, and raccoon for extra spending money. Henry was especially enamored by the fox and decided that raising foxes might be a profitable undertaking—although his farmer father thought little of the idea.

The Fromm brothers (Henry, John, Edward, and Walter) learned in *Hunter Trader Trapper* magazine that wild ginseng root was selling for six dollars per pound and quickly decided that raising ginseng might get them the money they needed to begin raising silver foxes. They built their first ginseng bed in the shade of their woodshed and planted 150 ginseng plants they dug up in the forest.[18]

In 1909, five years after they set out their first ginseng plants, the Fromm brothers sold their first crop of roots for twenty-four dollars, which they used to buy silver fox breeding stock. By 1919, they were Marathon County's leading ginseng producers. That year the Fromms organized the National Cultivated Wild Ginseng Growers Association. The Fromms combatted wildly fluctuating prices and ginseng diseases such as leaf blight and crown rot, eventually owning seventeen thousand acres of land and growing about five hundred acres of ginseng.[19]

In 1919, Wisconsin became the number-one state in the nation in the production of ginseng, and by 1920 ginseng beds could be found in most Wisconsin counties.

Wild Ginseng

Wild ginseng is defined as ginseng that is not grown or nurtured by a person, which means that it has not been watered, weeded, fertilized, or cared for in any way. According to Wisconsin regulations, anyone harvesting or digging wild ginseng on land they do not own is required to have a license. Those digging ginseng on their own land and selling it can obtain a free license. The harvest season for wild ginseng is September 1 through November 1. Wild ginseng doesn't reach a marketable size until it is six to ten years old, so the Department of Natural Resources provides detailed guidelines to those digging the root. Wild ginseng commands a higher price on the market than cultivated ginseng, and no caring for the crop is involved. By following the rules and regulations, it's possible to legally harvest and sell wild ginseng. Unfortunately, there continues to be an illegal trade in ginseng.

Hsu Ginseng Farm of Wausau markets both farm-raised ginseng and wild ginseng grown among forested vegetation, as seen here.
USED BY PERMISSION OF THE UNIVERSITY OF WISCONSIN FOUNDATION, DANA CRARY, PHOTOGRAPHER

NOTES

"Wild Ginseng: Regulations and Guidelines for Sustainable Harvest," Wisconsin Department of Natural Resources, http://dnr.wi.gov/files/PDF/pubs/LE/LE-005_13.pdf?o=n.

Marathon County, Ginseng Mecca

By the early 1960s, 200 of the estimated 300 acres of cultivated ginseng grown in the United States were grown in Marathon County in central Wisconsin. As more farmers learned of the potential profit for raising ginseng root, the industry expanded rapidly. From 1970 to 1983, the number of growers in Marathon County increased by ten times; from 1983 to 1997, grower numbers doubled once more, to 827 growers and 2,125 acres. But with declining prices and worldwide competition, Marathon County's ginseng grower numbers declined to 402 with 1,070 acres grown in 2002. Statewide, the number of acres decreased from about 4,000 in 1996 to 2,135 in 2002. Nonetheless, Wisconsin remains the leading producer of cultivated ginseng in the nation.[1]

To assist with the promotion and marketing of Wisconsin's ginseng, the Ginseng Board of Wisconsin, with offices in Marathon County, was established in 1986. Funded through a mandatory assessment of ginseng acreage under shade, the organization created a Wisconsin Ginseng Seal in 1991 to identify ginseng grown in Wisconsin.[2]

NOTES

1. Len Cheng and Paul D. Mitchell, *Status of the Wisconsin Ginseng Industry* (Madison: University of Wisconsin–Madison Department of Agricultural and Applied Economics, 2009), pp. 5, 8.

2. Ginseng Board of Wisconsin, www.ginsengboard.com.

Workers prepared ginseng beds in northern Wisconsin, circa 1938.
WHI IMAGE ID 25059

During World War II, when many ginseng growers in other states dropped out of the business because of labor shortages and the cutting of access to Asian markets, Wisconsin persevered. Today the state produces 95 percent of the cultivated ginseng grown in the United States.[20]

MUCK FARMING

In many parts of Wisconsin, the glacier not only left behind stone-studded fields, rivers, lakes, hills, and valleys, it also created enormous lowlands that were rich in organic matter but too wet to farm in their original state. In the early 1900s, farmers drained many of these wetlands and began planting crops on them, including potatoes, onions, carrots, lettuce, and cabbage. They also found the muck soils to be good ground for growing two very specialized plants that grew in the wild: mint and sphagnum moss.

Wisconsin's Indians knew about sphagnum moss long before the first pioneers arrived. They harvested the dense moss—which holds up to twenty times its weight in water—from wet marshy areas and used it for baby diapers and for dressing wounds. During the Civil War and World War I, military hospitals used sphagnum moss to dress surgical wounds. Today it is used primarily in the gardening and nursery business for lining hanging baskets, transplanting seedlings, mulching gardens, and as a decorative soil covering.

Harvesting onions in
Outagamie County, 1965
WHI IMAGE ID 83658

On the rich soils of Gumz Muck Farms in Endeavor (Marquette County), the fourth generation of Gumzes grow potatoes, corn, onions, soybeans, carrots, spearmint, and peppermint. Here a worker cut mint in the field.
COURTESY OF GUMZ MUCK FARMS

Long-fibered sphagnum moss is a perennial plant, and like other mosses it propagates with spores. It is not cultivated and is harvested only from naturally growing plants; then it regenerates. After the moss is harvested, it takes from three to seven years before a marsh is mature enough to cut again. The harvest season runs from spring until the marshes freeze in the fall. Harvesting the moss involves raking it, drying it, and bailing it for shipment to garden supply centers.[21]

Wisconsin is the only state with a commercial sphagnum moss industry. The plant grows mainly in Jackson, Monroe, Wood, and Clark Counties—notoriously sandy, dry counties that also have wet, marshy areas. Founded in 1932, the Mosser Lee Company of Millston (Jackson County) is the largest moss harvester in the state.[22] By obtaining permits from the DNR, moss harvesters compete for access to over five hundred acres of sphagnum bogs in the Black River State Forest (where only about seventy acres are harvested in a given year) and in the Jackson County Forest.[23]

Like moss, mint has been grown commercially in Wisconsin for a relatively short time, but its history has much deeper roots. Humans have used mint for thousands of years, for a variety of purposes. Spearmint was commonly grown and used for its medicinal qualities. In his history of the mint industry in the United States, James Landing described how the herb was employed over the centuries to "heat a cold liver, . . . aid in childbirth, cure leprosy, scurvy, dog and snake bites . . .

Muck Farms Return to Their Natural State

Some Wisconsin muck farmers sold their farms and allowed them to return to their natural state, providing a haven for wildlife. Felix Zeloski bought 1,496 acres of land in the London Marsh near Lake Mills in the 1940s and, with the advice of UW–Madison agriculture professors, drained the land and began farming the rich muck soils, raising mint, potatoes, onions, carrots, corn, and soybeans. Felix's son Dennis took over the farm in 1973. With urban development in the nearby city of Sun Prairie leading to an increase in roads, buildings, and parking lots, runoff from the area rushed into Koshkonong Creek and eventually flooded Zeloski's farm. When this had happened more than once, Zeloski sold his wetlands and allowed them to be restored to their original state as a wildlife wetland area.[1]

Another interesting example of drained land returning to its natural state is the thirty-three-thousand-acre Horicon Marsh, located in southern Dodge County and northern Fond du Lac County.[2]

Horicon Marsh is the largest intact freshwater marsh in the country. It is home and migratory staging area for more than three hundred bird species.
RJ & LINDA MILLER, COURTESY OF THE WISCONSIN DEPARTMENT OF TOURISM

When the early settlers arrived and saw this vast wetland, they damned the river running out of it to create waterpower for a sawmill, a gristmill, and an ironworks. The dam created fifty-square-mile Lake

bad breath, colic and dandruff." Mint was also found useful as a preservative for meat and cheese.[24]

Cultivated mint came to the United States with some of the earliest European immigrants and was planted in Massachusetts Colony gardens. Neither spearmint nor peppermint is native to the United States, but the plant quickly adapted to its new land, and in the 1790s, a few farmers began growing peppermint commercially in Massachusetts. They not only grew the plant but processed it as well, extracting the powerful peppermint oil and marketing it. As settlers moved west, they carried mint plants with them. By 1845, New York, Ohio, and Michigan had become major producers of mint oil, with New York state leading the nation.[25]

Wisconsin farmers have grown mint commercially since 1943. In that year, a few farmers began growing peppermint on a trial basis to determine whether Wisconsin

Muck Farms Return to Their Natural State

Horicon. Nearby farmers claimed the dam flooded their land, making farming impossible, and in 1869 they took their complaint to the state supreme court. They won the lawsuit, and the dam was removed in 1869. The area became a vast marshland once more.

By 1916, much of Horicon Marsh was ditched and drained, and farmers began raising onions, carrots, and potatoes on the black, organic soil. Farmers soon discovered that the land still retained water in the spring and thus they had to delay planting their crops. Heavy fall rains often delayed or prevented harvesting. Farming in the area faded, and the marsh was abandoned. Left exposed by farmer's plows, the peat dried out, and peat fires became common. In 1927, the Wisconsin legislature passed the Horicon Wildlife Refuge Bill, which provided funds to purchase the land and reconstruct the dam. In 1934, the dam gates were once again closed, and water levels in the marsh were restored. Soon native marsh grasses and plants began returning.

A total of eleven thousand acres comprising the southern third of the marsh is now a state wildlife area managed by the Wisconsin Department of Natural Resources. The northern two-thirds (twenty-one thousand acres) is a national wildlife refuge administered by the US Fish and Wildlife Service. The restoration returned the Horicon Marsh basin, which is about 13.5 miles long and 5.5 miles wide, to close to its original state.[3]

NOTES

1. Mark Martin and Charles Kilian, "From Muck Farm to Marsh," http://joomla.wildlife.org/index.php?option=com_content&task=view&id=831.

2. "Horicon," US Fish and Wildlife Service, www.fws.gov/midwest/horicon.

3. Bill Volkert, "Horicon Marsh Is Wild Again," www.enjoyhoriconmarsh.com/about_the_marsh/stories_of_the_marsh/wildagain.htm.

soils and climate could sustain the crop.[26] Not long after that, farmers in Sauk, Walworth, Jefferson, Dane, Columbia, Marquette, and Green Lake Counties began growing it. In 1948, Wisconsin peppermint growers harvested one hundred acres.

The mint plant, a perennial, produces no seeds. New mint fields, usually located in low, muck soils, are planted with rootstock, or runners, from existing plants. Mint is planted in rows; by the second year of growth it spreads out, creating a solid mint field. Every three to five years a mint field is rotated with another crop, and then the planting cycle begins once more.

In the second half of the twentieth century, most of the mint-production industry moved to the Pacific Northwest, and today only about fifteen mint growers remain in Wisconsin. One of the largest is Gumz Muck Farms near Endeavor, Marquette County.[27]

17

HONEY, MAPLE SYRUP, CHRISTMAS TREES, AND FUR FARMS

As Wisconsin farmers continued their experiments in diversified agriculture, they learned to not simply endure but embrace the region's often challenging weather and growing conditions. With cold, snowy winters and cool summers, Wisconsin's climate makes for excellent maple syrup production and Christmas trees farms. Its northern locale also makes it a comfortable home for fur-bearing animals, leading to a vigorous fur-farming business, and honeybees, important for the pollination of fruit crops in addition to providing a commercial honeybee industry. All have been important contributors to Wisconsin's agricultural economy.

HONEY

Beekeeping, or apiculture, traces back to 7000 BC, as evidenced by bees depicted in drawings on Egyptian tombs. Honeybees are not native to North America; Europeans introduced them here around 1620. By 1640, beekeeping was prevalent in Virginia.[1]

Honeybees found this new land quite hospitable. Many hives escaped from settlers as they moved westward, and by 1810 honeybees could be found as far west as Texas, Iowa, Illinois, and Wisconsin. Both Indians and early settlers in Wisconsin harvested honey from bee trees, and it was possible to earn a handsome bit of money from doing so; as University of Wisconsin bee specialist Walter Gojmerac explained, "There are many reports of trees yielding 25 to 50 gallons of honey. During this

Local honey for sale at the Dane County Farmers' Market, Madison
PHOTO BY BILL LUBING

period [early 1800s] honey sold for 25 to 37 cents per gallon. It was not unusual for a honey hunter to make $170.00 per season."[2] Later, some farmers captured swarms to keep in makeshift homemade "hives" for both honey production and crop pollination.[3] It wasn't until the mid-1850s that beekeepers learned enough to manage bees successfully.

By 1885, scientists in the US Department of Agriculture were researching bees and beekeeping, including how to control various diseases that afflicted them. The 1910 agricultural census reported 95,000 bee colonies in Wisconsin credited with producing more than 2.1 million pounds of honey and 55,000 pounds of beeswax.[4]

One of the oldest honey producers in Wisconsin is Honey Acres, established in Milwaukee 1852 by C. F. Diehnelt, who brought beekeeping talents with him from Rosswein, Germany. C. F.'s son August and grandson Walter later joined the business, which in 1930 moved to Menomonee Falls. In 1980, the business, which today sells

Beehives on the farm of Bernard Volkering in East Farmington (Polk County), circa 1895

WHI IMAGE ID 93520

honey and products made with honey and beeswax, moved to a rural site near Ashippun, Dodge County.

In 1977, the Wisconsin state legislature designated the honeybee as Wisconsin's state insect. In 1993, a peak year for Wisconsin honey production, 100,000 colonies produced some 8.2 million pounds of honey. In 2011, Wisconsin ranked ninth nationally in honey production, with North Dakota (460,000 colonies) in first place and California (370,000 colonies) in second.[5]

In addition to producing honey, bees perform an important role in the pollination of Wisconsin's fruit crops, especially cranberries, cherries, and apples. Pollination by honeybees is especially important for a good cranberry yield. Some growers have as many as ten beehives per acre of cranberries, employing commercial beekeepers to move the hives from their bee yards to the cranberry marshes.[6]

The Wisconsin Honey Producers Association and the Honey Queen

Like many other specialists, beekeepers organized trade associations for educational and marketing purposes; the Wisconsin State Beekeepers Association was formed in 1864. The group crafted a legislative bill in 1895 that created an apiary inspection program and 1919 began publishing a newsletter, *Wisconsin Beekeeping,* which in 1922 became a supplement to the Wisconsin Horticultural Association's monthly journal. At its 1922 annual conference, the association vowed to "redouble our efforts to put Wisconsin on the beekeeping map, to the end that our industry shall move up in the scale of importance, from the tenth rank in Wisconsin industries to the seventh or eighth and ultimately make for the individual success of all legitimate honey producers."[1]

Wisconsin's Honey Queen and Alice in Dairyland made a joint appearance in the early 1960s. WHI IMAGE ID 34039

The State Beekeepers Association was renamed the Wisconsin Honey Producers Association in 1965. Today the WHPA continues its mission of assisting Wisconsin beekeepers in marketing their products and providing educational programs for its members and the public. In addition, each year the WHPA selects a young woman to serve as the Wisconsin Honey Queen. The Honey Queen travels the state, appearing at county fairs, festivals, and farmers' markets and speaking about honey to students, agriculture groups, and youth and civic groups.[2]

The WHPA remains a strong advocate for the honey industry, working to protect it from policies and environmental changes that might have a negative impact on the business.

NOTES

1. "Wisconsin Beekeepers Conference and Field Meet," *Wisconsin Beekeepers,* supplement to *Wisconsin Horticulture,* September 1922, p. 31.

2. "Wisconsin Honey Queen," Wisconsin Honey Producers, www.wihoney.org/wihoney-queen.

Hobby Beekeepers

Tom Borchardt of Middleton (Dane County) has a longtime interest in honeybees and beekeeping. Borchardt's small business, Borkarts' Bees, places and manages beehives on other people's property (at their request), extracts the honey, gives some to the landowners, and sells the rest at local farmers' markets. Borchardt keeps more than twenty hives at locations around Wisconsin, all in rural settings. The benefits of his hobby are several, according to Borchardt: "The obvious benefit is lots of absolutely delicious, natural, local unadulterated honey. I have learned that each hive produces its own distinct honey, differing in taste, aroma, and color. . . . Beekeeping also connects the beekeeper to the natural world in unexpected ways. You begin to take notice of what trees and wildflowers are blooming by what you see around you and what you see the bees bringing back to the hive—pollen from different flowers in a variety of colors."

Small-scale beekeeping has its challenges as well. Borchardt said,

> Beekeeping is an agricultural endeavor, and the bees are "livestock." In this way, beekeeping is similar to other agricultural activities, just on a smaller scale with very low capital investment and with insects rather than mammals. Food (nectar and pollen), shelter (the hive), disease, pests, predators, and weather are all

In 2015, the Wisconsin Honey Producers Association estimated that there were more than two thousand beekeepers in the state, most of them hobbyists. COURTESY OF KENT PEGORSCH

concerns for the beekeeper. There is a vast body of knowledge about beekeeping (it is an ancient practice), but individual judgment and good decisions concerning each hive are critical to each colony's survival and productivity. New beekeepers need to be willing to sort through lots of conflicting information and advice, and also be willing to accept that mistakes will be made and to learn from those mistakes.

NOTES

Personal correspondence from Tom Borchardt, June 19, 2012.

MAPLE SYRUP

Wisconsin's "maple tree belt" stretches from east to west across the center of the state, where hard maple trees have naturally grown for centuries. Maple syrup and maple sugar were enjoyed by Native Americans, who tapped trees with cedar spikes and cooked down the sap.[7] Maple sugar became, according to historian Lucy Eldersveld Murphy, "a commodity of major importance for Indians in the region"; indeed, "Indians of northern Illinois and southern Wisconsin sold seventy thousand pounds of it in 1816 not counting what they made for their own consumption."[8]

The Menominee Indians have a long history of harvesting and using maple sap, and it is deeply embedded in their culture. According to regional foods expert Terese Allen, "Myth has it that granulated maple sugar—not syrup—is what came out of maple trees originally. According to Menominee lore, maple sugar was a source of concern to the tribal hero named Manabush. He worried that his tribe would grow lazy if obtaining such sweetness with too little effort. So he turned the sugar into a liquid."[9]

Newly arrived settlers made maple syrup and sugar as well, some for trade and some for home use.[10] Agricultural economist Frederick Merk, discussing settlement of the central and northern regions of the state in the 1860s and 1870s, wrote, "Among the minor products of the northern forest and marshes were maple sugar, furs, cranberries, and ginseng."[11] By the late 1800s, maple syrup producers became

Seth Eastman's sketch, created circa 1850, of an Indian sugar camp

WHI IMAGE ID 9829

commercial—meaning they were tapping trees, boiling down the sap, and selling the syrup and products made from it. The process began in March, when the daily temperatures began rising above freezing and returned to freezing at night, conditions that made the maple sap rise. A metal tap was pounded into the tree and a pail attached to it. The sap dripped into the pail and was periodically collected and dumped into a large shallow pan set over a wood fire. The sap was boiled until it reduced into a thick, sweet syrup. (It takes forty gallons of maple sap to yield one gallon of maple syrup.)

By 1920, Wisconsin maple sugar operations were yielding 113,000 gallons of syrup. In 1932, producers formed the Wisconsin Maple Syrup Producers Association, a membership organization that promotes maple syrup products and sponsors annual meetings. The organization includes both commercial and hobbyist maple producers.[12]

Collecting maple sap near Granton (Clark County), circa 1945
WHI IMAGE ID 36461

Maple syrup production, like so much of agriculture, depends on the weather. Production has fluctuated over time, from a low of 29,000 gallons in 1945 to several years when production topped 100,000 gallons. In 2009, Wisconsin produced 200,000 gallons of syrup, making it the fourth-largest producer in the nation after Vermont, New York, and Maine.[13]

While Wisconsin's maple syrup production reached 155,000 gallons in 2011, production plummeted by 68 percent to 50,000 gallons in 2012. The 2012 maple syrup season began in late January and lasted only ten days, eighteen days shorter than in 2011. Producers reported that the season was too warm for good sap production.[14] An exceedingly warm March fooled the maple trees into budding—and once the buds appear, the sap turns bitter and the season is over. Many producers, expecting several weeks of sap run, had only a few days of sap. For some the maple syrup season lasted just one day.[15] Climate change, with the possibility of warmer winters and wildly fluctuating temperatures, will be an important factor in maple syrup production in the years ahead. (For more on climate change, see page 267.)

CHRISTMAS TREE FARMING

Wisconsin's Christmas tree history began with the harvesting of native and naturally growing balsam fir, black and Norway spruce, and red pine—all growing in abundance in Wisconsin's vast North Woods. In the early 1920s, city dwellers bought Christmas trees, primarily spruce, from retailers such as grocery stores, who imported them from Vermont, New Hampshire, and Maine. Then in 1925, George Blaesing of Rhinelander began marketing Christmas trees in a retail lot in Milwaukee, competing with trees from New England. By the 1930s, Wisconsin's native balsam and spruce were becoming common in city markets.[16]

It wasn't until after World War II that Wisconsin saw the emergence of extensive Christmas tree plantations—trees planted especially for the Christmas tree market. In 1954, with the assistance of UW–Extension forester Fred Trenk, the Wisconsin Christmas Tree Producers Association was organized, with seventy-three charter members. Three years later, Wisconsin was producing about 1.3 million Christmas trees, many of them shipped out of state. The counties harvesting the largest numbers were Waushara, Lincoln, Oneida, and Douglas, and balsam fir, most cut from wild lands, accounted for about half of the total number of trees cut. Twenty-six percent were pine, almost all from plantations.[17]

With the emergence of Christmas tree plantations after World War II, many of them on the sandy soils of central Wisconsin in counties like Waushara, Scotch pines became popular. Pine tree nurseries imported Scotch pine seeds from Austria, Germany, Poland, and other European countries; the trees grew rapidly, sometimes reaching market height of eight feet in less than ten years. Scotch pines held their needles well and could be pruned so they were uniformly shaped and fully formed.

Loggers with horses and oxen cut fir trees in Jackson County to take to market, circa 1895.

WHI IMAGE ID 60429

Christmas tree pruning provided summer jobs for migrant workers and high school and college students.

Christmas tree plantations continued to expand in the 1950s and 1960s, and then artificial trees became available. As one Christmas tree grower said, "I don't recognize these metal things as Christmas trees, but surely recognize them as competition." By 1962, a dyed green polyethylene tree appeared on the market, with the sales line "No fuss, no fire . . . and it will last for years." By 1970, artificial trees were selling at the rate of 3.6 million per year.[18]

In 2007, Wisconsin Christmas tree growers harvested 950,000 trees cut from 1,136 farms comprising 33,458 acres, making Wisconsin the fifth-largest producer of Christmas trees in the nation. By 2012, although both acres and number of trees had fallen, the state remained in fifth place in sales, with 611,387 trees cut from 23,651 acres.[19]

FUR FARMS

The French trappers who traveled Wisconsin during the seventeenth and eighteenth centuries knew the value of the thick furs produced in this northern climate. They trapped wild animals, mostly beaver, for their furs, some for trade with Wisconsin's Indians and some for shipment to Europe.

Of course, many a pioneer trapped wild animals for their furs, and in some cases for food. The furs of muskrat, beaver, raccoon, fox, and wolf were made into clothing and blankets and were sold to fur dealers to earn the trapper some money. But fur farming—the breeding, raising, and harvesting of animals for their furs— didn't become a business in Wisconsin until the early 1900s.

The Fromm brothers of Hamburg, Marathon County, were among the state's first fur farmers. With twenty-four dollars raised from selling ginseng, the four young men bought seven foxes to get started; Henry Fromm also trapped wild red foxes to add to the fledgling fox farm. But he was especially interested in silver foxes. By 1917, with additional purchases and careful breeding, the Fromms had sixty-five silver foxes; ten years later the farm had seven thousand foxes.[20]

A 1936 *Time Magazine* article reported that the Fromms had two thousand foxes at Hamburg and another four thousand on a ranch near Milwaukee. The six thousand foxes were valued at $1.5 million. In 1935, sales from the Fromm fox farming enterprise amounted to 10 percent of all the silver foxes sold in the United States.[21]

Many others farmers got into the business. Some of them succeeded, but many didn't. In some instances, unscrupulous fox farmers sold breeding stock for as much

John J. Werth held a platinum fox at Capitol Fox and Fur Ranch, circa 1932. John Werth's grandfather started fox farming in 1927 just south of Madison. At one time he had three hundred breeding female foxes. The family later dealt in mink, at their peak raising 2,300 females and selling 11,000 pelts in a year.
COURTESY OF JOHN WERTH

as $1,200 to $1,500 a pair, with the promise of much money to be made. Wisconsin is the nation's leading producer of mink pelts, but the number of mink ranches has been in decline. In 1968 there were 87; by 2014 the number had declined to 65.[22]

Some fox farmers added mink to their operations. Herb Magnuson's grandfather bought his first foxes in 1917. Twenty years later, Herb's dad traded a few dairy heifers for some breeding mink. Herb graduated from high school in 1946 and returned to the farm when he finished college. Due to demand for mink coats, the mink ranch grew while their fox farming declined. The family's peak years of operation were in the 1980s and 1990s, and their largest yield of mink pelts was fifty-five thousand one year in the early 1990s. Herb Magnuson sold the fur farm in 2009.[23]

Harry Erickson began working on a mink and fox ranch in Racine County when he was eighteen. In 1962, he and his family bought out a small mink rancher in Wild Rose, Waushara County. Erickson raised foxes for three or four years and then moved entirely into mink ranching. The Ericksons continue to raise mink today. Harry commented, "About 90 percent of our pelts go to China, which is our best market. Other good markets are Russia, Greece, and South Korea. These have been our best markets for the past seven or eight years."[24]

In 1997, Wisconsin boasted 120 mink ranches. In 2002, twenty-five Wisconsin counties had at least one mink ranch, led by Calumet, Taylor, Sheboygan, and Marathon.[25] Today Wisconsin leads the nation in the production of mink pelts; in 2011, Wisconsin mink pelt production accounted for 34 percent of the nation's total.[26]

Challenges in Fur

The animal rights movement has posed many challenges to the mink ranching industry. As Herb Magnuson explained, "Prices have been a roller coaster all the time. Two good years and then not good. Right now [2012], fur prices are high. Good male pelts are bringing over one hundred dollars per pelt. They used to bring twenty-five to thirty each. Milk prices are stable compared to mink pelt prices."

NOTES
Interview with Herb Magnuson, February 16, 2012.

PART V

TWENTIETH-CENTURY TRANSFORMATIONS

18
THE GREAT DEPRESSION AND THE NEW DEAL

On October 29, 1929, the US stock market collapsed, plummeting the nation into the Great Depression, which would last for more than a decade. From August 1929 to November 1930, employment in Wisconsin's manufacturing industries fell by nearly 25 percent. The state's gross farm income dropped from $438 million in 1929 to $357 million in 1930; by 1932 it had slipped to $186 million. Land values also dropped; in 1929 Wisconsin farmland was valued at an average of $69.38 per acre. By 1932 it had fallen to $36 per acre.[1]

Farm prices also fell as struggling consumers tried to reduce expenses by cutting food purchases. In 1919, the average price Wisconsin farmers received for a hundredweight of milk was about three dollars; that number fell to two dollars in 1929 and less than one dollar in 1932. With the hope of increasing prices, some farmers withheld their milk from the market, effectively going "on strike." In 1933, some desperate milk producers went so far as to dump their milk rather than sell it. Violence broke out; one striker was killed by gunfire from a passing vehicle, and at least seven cheese factories were bombed.[2]

The number of Wisconsin farms peaked in 1935 at 199,877. One reason behind the increase of 18,110 farms from 1930 to 1935 was the number of unemployed workers moving back to the country. (From 1940 to 1950, farm numbers would decline by nearly 10 percent.)[3]

By the time that President Franklin Delano Roosevelt took office on March 4, 1933, the Depression had worsened. Banks had closed, unemployment was soaring, factories had shut down—and farmers, although they had food and shelter, suffered

Producers dumped their milk in protest near Burlington in 1934.
WHI IMAGE ID 2038

A Farm Security Administration county supervisor reviewed a plan with a borrower and his family in Grant County, 1939.
WHI IMAGE ID 25048

with low incomes and the fear of losing their farms to foreclosure. During his first one hundred days in office, FDR initiated his New Deal legislative proposals, tagged "recovery legislation." Two of the early programs resulted in the formation of the Agricultural Adjustment Administration (AAA), created to support farm prices, and the Civilian Conservation Corps (CCC), designed to employ young men in conservation work, including flood control and soil conservation.

The Oleo Wars

During the Depression years, oleomargarine—which was less expensive than butter—began replacing butter on many dinner tables, much to the dismay and outright anger of Wisconsin's dairy producers, who had successfully supported legislation outlawing the use of this butter imitator.

Oleomargarine was developed in France in 1869 by chemist Hippolyte Mège-Mouriès, who made it by churning beef tallow with carbonate of potash, milk, and water (today's margarine has a vegetable base). Mège-Mouriès won a prize from Emperor Napoleon III for developing a cheap butter substitute. In 1871, he shared his process with Dutch company Jurgens, which added yellow coloring to the otherwise white product and began shipping it around the world. By 1873, the Oleo-Margarine Manufacturing Company of New York was producing the product, and by 1886 there were thirty-seven oleomargarine plants in the United States.[1]

Dairy producers in Wisconsin and other states recognized the threat that the cheaper oleo presented to the sale of butter and sought legislation to stop the intruder. Wisconsin passed anti-oleomargarine laws as early as 1881 and passed even more comprehensive legislation in 1885 (Wisconsin Statutes 97.18). In 1886, the US Congress passed the Oleomargarine

Act, which imposed a two-cent-per-pound tax on colored oleomargarine. It would remain in effect until 1950.[2]

This cartoon from the May 14, 1887, issue of *The Rural New-Yorker* captured farmers' fears about margarine as a threat to their livelihood.

THE RURAL NEW-YORKER; WHI IMAGE ID 42825

The Farm Security Administration (FSA), also a New Deal program, was organized as a subagency within the US Department of Agriculture. The FSA worked through county offices that reported to state directors and provided loans to farm families who could not obtain credit elsewhere. The loans could be used for purchasing land, equipment, livestock, and seed. The FSA also offered a health care program and promoted educational programs for farmers. The Farmers Home Administration (FHA) replaced the FSA in 1946.[4]

The Oleo Wars

Although the sale of colored oleomargarine was a criminal offense in Wisconsin, people sneaked across the border to neighboring states where they could easily purchase the yellow butter substitute. During the depths of the Depression, Wisconsin dairy farmers were so agitated by the influx of contraband oleomargarine in the state that in 1931 a group of them marched on the state capitol in Madison. Headlines in the December 16 *Wisconsin State Journal* read, "Down with Oleo! Farm Crusaders Cry."[3]

By the 1950s and 1960s, smuggling of colored oleo from nearby states reached epic proportions. If caught, oleo smugglers could be punished with a fine and even imprisonment, but they were not deterred.

By the mid-1960s, a movement grew to repeal the ban on colored oleo in the state. Democratic state senator Martin Schreiber proposed the repeal but faced a firestorm of opposition led by rural Republicans. Schreiber suggested a blind taste test to challenge Republicans who believed that butter tasted better than oleomargarine. Republican senator Gordon Roseleip of Darlington, an ardent supporter of the existing regulations, agreed to take the test—and chose margarine as the better-tasting product. Two years after the test, in 1967, the Wisconsin legislature repealed the ban on colored oleo. It was the last state in the nation to do so.[4]

But remnants of Wisconsin Statute 97.18 remain. The statute includes detailed rules for the packaging of oleomargarine. All public eating places in Wisconsin must serve butter unless customers specifically ask for margarine. Students, patients, and inmates of any state institution must be served butter. The fines are stiff if these regulations are violated. Although it may look and even taste like butter, oleomargarine is not a butter substitute for many people living in Wisconsin. For them, nothing can replace butter.

NOTES

1. Gerry Strey, "The Oleo Wars: Wisconsin's Fight over the Demon Spread," *Wisconsin Magazine of History*, Autumn 2000, p. 3.

2. "Historical Highlights: The Oleomargarine Act," US House of Representatives, http://history.house.gov/HistoricalHighlight/Detail/15032395622.

3. "Battle of the Bread Spreads," Portalwisconsin.org, http://portalwisconsin.wordpress.com/2010/11/18/battle-of-the-bread-spreads.

4. Ibid.

1930S LEGISLATION AND FARM SUBSIDIES

The AAA created the first major price supports and acreage reduction program for farmers. Acreage reduction was achieved through voluntary agreements with farmers, who were paid to limit the amount of crops they grew or destroy crops they had already grown. The federal government also bought farm animals and slaughtered them with the intent of raising farm prices.[5]

Workers at the CCC camp at Devil's Lake State Park near Baraboo
WHI IMAGE ID 64448

The CCC provided jobless single men between the ages of eighteen and twenty-five paid work on conservation projects that ranged from tree planting to fire prevention, soil conservation, and flood control. Of the forty-five CCC camps in Wisconsin at the peak of the program in 1938, thirteen of them, run by the Soil Conservation Service, were "primarily concerned with preventing soil erosion through terracing, drainage control, tree planting, and other such measures," according to Paul Glad's history of Wisconsin.[6] The program ended in 1942, during the early years of World War II, when young men were needed in the armed forces.

SOIL CONSERVATION SERVICE

In 1935, the US Congress passed Public Law 74–46, which established the Soil Conservation Service (SCS) as a permanent agency in the USDA. County SCS offices were established throughout Wisconsin, with offices at county seats. Employees of the SCS worked closely with county-based Cooperative Extension agricultural agents to assist farmers with soil conservation efforts. Money became available for farmers to carry out such soil-saving projects as strip cropping, contour farming, and the establishment of windbreaks to prevent wind erosion. (The name of the agency was changed to Natural Resources Conservation Service in 1994.)[7]

Southwestern Wisconsin, the nonglaciated area of the state, is a region of rich soils. But it also features many steep hills, a feature that contributes to soil loss when the land is tilled and subsequent rains carry away valuable topsoil. The SCS established the first large-scale soil and water conservation experiment near Coon Valley, in Vernon County. The program included contour farming (farming around the hills), strip cropping (planting crops such as corn, oats, and hay in relatively narrow strips on the established contours), and creating flood-control dams. The experiment proved highly successful, and soon many farmers living on hilly farms, especially in southwestern Wisconsin, were using these new soil conservation practices for preventing soil erosion.[8]

To further challenge Wisconsin farmers who were suffering through the Depression, rainfall in the years 1930 and 1932 was less than twenty-six inches, more than

An aerial view of Wisconsin fields planted using the contour farming method (that is, crops planted parallel to sloping land rather than perpendicular), 1949

WHI IMAGE ID 58837

In the US Department of Agriculture photo below, depicting strip cropping, the fields were planted with corn, grain, alfalfa, grain, alfalfa. Working with the Soil Conservation Service, Wisconsin was a national leader in the development of strip cropping.

WHI IMAGE ID 2186

six inches below normal. As a result, hot, dry winds blowing from the southwest lifted Wisconsin's sandy soils, especially in the central region, creating vast clouds of dust, ruining crops, and destroying hopes in a situation not unlike the Dust Bowl in the country's Southwest. The SCS, sometimes with the assistance of CCC boys, planted long rows of windbreaks to stop the relentless wind.

Five years after the passage of the original Agricultural Adjustment Act, FDR signed the Agricultural Adjustment Act of 1938. Upon its signing, the president said, "By experience we have learned what must be done to assure to agriculture a fair share of an increasing national income, to provide consumers with abundant supplies of food and fiber, to stop waste of soil, and to reduce the gap between huge surpluses and disastrous shortages. . . . As we go ahead under the new Act, let us resolve to make it an effective instrument to serve the welfare of agriculture and all our people."[9]

The second AAA provided for acreage allotments, payment limits, and protection for farm tenants. This set of laws also included the first comprehensive price-support legislation, with marketing quotas established for several crops. The goal was to gradually increase the subsidy to farmers until farm prices reached their pre-1914 levels.[10]

Milk marketing orders were put in place by the US Department of Agriculture in 1933 to help dairy farmers who faced low prices because of overproduction. Federal milk marketing orders, designed for specific geographic regions of the country, established minimum prices that a milk processor, such as a cheese factory, had to pay a farmer for his milk. The milk price varied, depending on whether the product was sold as fluid milk on grocery shelves (which commanded the highest prices) or as milk used for cheese, butter, or dry milk (the lowest prices).[11]

The federal government also authorized crop insurance for farmers in the 1930s, which resulted in the establishment of the Federal Crop Insurance Corporation in 1938, designed to help farmers recover from the combined effects of the Dust Bowl and the Great Depression. The program was mostly limited to major crops such as wheat, corn, cotton, peanuts, rice, and tobacco. The program would remain an experiment until the passage of the Federal Crop Insurance Act of 1980 (see page 228).

THE RURAL ELECTRIFICATION ADMINISTRATION

By 1910, many Wisconsin villages and cities had electricity. City dwellers in central and southern Wisconsin had electricity thanks to the mills that ground the wheat into flour: rivers and streams were dammed to form millponds, which in turn provided waterpower for the turbines that turned the millstones. With the construction of the first hydroelectric plant in Appleton in 1882 and the refinement of water-powered turbines and electrical generators, many flour mills installed generators, and the village and cities surrounding them enjoyed electricity.

By the 1930s, 90 percent of urban dwellers had electricity, while only 10 percent of rural dwellers did. Farm organizations such as the Farm Bureau and Farmers Union had been advocating for electricity on the farm for several years, and in 1935 President Roosevelt signed an executive order establishing the Rural Electrification Administration (REA), which provided loans to local electric cooperatives. Almost immediately, these co-ops began organizing all over the country, often with the help of county agricultural agents.[12]

The REA was poised to bring electricity to rural locations. But after the United States was pulled into World War II in 1941, the newly organized REA cooperatives were unable to obtain necessary supplies, such as copper wire, or to find a sufficient labor force. It was not until after the war that many farmers would see electricity, with all its benefits, come to their farms. (For more on the arrival of electricity on farms, see page 216.)

With electricity now on the farm, a huge cultural gap between rural and urban

Electricity would eventually revolutionize life on the farm—for all members of the household.

WHI IMAGE ID 82228

dwellers closed. Electrical suppliers quickly learned that their farm customers used far more electricity than the suppliers had anticipated. For farmers, the light bulb was probably the least of what they prized. It was electric motors, electric heaters, milking machines, silo unloaders, milk refrigeration units, and more that farmers found so convenient and labor saving.

At a deeper level, farmers' lives had long been seen—at least by some of their urban neighbors and relatives—as less rich and fulfilling because they had no electrical power. Now farmers had access to the same electrical conveniences as people living in the cities.

The Farmers Union

The National Farmers Union was started by a group of low-income farmers in Texas in 1902. The organization quickly spread throughout much of the country, and by 1940 it had affiliates in twenty-one states. In an interview that year, National Farmers Union president John Vesecky explained the organization's work as follows: "The Farmers Union is trying to organize farmers into their own group, to educate them in economics, production, and cooperation, and to develop cooperatives, beginning with local cooperatives and going on through processing and handling and all the way to consumers."[1]

The group prided itself on being a grassroots organization, with decisions made at the local level. At the 1939 annual convention in Omaha, Nebraska, the organization reaffirmed what it called its "historic principles," stating, "A system of cooperative business, owned by producers and consumers, is the only means by which the potential abundance of this nation may be made available to all its people, and by which true democracy may be maintained and safe-guarded. We urge that our membership continue actively to encourage and promote the development of cooperative business institutions."[2]

Throughout its history, the Farmers Union has advocated for farmer-producers and emphasized the importance of the cooperative movement. The organization supported passage of the 1922 Capper-Volstead Act, which exempted cooperatives from many of the provisions of the Sherman Antitrust Act of 1890. It successfully lobbied for the establishment of rural electric cooperatives and rural and small-town telephone cooperatives. And the group made education a priority, especially for youth; it established a national Farmers Union Youth Education program in 1930.

Also organized in 1930, the Wisconsin Farmers Union began in the state's western and northwestern counties; the organization continues to have its state headquarters in Chippewa Falls. The WFU owns and operates Kamp Kenwood, built by volunteers in the 1940s on the shores of Lake Wissota near Eau Claire. There the organization conducts educational programs for people of all ages, who "come together to celebrate, to learn, and to enjoy family, friends, and nature."[3]

NOTES

1. United States Department of Agriculture, *Farmers in a Changing World: Yearbook of Agriculture, 1940* (Washington, DC: United States Government Printing Office, 1940), p. 950.

2. Ibid., p. 958.

3. "Kamp Kenwood," Wisconsin Farmers Union, www.kampkenwood.com/About.php.

CULTURE IN AGRICULTURE

By the early 1900s, scientific research with the goal of improved agricultural production had become widely accepted. Feeding trials, animal disease control and prevention studies, livestock management strategies, crop variety trials, and research into the genetic improvement of farm animals were carried out by University of

Wisconsin College of Agriculture researchers, with results widely applauded and accepted by Wisconsin farmers. But little was done to study rural communities, rural life, and the broader dimensions of cultural improvement in rural areas. The conveniences and cultural opportunities available to rural dwellers lagged behind those found in cities.

The University of Wisconsin recognized the need for research to understand and improve rural life as early as 1911, when the Department of Agricultural Economics hired the faculty's first rural sociologist, Charles Galpin. In 1930, the school established the Department of Rural Sociology.[13]

In 1931, Chris Christensen became dean of the University of Wisconsin's College of Agriculture. Christensen had studied at the Royal Agricultural College in Denmark and was an admirer of the Danish folk schools, which emphasized self-expression.[14] Concerned about the effect of the Great Depression not only on agricultural enterprises but on farm families as well, he stated that he was committed to putting "culture into agriculture."

Christiansen hired American Regionalist painter John Steuart Curry in 1936 as the college's artist in residence—the first such post at any agricultural college in the country. The Board of Regents voted to grant $4,000 a year for five years for the development of regional art, "as a force for rural culture."[15]

During his residency, Curry painted while on campus and taught painting around the state, with the administrative support and encouragement of UW rural sociologist

One section of Curry's three-panel work *The Social Benefits of Biochemical Research,* painted during his UW–Madison residency

COURTESY OF ROBIN DAVIES, UW–MADISON BIOCHEMISTRY MEDIALAB

John Rector Barton. Barton and Curry helped organize the Wisconsin Rural Art Program, and regional art groups soon emerged in rural communities around the state. The first Rural Art Exhibit was held at the UW Memorial Union during the College of Agriculture's Farm and Home Week in 1940. The book *Rural Artists of Wisconsin,* written by Barton, was published in 1948.[16] Curry died in 1946, and Aaron Bohrod followed him as artist in residence, holding the position until 1973.

Robert E. Gard was another giant in promoting culture in Wisconsin's rural communities. A Kansas farm boy with a degree in theater from Cornell University,

Gard joined the faculty of the UW's College of Agriculture in 1945.[17] Gard valued telling and writing stories not only as entertainment but also as ways to help people understand the importance of place. He traveled the state, leading drama and writing workshops and encouraging farm people to write, paint, participate in community plays, and in other ways to be active in the arts. Gard founded the Wisconsin Regional Writers Association and guided the organization for more than thirty-five years. He also helped organize the Council for Wisconsin Writers in 1964 and wrote more than thirty books, most about Wisconsin.

Robert Gard talked with Wisconsin farmers, circa 1950. The door on his truck read "Wisconsin Idea Theatre," referring to the cultural outreach program he founded in 1943.
IMAGE COURTESY OF THE UW–MADISON ARCHIVES, #S15183

President Roosevelt's New Deal programs also shone a light on the cultural lives of the nation's agricultural communities. As part of the US Work Progress Administration (WPA), the Federal Writers' Project was created in 1935 to provide jobs for writers and other white-collar professionals, including teachers, historians, and librarians. The writers conducted interviews and wrote life histories of ordinary citizens, many of them rural people, thereby helping to forge a broader understanding of rural life and the importance of documenting it. Many of the manuscripts the writers produced are available online through the Library of Congress (LOC). According to the LOC, the collected FWP material "provides the raw content for a broad documentary of both rural and urban life, interspersed with accounts and traditions of ethnic group traditions, customs regarding planting, cooking, marriage, death, celebrations, recreation, and a wide variety of narratives."[18]

19
WAR BRINGS CHANGE

With the bombing of Pearl Harbor by the Japanese on December 7, 1941, the United States was once more at war, this time with Japan, Germany, and Italy. Almost immediately, World War II created challenges and change for everyone in Wisconsin, no matter where they lived. Where there had been farm surpluses during the Depression years, now the call was for greater farm production. While millions of workers could not find jobs during the long, dreadful years of the Depression, now, almost overnight, there was a shortage of labor in both town and country. And rationing affected everyone and caused long-term changes in eating and living habits.

LABOR SHORTAGES

After President Roosevelt signed the Selective Service Act into law in 1940, all young men ages twenty-one to thirty-six were required to register for the military draft. The law was expanded to include ages eighteen to thirty-eight in 1943. Eventually, more than 330,000 Wisconsin men and 9,000 Wisconsin women served in the war. Servicemen and servicewomen came from every county in the state, from the farms, village, and cities.[1]

Wisconsin farms saw a severe labor shortage. Many of the young men had gone off to war; others, attracted by the higher wages in industrial jobs, moved to the cities. In the spring of 1943, Arlie Mucks, supervisor of the state's emergency farm labor program, estimated that Wisconsin farms would be short some one hundred thousand men. The problem persisted throughout the war. In January 1945, Mucks

A German POW pitched pea vines at a Columbia County cannery, 1945.
WHI IMAGE ID 43581

said the state's farmers needed an additional fifty thousand farm-workers to harvest crops and work on dairy farms.[2]

Although many farm boys were drafted during the early years of the war, by 1943 the local draft boards, aware of the shortage of farmworkers, were more apt to grant a deferment for farmers, calling farmwork essential for the war effort.[3]

Prisoners of war also helped to solve some of the labor shortage, both on farms and in vegetable canning plants. In the fall of 1942, the United States began accepting German POWs captured by Great Britain. By late spring of 1944, more than 5,000 Japanese, 371,000 Germans, 51,000 Italians, and smaller numbers of other nationalities were housed in United States POW camps. An abandoned Civilian Conservation Corps camp at Camp McCoy in Monroe County was one of the first sites in the country to house POWs. At its peak, Camp McCoy held nearly 3,500 Japanese, 5,000 Germans, and about 500 Koreans.[4]

In addition to the larger and more permanent base camps like the one at Camp McCoy, branch camps were established close to areas of potential labor shortages. Only German POWs were assigned to branch camps. In 1944–45, Wisconsin had thirty-eight branch camps open during the summer and fall months. For example, Camp Ripon near the Central Wisconsin Canning Company site housed as many as 650 POWs, who worked in the cannery and also assisted farmers in harvesting peas, sugar beets, and sweet corn. Camp Markesan was located on the site of the Grand River Canning Company property and housed up to 637 POWs, who worked in Markesan, Fairwater, and Fall River canneries and fields.[5] Because Wisconsin had so many German-speaking residents, some POWs felt almost at home, especially when helping a Wisconsin German farm family harvest its crops.

As writer Betty Cowley explained, the program expanded beyond farm fields and canneries: "In Wisconsin [POWs] were contracted to the canning companies to help harvest and process crops that would have gone to waste, to bale hemp, and to work in nurseries, tanneries, dairies, and some industrial factories."[6]

Boys and girls of high school age provided another source of temporary labor for farmers, especially during times when vegetable and fruit crops were ready for harvest. A farm labor recruitment official estimated that in 1943 some five thousand teenagers would be necessary to assist with the Door County fruit harvest. For the state as a whole, the number of teenagers to be recruited for emergency farmwork that year would reach sixty thousand.[7]

With farmworker deferments, POW help, teenage labor, and the efforts of the women who stayed on the homefront, farmers managed to make it through the war, even though many of them continued to farm with horses and had no electricity or indoor plumbing. Even with the labor shortage, Wisconsin farmers increased production levels—a tribute to their commitment to the war effort and their hard work.[8]

RATIONING

With the start of World War II, the economy immediately shifted to an emphasis on war production. Consumer goods took a backseat to the production of guns, ammunition, airplanes, bombs, and all that was necessary to fight a war. In May 1942, the US Office of Price Administration (OPA) froze prices on everyday consumer products, beginning with sugar and coffee.[9]

Marion Rentschler and Eileen Frederick, members of the Madison Women's Club, proudly displayed their victory garden produce, 1944.
WHI IMAGE ID 40293

Ration books were issued to each family member, indicating how much gasoline, how many tires, and what quantities of other items could be purchased. The first nonfood item rationed was rubber, as the Japanese had taken over the rubber plantations in the Dutch East Indies, which supplied the United States with 90 percent of its raw rubber.[10]

People were encouraged to contribute scrap iron and rubber for recycling. Schoolchildren collected milkweed seedpods for use in making lifejackets. Everyone, whether in the country or the city, was encouraged to grow a victory garden to produce as much of their own food as possible and donate any excess to the war effort. In Wisconsin, the growing of sweet sorghum saw renewed interest after sugar was rationed. Although after the war sorghum became more of a novelty than a necessity, some home cooks continued to use sorghum in their baked goods, having grown accustomed to the syrup's subtle, sweet flavor.

Rationing led to bartering, as people traded labor for hard-to-come-by meat and other goods. Historian and author Richard Haney, who grew up in Janesville, Wisconsin, recalled that during the war his grandpa "devoted several hours of his spare time each month to doing all the bookkeeping and accounting work for a lifelong friend who operated a small family-run creamery. In exchange, Grandpa received butter for his family's personal use."[11]

Items Rationed during World War II

- **Tires:** January 1942–December 1945
- **Cars:** February 1942–October 1945
- **Bicycles:** July 1942–September 1945
- **Gasoline:** May 1942–August 1945
- **Fuel oil and kerosene:** October 1942–August 1945
- **Solid fuels:** September 1943–August 1945
- **Stoves:** December 1942–August 1945
- **Rubber footwear:** October 1942–September 1945
- **Shoes:** February 1943–October 1945
- **Sugar:** May 1942–47 (month varied around the country)
- **Coffee:** November 1942–July 1943
- **Processed foods:** March 1943–August 1945
- **Meats and canned fish:** March 1943–November 1945
- **Cheese, canned milk, fats:** March 1943–November 1945

The Office of Civilian Defense encouraged people to can their own food in support of the war effort.

WHI IMAGE ID 66866

NOTES

"World War II Rationing on the US Homefront," Ames (Iowa) Historical Society, www.ameshistory.org/exhibits/ration_items.htm.

A POULTRY INDUSTRY ARISES

World War II brought an increased demand for dairy products, beef, and pork, which led to the emergence of a commercial poultry industry in Wisconsin. Many of the state's early settlers raised chickens, both for food for the family table and for eggs to sell or barter, but income from poultry and eggs was a minor contributor to farm income until the mid-twentieth century. The commercial poultry industry today owes much of its success to World War II, as not only did chickens, eggs, broilers, and turkeys provide an alternative to pork and beef during the war years, but consumers developed a taste for these products that has created strong market demand ever since.

Wisconsin's peak year for chickens for egg production and broilers for meat was 1944, when 19.8 million chickens were reported. Throughout the war years, poultry numbers were concentrated near large markets: Trempealeau, Pepin, and Pierce Counties in the west; Sheboygan and Fond du Lac in the east; and Dane, Dodge, and Jefferson Counties in the south.[12]

Edna Kern tended to laying hens on her Green County farm, 1956.
WHI IMAGE ID 25078

Workers at the Frank Lyons Turkey Farm, Verona (Dane County), 1947
WHI IMAGE ID 34551

Turkey Leader

Wallace Jerome had liked turkeys ever since he was a child. Born in 1909 in Spooner, Wisconsin, Jerome owned one hundred turkeys by the time he graduated from high school in 1928. He went on to study poultry science at the University of Minnesota and graduated from the University of Wisconsin in 1941. In the late 1940s, he purchased an abandoned pea cannery in Barron, Wisconsin, and started a turkey processing company, Jerome Foods.

The company was later renamed the Turkey Store Company and in 2001 merged with Jennie-O Foods to become Jennie-O Turkey. With 2,500 employees and processing plants in Barron, Wisconsin, and in Altura and Faribault, Minnesota, the company processed more than forty-five thousand turkeys per day. Wallace Jerome helped develop a year-round market for turkey products such as turkey steak, turkey tenderloins, ground turkey, turkey ham, and many kinds of turkey sausages.

NOTES

"Our History," Jennie-O, www.jennieo.com/content/our_history; and "Wallace Jerome," Wisconsin Meat Industry Hall of Fame, www.ansci.wisc.edu/Meat_HOF/index.htm.

Before World War II, there was no commercial broiler production in Wisconsin. In 1934, the state produced but 350,000 birds. But by 1945, the number of broilers raised in Wisconsin soared to more than 3.9 million. Beef and pork supplies were limited during the war years, and chicken was an affordable alternative. Demonstrating the long-lasting effects of the war years, broiler numbers continued to rise in Wisconsin after the war. In 1934, less than 1 percent of the state's total gross farm income came from commercial broiler production; in 1953 it was 10 percent.[13]

The war also launched a commercial turkey industry. Only about 350,000 turkeys were raised in Wisconsin in 1933, yet by 1953, turkey numbers reached 1.6 million birds.[14]

Although farmers had to deal with rationing and labor shortages, in general their economic situation improved considerably during the war compared to the dreadful Great Depression years. Farm prices were up, and the demand for farmers' products was high. And farmers were held in high esteem as major contributors to the war effort. But after the war, surpluses once more became a problem, and the public's attitude toward farmers would change.

FARMING AT MIDCENTURY

The first agricultural revolution, which began in the 1830s, saw the heavy draft horse breeds replace the sturdy oxen that had done the heavy work on the farm since colonial days. And then, for many Wisconsin farmers, farming methods remained relatively unchanged for a long time to come—nearly a century, for some.

The next big changes in agriculture began during World War II and became more evident in the years immediately following. This revolution was marked by electricity replacing lamps and lanterns and tractors putting horses out to pasture. Agriculture was evolving in other ways as well, but electricity and mechanization were the core of sweeping changes. As historian William F. Thompson wrote,

At midcentury, many Wisconsin farms looked a lot like the one depicted in this 1948 State Fair mural, with a red dairy barn, house, and well-kept outbuildings. But another set of enormous changes were already on the horizon for Wisconsin farmers. (For more on the state fair mural project, see page 76.)

WISCONSIN HISTORICAL
MUSEUM 2010.156.1.8

"There was much that was familiar throughout Wisconsin in that last full year of peace before the war. The climate and seasonal rotation remained much as they had been at the time of settlement, varying only slightly from year to year. . . . Few people foresaw sprawl or pollution, much less a rate of change in their physical and social surroundings that was governed only by its own momentum."[1]

ELECTRICITY COMES TO THE COUNTRY

Arguably, electricity influenced farm operations and farm family life more than any other technological innovation—before or after. With electricity in his barn, a farmer no longer needed a pocket of matches to strike the wicks of the lamps and lanterns that had lighted his way for years. With the pull of a lever, a pump motor came alive and began pumping water. Turn another switch, and the milking machine began pulsing, allowing the farmer to add several more cows to his dairy herd. And with yet another switch, a barn cleaner automatically moved the animal waste to the manure spreader standing outside the barn, without the farming having to touch a shovel or fork. On my home farm, we no longer had to hope for a bright moon to light our way to the barn for morning and late-afternoon chores; now a yard light showed the way. And I stopped carrying a lantern up to the haymow, for with the flip of a switch, the haymow was as bright as day.[2]

Men and women examined a six-can milk cooler promoted by the McCormick-Deering company in the late 1930s.
WHI IMAGE ID 54516

According to the report *Wisconsin Agriculture in Mid-Century* prepared in 1953 by the Wisconsin State Department of Agriculture, electricity was "one of the best and cheapest workers on Wisconsin farms. . . . It is used in the performance of numerous farm tasks as well as providing light, power and fuel for the farm home. The water that flows in the barn is often supplied by an electric pump. Electricity is used for the milking machine, milk cooler, feed grinder, fans, radios, washing machines and many other items." By 1950, 93 percent of the farms in Wisconsin had electricity, paying an average monthly bill of $9.74.[3]

MECHANIZATION ARRIVES ON THE FARM

After essentially replacing oxen in the mid-nineteenth century, horses continued to handle the heavy work on the farm through the Depression years. Many farmers didn't purchase their first tractor until after World War II. During the Depression, when gas tractors became available, many farmers simply couldn't afford them. (A handful of farmers owned steam tractors, mostly used for powering threshing machines.) Most farmers were accustomed to farming with horses and enjoyed working with the animals.

In the 1950s, prosperity led more farmers to add tractors to their farm equipment. And with tractors came a new generation of tractor-powered farm machinery.

Tractors allowed farmers to harvest their corn crop without the use of a corn binder, without a stationary silo filler, and without a corn shredding bee to husk the corn. New tractor-drawn implements did this work quickly, efficiently, and with much less labor required.

WHI IMAGE ID 88518

Dairy farmers needed a barn full of hay to feed their hungry cows throughout the long winters, and hay making with horses was slow, tedious, dusty, and dirty work. Thankfully, tractor-pulled hay balers allowed the farmer to forgo bunching newly raked hay by hand, pitching it onto a horse-drawn wagon, and then forking it into the haymow.

With tractors and newly developed forage harvesters, corn binders were eliminated, and tractor-pulled grain combines eliminated the need for grain binders, for shocking grain by hand, and for the threshing crews that moved from farm to farm. In the wake of these technical innovations, communal work gatherings such as silo-filling bees and threshing bees disappeared. These work bees not only helped neighbors with the harvest, but were social events and a way to tie rural communities together.

CHANGES IN RURAL COMMUNITIES

This second revolution affected farming practices and had profound structural effects on rural communities. The most obvious was the decline in the number of farms. With tractors, electricity, and new disease-resistant and higher-yielding crop varieties, Wisconsin farmers could grow more crops and milk more cows with less human power than ever before. As a result, farmers, and especially farmers' children, had fewer opportunities in farming. Starting in the late 1940s, with more young people

Rural Rock County students boarded a bus for the Janesville consolidated schools, circa 1950.

WHI IMAGE ID 41159

having completed a high school education, many of them left the farms for work in the cities. Some of the more fortunate young people left to attend college. The number of Wisconsin farms had peaked in 1935 at around 200,000; by 1950 that number was down to 168,561 and falling. At the same time, the average size of a Wisconsin farm increased from 117 acres in 1935 to 138 in 1950. In 1910, 35.7 percent of Wisconsin's citizens lived on farms; by 1950, that percentage had fallen to 21.3.[4]

As the number of farms shrank, farms themselves became larger, and the farm population declined, rural communities changed dramatically. One-room country schools, a prominent feature in all Wisconsin communities, were mostly closed by the mid-1950s, as school buses transported the remaining young people on farms to the consolidated schools in the nearby villages and cities.[5] Many country churches closed as well. Crossroads cheese factories ceased operations as trucks and improved roads made travel from farm to market easier. And with better roads and better cars, people traveled farther to large retail centers for their purchases, causing smaller villages to lose business.

WISCONSIN'S FARM ECONOMY AT MIDCENTURY

Income from Wisconsin's dairy industry grew steadily during World War II, reaching $300 million in 1943 and more than $500 million in 1946, increases due mainly to the greater demand for dairy products during the war. In 1948, Wisconsin's dairy income reached $590 million; it dipped to $580 million in 1952.[6]

One reason for the increased income from milk was how it was priced. Milk pricing in the United States was affected by milk marketing orders, which were instituted in 1949. These milk marketing orders provided a floor for the amount of money dairymen received for their product. When there was more milk than the market required, the government stepped in and bought dairy products, thus keeping milk prices from falling as far as they otherwise might.[7]

The sale of cattle and calves was the second major source of Wisconsin farm income at midcentury, reaching $200 million in 1951. The sale of hogs ranked third ($129 million) and poultry fourth ($111 million).[8]

THE UW'S MAJOR CONTRIBUTIONS AT MIDCENTURY

The University of Wisconsin continued to have great impact on agricultural practices during the mid-twentieth century. Plant breeders at the UW's College of Agriculture and other ag colleges were discovering new and improved varieties of grain by the mid-1900s; one such development was faster-maturing hybrid seed corn, created by crossing two genetically different corn plants. From 1900 to 1939, the average corn yield for Wisconsin farmers held steady at 38.5 bushels; by 1971, corn acreage yields shot up to nearly 100 bushels per acre.[9]

During this era the university also developed new, high-protein varieties of alfalfa, which provided greater yields and were winter hardy. Research on high-yielding grasses led to new varieties of brome grass with increased yields.

In 1940, the UW College of Agriculture's Dairy Husbandry Department established an experimental bull stud program to supply semen for dairy farmers in southern Wisconsin counties. The department conducted research "on optimum time for breeding, comparison of semen diluents, age of semen in relation to fertility, and positioning of semen in the female tract." They also studied techniques for the collecting of semen, including "electrical stimulation, [and the] use of artificial cows or cows in heat or infertile animals with hormone injections."[10]

This 1939 brochure promoted International Harvester Company's hybrid seed corn.
WHI IMAGE ID 86791

In 1939 and 1940, biochemistry researchers Paul Phillips and Henry Lardy experimented with an egg yolk buffer medium for preserving bull semen. This buffer extended the life of the semen and allowed it to be stored as long as 150 to 180 hours.[11] Research continued on best practices for collecting and storing semen, and by the 1950s frozen semen that could be stored for years became available. Frozen semen gave farmers access to semen from the highest-quality bulls available, and by signing up for an artificial breeding service, they could now improve the genetics of their dairy herd. Additionally, they no longer had to keep an unpredictable (and sometimes dangerous) bull on the farm.

As the UW continued its research into best farming practices, it also continually worked to improve the marketing and selling of farmers' products. In 1952, Henry Ahlgren, the College of Agriculture's associate dean and chair of the UW's annual on-campus Farm and Home Week, envisioned an off-campus opportunity for people not able to travel to Madison. The first event held as part of Ahlgren's plan was a state plowing contest in 1953 near Augusta. The next year, a two-day show called Farm Progress Days was held in Waupaca County, and articles of incorporation for the new program were approved. The show was held in different counties over the years and moved to a three-day format beginning in 1957. In 1961, the show was held in Rock County; 250,000 people attended.[12]

With its Farm and Home Week, the University of Wisconsin offered an opportunity for farm families from around the state to come to Madison for one or more days to learn about new agricultural research findings and meet with College of Agriculture staff.

WHI IMAGE ID 100927

By the 2000s, the program, now called Farm Technology Days, would be the largest agricultural show in Wisconsin and one of the largest in the nation. The show is coordinated and managed by the host county's University of Wisconsin–Extension office in cooperation with a local Farm Technology Days committee and from seven hundred to a thousand volunteers.[13]

LIFE ON A WISCONSIN FARM, 1950

By the mid-twentieth century, many Wisconsin farm homes were beginning to see the transforming effects of modern conveniences including indoor plumbing, central heating, and electricity. A writer for the Wisconsin Crop and Livestock Reporting Service described the farm home at midcentury as being

surrounded with evidence of an advancing agriculture. The springhouse is replaced by the refrigerator, and modern methods of food distribution and the deepfreeze have eliminated much of the necessity for home canning. Telephones, electricity, radio, television and automobiles have all contributed to improved rural life in Wisconsin. . . . By 1950, 87 percent of Wisconsin farmers had electric washing machines. . . . Forty percent of the farm home wood heaters had been replaced with central heating. About fifty percent had water piped into the home.[14]

Not all farm families, however, wanted—or could afford—to upgrade their operations, and many Wisconsin farms stepped into the second half of the 1900s with one foot firmly planted in the past. David Shekoski recalled that in the 1950s, his grandparents Gustav and Elizabeth Fritz heated their farmhouse near New London with wood-burning stoves, including the ancient, massive one in the kitchen. "It was amazing what my grandmother could do with that stove," he remembered. "If the cooking temperature was a little too hot or too cool, she knew exactly where to slide the kettle to achieve the correct cooking temperature. There were no temperature settings to adjust except the stove vents on the firebox and the damper in the stove pipe." In summer, Elizabeth prepared meals on a kerosene stove in the summer kitchen to avoid heating the house. And indoor plumbing remained "something only to be dreamed about." Yet apart from that,

[T]he house was equipped with all of the conveniences of modern times. Running water was fed directly into the kitchen by a hand pump mounted next to the sink. (Apparently the well was drilled and the house was built around it. There was another pump in the back yard between the house and the barn.) Electricity was brought to the house through wires that extended from a pole next to the road and entered the house through the kitchen wall. The extent of electrical service was one outlet in the kitchen (which operated the refrigerator and the radio, which sat on top of the refrigerator), a wire that ran to the ceiling for the kitchen light, and another wire that ran along the wall to the single outlet in the living room.[15]

By midcentury, many homes, both rural and urban, had installed electric appliances. This refrigerator, advertised in 1949, was manufactured by the International Harvester company, which got its start making agricultural machinery at the turn of the nineteenth century.

WHI IMAGE ID 60040

Changes in Wild Rose, Wisconsin

Located in Waushara County and incorporated as a village in 1873, Wild Rose served the surrounding farm community for more than a hundred years, similar to hundreds of other villages scattered across the state.

In 1950, the village, with a population of about six hundred, offered these businesses and services: a gristmill, a cheese factory, a feed store and lumberyard, the Midland Cooperative (which sold grease, oil, fertilizer, and farm seed), a small hotel, three taverns, several churches, the high school and consolidated grade school, a hospital, a welding shop, a hardware store, a sawmill, a cucumber salting station, two small restaurants, a mercantile that sold everything from shoes to groceries, an ice cream shop, a pharmacy, a dentist's office, a harness shop, a clothing store, a butcher shop, a bank, a post office, two car dealers that also did auto repairs, and a small public library.

This photo of my home farm, located four and a half miles west of Wild Rose, was taken in the late 1950s or early 1960s. My parents, Herman and Eleanor Apps, sold the farm in 1973 and moved into Wild Rose. The land was no longer farmed and would eventually be sold to seven different families, several of whom built homes on the property. With one or two exceptions, all of the neighboring farms met a similar fate. As farmers left the land, the need for village services diminished, and the villages changed as well. Wild Rose was no exception.
WHI IMAGE ID 95832

Over the next fifteen years, the village changed as the farming community changed. The gristmill closed and became a home. The cheese factory closed and was torn down. The mercantile became an antiques store. The car dealers closed, as did the harness shop, dentist office, clothing store, butcher shop, feed store/lumberyard, ice cream shop, and pharmacy. The Midland Cooperative became a convenience store that sold gas, a few groceries, and other necessities. The taverns remained, as did three restaurants and a small grocery store. The high school and grade school continued. Two nursing homes were added. The hospital remained open, making it the only one in Waushara County. Patterson Memorial Library expanded, added a community room and kitchen, and served as the community's meeting center.

Better than many small farm-service villages, Wild Rose, because of its proximity to many lakes with

(continued on next page)

Changes in Wild Rose, Wisconsin

(*continued from page 223*)
surrounding cottages and summer visitors, moved from being primarily a village serving farmers to one relying on tourists. But the transition has been a struggle. The population of the village has grown to more than seven hundred, but the village is challenged to provide basic services with a limited tax base. Also, with few employment opportunities, many young people leave the community upon graduating from high school. Nonetheless, with strong local leadership and vibrant service clubs, the village is facing the future with enthusiasm, as seen in the several communitywide events held during the year that attract hundreds of visitors.

NOTES

Jerry Apps, *Village of Roses* (Wild Rose, WI: Wild Rose Historical Society, 1973).

When farm families did decide to make improvements, those upgrades often took place in the barn before the house. At my home farm, we installed running water in the barn twenty years before we had indoor plumbing in the house. As my father often said when I asked why conditions in the barn seemed better than in the house, "There is no income coming from the house."

The years from the end of World War II into the early 1960s were a time of tremendous change in Wisconsin agriculture. Not only did total farm numbers continue falling from their peak in 1935, but the number of dairy farms declined as well. In 1965, Wisconsin had 86,000 dairy farms (124,000 total farms). By 1970, the number of dairy farms would fall to 64,000 (110,000 total farms).[16]

Many young people left the land to find employment in cities. Those remaining on the farm now felt the need to purchase more land and invest in the mechanization required to farm more acres. Dairy farmers purchased more cows and built larger barns and silos, and their debt levels rose. Some left dairy farming to concentrate on raising cash crops—mainly corn and later soybeans—for sale off the farm. Others left dairy farming to grow vegetables and other specialty crops.

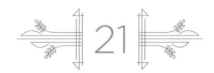

NEW CHALLENGES, MODERN SOLUTIONS

With advances in technology, including ever larger and more sophisticated farm machinery, chemical weed control for crops, hybrid crop varieties, and improved genetics for livestock, Wisconsin farms continued to become larger during the second half of the twentieth century. However, as farm sizes increased, the overall number of farms continued to fall. Wisconsin had 138,000 farms in 1960; by 1997 the number had declined to 79,000. The average size of a farm in 1960 was 160.9 acres; in 1997 the average was 213 acres.[1]

From 1987 to 1997, Wisconsin lost almost 13 percent of its farms, as many farms near major urban centers became housing developments and shopping centers, and less-productive farms became recreational land for hunters and second-home owners. Diversified farms—those relying on more than one income-generating enterprise—also began to disappear. For example, during that decade the number of Wisconsin farms raising hogs as part of a larger operation dropped by almost 60 percent.[2]

Both in response to the increasing amount of farmland becoming available for sale and to prevent ownership of Wisconsin agricultural lands by large corporations and foreign countries, the state legislature in 2010 created a law that prevents corporations and trusts from "owning or carrying on farming operations" (2010 Wisconsin code: Chapter 182.001). (A corporation is defined as having no more than fifteen shareholders or beneficiaries. A second statute, 710.02, prevents "aliens not residents of the United States" from owning or holding any interest in more than 640 acres of land in the state.)

A housing subdivision arose at the edge of farmland near Theresa (Dodge County), 1978.
WHI IMAGE ID 87186

Significant changes occurred in dairy farming in the 1960s, as dairy farmers moved their cattle from the old dairy barns constructed in the late 1800s and early 1900s to loose housing operations, where the cattle were confined indoors all months of the year and had their feed hauled to them. The next decades saw a dramatic decline in dairy farm numbers in the state: from 53,000 in 1974 to 25,000 in 1997. Farm auctions were held throughout the state, hundreds each year, with all of the stress and emotion associated with families selling their farm animals and leaving their land. Many tears were shed as the auctioneer banged his gavel, announcing the sale of a prize dairy cow, well-worn implement, or the farm itself.

At the same time that farm numbers were decreasing, with improved dairy cattle genetics and better understanding of animal nutrition and dairy cattle management the average annual milk production per cow increased from 5,380 pounds in 1935 to 16,057 pounds in 1997.[3]

It wasn't only new farming practices that led to changes in the dairy industry. In the 1970s, political maneuvering resulted in artificially high prices, with price supports soaring from $5 per hundredweight of milk to $13 per hundredweight. The result was unsustainable growth of the dairy industry in Wisconsin and elsewhere. Farmers expanded their herds, bought new equipment, and took on considerable debt—and they produced more milk than the market could handle. The federal government bought the excess cheese, butter, and powdered milk under the Dairy Price Support Program. Soon the federal government ran out of storage space and began giving away cheese as a part of food assistance programs. The system was out of control.[4]

The federal government tried several programs to eliminate excess dairy production. In 1983, the US Congress enacted the Milk Diversion Program, in which the federal government paid farmers to reduce production for a fifteen-month period in 1984–85. The program was unsuccessful, as farmers circumvented the restrictions by selling their low-producing cows to meet the required cutback and delayed breeding heifers so the cows began to produce milk after the program terminated in March 1985. Milk production declined little, and it rebounded completely as soon as the program ended.[5]

In 1986–87, the US government implemented the dairy whole-herd buyout program. Farmers who participated sold their entire herds for slaughter or export, with a government subsidy established through a bidding process. Farmers signing up for the program agreed to stay out of dairy farming for a minimum of five years. The program lasted just over a year and did help reduce production. The most successful way to control overproduction was a gradual lowering of the milk support price so it was no longer an effective inducement for increasing production.[6]

In large loose-housing barns, several hundred dairy cows can move about easily. By the twenty-first century, these would be fairly common. The little hutches in front of the barn seen here house young calves.
STEVE APPS

World Dairy Expo

In mid-1960s, dairy cattle shows across the country were facing shrinking audiences. Wisconsin dairy leaders, including farmers and University of Wisconsin–Extension dairy specialists, began discussing holding an international show in Wisconsin with the purpose of promoting the dairy industry. The group formed a corporation called the World Food and Agriculture Foundation, with Wilbur N. Renk as its first president. The first World Food Expo was held September 15–24, 1967, at the newly completed Dane County Memorial Coliseum in Madison. In 1970, with strong interest from the dairy industry nationwide, the group changed its focus solely to dairying and changed the name of the exposition to World Dairy Expo.

The expo has grown ever since. The dairy cattle show, where elite dairy farmers bring their cattle to Madison, also attracts companies (810 in 2011) related to the dairy industry. Total attendance at World Dairy Expo in 2011 was 68,000 people including more than 2,700 from 90 different countries.

NOTES

Adapted from "History Summary of World Dairy Expo," World Dairy Expo, http://www.worlddairyexpo.com/file_open.php?id=194.

Starting in the 1990s, competition for milk products and growth in cheese sales began to overcome the inequities in the milk marketing order system. Unfortunately, dairy legislation, like other farm-related legislation, became highly politicized. As agricultural economist Ed Jesse has argued, "The pricing system needs to reflect current market conditions, not political interests. . . . From Wisconsin's perspective, the fundamental objective is simple: eliminate or at least minimize artificial (non-market) milk production incentives. . . . Economic forces will treat Wisconsin dairy farmers and processors more favorably than political forces."[7]

FOOD SECURITY ACT OF 1985

By the 1980s, farmers were taking advantage of guaranteed price supports. For instance, the Federal Crop Insurance Act of 1980 expanded crop insurance to farmers, making more crops eligible for coverage.[8] Farmers began farming marginal land that was susceptible to soil erosion both by wind and water. As Sierra Club spokesman Douglas Scott has noted, "Farmland washes and blows away at the rate of 3 billion tons a year, more than twice as much as gets replaced by nature. . . . Soil erosion in the nation is today as bad as, and in many places dramatically worse than it was at the height of the Dust Bowl of the 1930s."[9]

The Sierra Club, the American Farmland Trust, and other environmental groups pushed for stronger conservation measures in the Food Security Act of 1985 (also known as the 1985 Farm Bill). In addition to provisions in support of dairy, wool and mohair production, wheat, feed grains, cotton, rice, peanuts, soybeans, sugar, agricultural research, cooperative extension, food stamps, and ag marketing, the bill included Title XII, or the Conservation Provision. Sometimes called the Swampbuster Law, this section of the legislation was included to discourage the conversion of wetlands to agricultural production. Those farmers who converted wetlands to cultivated land after December 23, 1985, were denied federal farm program benefits. Other provisions of Title XII created the Conservation Reserve Program (CRP) and the Conservation Enhancement Program (CREP), intended "to help agricultural producers safeguard environmentally sensitive lands by planting long-term, resource-conserving covers that would control soil erosion, improve water and air quality, and enhance wildlife habitat."[10]

The Food, Agriculture, Conservation and Trade Act of 1990 gave the 1985 Farm Bill additional teeth by preventing those who converted wetlands into cropland from receiving farm program benefits for the year of the violation and for all subsequent years as well.[11]

By the 1980s, the number of working farms was dropping rapidly, and those that remained by and large were bigger and more heavily mechanized, making it increasingly difficult for a new generation to become farmers. The financial challenges of entering farming had become enormous.

WHI IMAGE ID 9267

AGRIBUSINESS ORGANIZATIONS EMERGE

The word *agribusiness* is believed to have come into use around 1955. Simply put, it refers to the range of activities that arise at the intersection of agriculture and business. The nonprofit Wisconsin Agri-business Association was organized in the 1960s to bring together agriculture manufacturers, wholesalers, and distributors; implement dealers; seed dealers; granaries; farm supply retailers; agricultural consultants; custom applicators; soil-testing-lab representatives; insurance companies; and legal firms—all with interests in agriculture. The organization's mission is to "represent, provide programs and services, educate, train, manage regulatory and legislative affairs, and to be a strong unifying voice for agribusiness industries of Wisconsin."[12]

The Farm Press Meets Changing Needs

As agriculture changed, Wisconsin's farm press adapted. Not only did farm publications add color and contemporary graphic design, they kept their readers informed of new agricultural research, explained changes in farm-related laws and regulations, and shared stories of successful farmers and their operations. Almost paradoxically, as farm numbers decreased, the farm press grew.

Central Wisconsin Farmer, which later became *Wisconsin State Farmer,* was launched in 1956 by Carl Turner, publisher of the *Waupaca County Post.* Turner told his readers that the paper would be "devoted exclusively to bringing you news and pictures—lots of them—of Central Wisconsin farm families. . . . Special emphasis will be placed upon pictures pertaining to farm families. . . . Since *Central Wisconsin Farmer* is a regional publication, it will bring its readers news and pictures of people they know—their neighbors and themselves."[1]

The first issue consisted of six broadsheet pages and carried ads from local commercial advertisers, the same ones who advertised in the *Waupaca County Post.* In 1963, when Frances Turner was publisher and Hubert Mocadlo was editor, the paper went statewide, changing its name to *Wisconsin State Farmer.* Stories in the paper at that time included weed control, dairy news, hog news, crabgrass control, and a humor column, "Uncle Lem Says." In 2009, *Wisconsin State Farmer* (along with the *Waupaca County Post* and *Wisconsin Horseman's News*) was sold to Journal Communications in Milwaukee, publishers of the *Milwaukee Journal Sentinel.*[2] Today it is published by parent company Journal Community Publishing Group.

Partners Jerry Petcher, Bryan McNeely, Jim Brayer, and Emil Radeztsky started *Agri-View* as *Dairyland Agri-View* in Marshfield, Wisconsin, in 1975 with a circulation of about seventeen thousand in ten counties. The publication set out to reach

The Wisconsin Agribusiness Council, organized in 1971, includes a broad range of members, from representatives of educational institutions to farmers, from agricultural press representatives to agricultural cooperative officials. The organization is "a statewide league dedicated to improving the business environment for agriculture in Wisconsin."[13] The council keeps members informed about proposed laws and regulations that might affect their business, trains members in the legislative process, and brings together a broad array of agricultural industry leaders to share ideas and work toward change.

PRECISION AGRICULTURE

Global positioning system (GPS) technology has its roots in the Cold War days of the 1960s, when the United States launched five earth-orbiting satellites. Between 1978 and

The Farm Press Meets Changing Needs

active farm producers interested in new farm equipment and farm-related products and services. A southern edition debuted in 1976, with another nineteen thousand subscribers. By 1979, the publication was available statewide, reaching some seventy-five thousand farm families. In 1990, Krause publications bought *Agri-View,* moving its offices to Iola. Capital Newspapers purchased *Agri-View* in 1996 and moved it to Madison. Today *Agri-View*'s circulation is thirty-two thousand readers throughout Wisconsin and in Minnesota, Michigan, Illinois, and Iowa. The paper includes sections on calf care, nutrient management, dairy herd health, farm construction, and money matters.[3]

The first edition of *The Country Today* came off the presses on January 26, 1977. With offices in Eau Claire and owned by the *Eau Claire Leader-Telegram,* the paper calls itself "the newspaper that cares about rural life." In addition to carrying farm and related agricultural news, the weekly paper also includes the popular "Country Life" section, which features historic farming photos and stories written by readers titled "Yarns of Yesteryear." The newspaper's niche is its diversity, with pages devoted to recipes, horses, outdoor news, woodlot-management tips, and rural feature stories. *The Country Today* has a full online version as well. When the newspaper celebrated its thirty-fifth anniversary in 2012, it boasted subscribers in forty-five states.[4]

NOTES

1. Personal communication from Trey Foerster, publisher, *Wisconsin State Farmer,* August 3, 2012.

2. Ibid.

3. Interview with Joan Sanstadt, September 2, 2011; and "About," Agri-View, www.agriview.com/site/about.

4. "35 Years and Counting," *The Country Today,* January 18, 2012.

1985, the nation launched eleven more satellites. The system was used exclusively by the military until 1983, when GPS became available for civilian applications, such as aircraft, shipping, and transport. By 2000, GPS was widely used for route finding by motorists, mapmakers, earthquake researchers, and climatologists as well as in agriculture.[14]

Precision agriculture refers to the use of GPS technology to micromanage crop production. With GPS, farmers can make precise applications of pesticides, herbicides, and fertilizers and as a result reduce expenses, produce higher yields, and avoid overuse of chemicals and fertilizers that can have adverse effects on the environment.

By 2014, drones (unmanned aerial vehicles, or UAVs) began to appear over some Wisconsin fields. Originally developed for military use, drones are regulated by the FAA and must fly under four hundred feet. They are most useful in flying low over crops to photograph or record what's below, gathering data that is then used to detect insect damage, measure crop heights, and determine germination rates.[15]

At its 2014 Potato Field Day, the University of Wisconsin–Extension's Hancock Research Station demonstrated drones for agricultural use.
SEVIE KENYON/UW-MADISON CALS

The controversies over genetically modified crops include the question of whether food products from animals who consume them (eggs from hens who eat modified corn, for example) should be labeled accordingly.
WOLFGANG HOFFMAN/UW-MADISON CALS

GENETICALLY MODIFIED (GM) CROPS

Building on the great strides agricultural plant breeders made, beginning with the development of hybrid corn tracing back to the 1940s and continuing with plant breeding to enhance production as well as resistance to disease and weather, GM crops represent a revolutionary idea in plant breeding. Also known as recombinant DNA technology, this process involves the genetic modification, or engineering, of plants, such as corn, soybeans, and more recently alfalfa, to make them resistant to herbicides and insects.[16]

The Monsanto Company has been a leader in the development of herbicide-resistant corn, soybeans, and alfalfa. Glyphosate, produced by Monsanto and sold under the trade name Roundup, essentially kills all weeds and grasses—except genetically modified crops. With GM crops, farmers can use minimal tillage, do not have to use mechanical cultivation, and generally experience higher yields.

Bt corn, genetically modified through introduction of a gene from the soil bacterium *Bacillus thuringiensis* (Bt), produces a protein that kills corn borers and root worms but appears harmless to other animal species. Bt corn was first commercialized in 1996; by 2004, Bt corn comprised 27 percent of the US field corn production. Its main benefits are increased yields and reduced pesticide use.[17]

The development of GM crops is not without controversy. Critics argue that insufficient research has been conducted on the possible side effects of using GM crops as foods. The World Health Organization said in a 2009 statement, "The movement of genes from GM plants to conventional crops . . . may have an indirect effect on food safety and food security. The risk is real, as shown when traces of a maize type which was only approved for feed use appeared in maize products for human consumption in the United States of America."[18]

In addition to food safety concerns, some critics also are concerned about a small number of corporate giants controlling the country's seed supply. As journalist Christopher Cook commented, "The genetic and proprietary control of our diets by a handful of companies (Monsanto, DuPont, and Syngenta combined own an astounding 47 percent of the global seed market) directly robs consumers and farmers of the most basic right to choose what they will eat and grow. The entire concept of creating and selling patented GM seeds is based on proprietary corporate control. The seeds are non-replenishing and must be purchased anew each season, eliminating the time-honored farmer tradition of saving and re-using seeds."[19]

Another issue swirling around GM crops and foods is whether foods produced from GM crops should be labeled as such. The labeling controversy pits consumer groups and the organic food industry against conventional farmers, agricultural biotechnology companies such as Monsanto, and the nation's well-known food brands such as Kellogg's and Kraft.[20]

A similar labeling controversy emerged following approval by the Food and Drug Administration (FDA) in 1994 of using recombinant bovine growth hormone (rBGH) on dairy farms. Bovine growth hormone, a synthetic form of a hormone naturally produced in all animals, helped increase milk production by 15 to 25 percent. But many concerned parents believed that rBGH caused premature puberty in children and other health risks for those who drank milk from cows treated with the hormone. The FDA has stood by its determination that such milk is safe, but studies and controversy continued into the 2000s. It is not difficult to find milk and other dairy products labeled as rBGH free as a result of the unease.

Biotechnology continues to be a hot research topic at agricultural colleges and at major agricultural firms. No doubt it will remain controversial as new GM crops emerge. In the meantime, the use of genetic modification of crops continues to grow; by 2012, 92 percent of the soybeans and 86 percent of the corn planted in Wisconsin were herbicide resistant.[21]

ORGANIC FARMING

Organic farming is a very old idea. Long before the creation of such agricultural technologies as commercial fertilizers and pesticides, farmers knew to return manure and other refuse to their soils to enhance them and ensure adequate crop production. The founding of the organic agricultural movement is attributed to Sir Albert Howard (1873–1947), an English agricultural educator. After spending twenty-six years in

Harvesting organic cabbages at Tipi Produce, Evansville
WOLFGANG HOFFMAN/
UW–MADISON CALS

India, Howard returned to England in 1931 and began teaching and writing about composting and soil fertility, health, and disease. He described his farming approach in his book *An Agricultural Testament,* published in 1943.[22]

The 1990 Farm Bill's Organic Foods Production Act (OFPA) established uniform national standards for the production and handling of foods labeled "organic." The act authorized the USDA National Organic Program (NOP) with the responsibility of establishing national standards for organic foods, from production to marketing. The legislation defined organic food as that "produced by farmers who emphasize the use of renewable resources and the conservation of soil and water to enhance environmental quality for future generations. Organic meat, poultry, eggs, and dairy products come from animals that are given no antibiotics, or growth hormones. Organic food is produced without using most conventional pesticides, fertilizers made with synthetic ingredients or sewage sludge; bioengineering, or ionizing radiation."[23]

Organic farming expanded rapidly in the 2000s. In 2013, Wisconsin had 1,257 certified organic farms, representing a 77 percent increase since 2005. Processors and handlers of organic crops numbered 233 in the state in 2013. Also in that year, Wisconsin ranked first in the nation in both organic dairy and organic beef farms

Organic Valley

In 1988, a group of southwestern Wisconsin farmers who believed in the importance of sustainable agriculture, family farms, and successful rural communities formed a cooperative with the intent of bringing organic farmers together. Officially known as Cooperative Regions of Organic Producer Pools (CROPP), the group began operations on March 13, 1988, with headquarters in La Farge (Vernon County).

In 2012, the cooperative, marketing its products under the brand name Organic Valley, included more than 1,766 farmer members in thirty-five states and three Canadian provinces, making it the largest organization of organic farmers in North America. Organic Valley produces organic milk, soy, cheese, butter, spreads, creams, eggs, produce, and juice and sells them through supermarkets, natural foods stores, and food cooperatives throughout the country. In 2011, the company's sales reached $715 million.

The Hemstead family farm, a fourth-generation farm near La Farge, is among the hundreds of farms that produce milk for Organic Valley.

© 2015 BY DAVID NEVALA FOR ORGANIC VALLEY

NOTES

"Organic Valley to Celebrate 25th Anniversary," Organic Valley, www.organicvalley.coop/newsroom/press-releases/details/article/organic-valley-to-celebrate-25th-anniversary.

and fourth in the total number of organic vegetable and melon farms. In organic oilseed and grain production, Wisconsin ranked second behind Iowa, with 198 farms. (The production of organic feed is necessary to meet the demand of the region's organic dairy and livestock industries, which are required to feed animals 100 percent organic grains and forages.) And Wisconsin ranked second in the nation for the number of farms with acreage in transition to organic production.[24]

Wisconsin's organic farms are clustered in western and southern Wisconsin, with the largest numbers in Monroe, Vernon, Grant, Lafayette, and Dane Counties. With only four exceptions (all in far northern Wisconsin), every county in the state had at least one organic farmer in 2013.[25]

22

DAIRY TODAY

The dairy industry has been the premier player in Wisconsin's agriculture since the early 1900s. And like the state's other agricultural pursuits, dairy has seen dramatic changes. By the early twenty-first century, Wisconsin led the nation in cheese production but not in the number of dairy cows or in the production of milk—in those two areas, California held the lead. Wisconsin's dairy herds continue to increase in size in the 2000s, with the average dairy herd comprising 114 milk cows in 2012. In that year, Wisconsin had 1.27 million dairy cows. The number of dairy herds, however, continues to fall. In 2008, Wisconsin had 13,962 dairy herds; by 2013 that number had slipped to 11,155.[1]

Percentage of Wisconsin Dairy Farms by Herd Size[2]

	1–29 head	30–49 head	50–99 head	100-plus head
1980	37.3%	39.1%	21.1%	2.5%
1990	23.3%	37.0%	32.7%	7.0%
2000	17.6%	29.5%	39.5%	13.3%
2007	14.8%	24.6%	40.8%	19.7%

In 2007, Wisconsin had 14,158 dairy farms. Seventy-one of them had 1,000 to 2,499 dairy cows, and seven had more than 2,500.[3]

According to the 2012 agricultural census, Wisconsin had 11,543 dairy farms. Of those, 1,298 milked 19 cows or fewer, 3,278 milked 20–49 cows, 4,181 milked

50–99 cows, 1,584 milked 100–199 cows, 815 milked 200–499 cows, 256 milked 500–999, 131 milked 1,000 or more cows.[4]

Wisconsin's Dairy Industry in 2014[5]

Number of dairy farms: 10,860

Number of dairy cows: 1,271,000

Total milk production: 27.5 billion pounds (13.7% of U.S. total; second to California)

Average number of cows per farm: 117

Total cheese production: 2.8 billion pounds (25% of US total; first in the nation)

Total specialty cheese production: (last measured in 2012) 611 million pounds

Total cheddar cheese production: 567 million pounds

Total other American cheese production: 268 million pounds

Total mozzarella cheese production: 962 million pounds

Total other Italian cheese production: 463 million pounds

Number of cheese plants in Wisconsin: 134

Nationwide in 2011, 3,400 dairy operations milked 500 or more cows, accounting for 62.9 percent of all the milk produced in the country. Eight hundred of these

With careful management and feeding, plus ever-improving genetics, modern dairy cows continue to produce milk at record levels.
WOLFGANG HOFFMAN/
UW-MADISON CALS

Wisconsin Milk Marketing Board

Wisconsin dairy farmers voted in 1983 to establish the Wisconsin Milk Marketing Board (WMMB), a non-profit organization owned and funded by Wisconsin dairy farmers with the purpose of promoting milk and milk products. For every 100 pounds of milk produced and marketed in the state, a farmer gives ten cents to WMMB. An additional five cents goes to the National Dairy Promotion and Research Board, which carries out dairy promotion at the national level.

The WMMB's mission is to "help grow the demand for Wisconsin milk by providing programs that enhance the competitiveness of the state's dairy industry." Those efforts include educating Wisconsin and national food-service operators and distributors about the varieties and styles of cheese produced in Wisconsin and year-round seasonal dairy promotions, including in-store demonstrations, advertising, and recipes featuring Wisconsin dairy products.

The work of the WMMB is directed by twenty-five dairy farmer board members who are elected by their peers for three-year terms. The WMMB supports the Wisconsin Center for Dairy Research, including serving as a partner in the Master Cheesemaker program. (For more on the Master Cheesemaker program, see pages 242–244.)

NOTES

"Who We Are," Wisconsin Milk Marketing Board, www.wmmb.com/Who-We-Are.

operations milked 2,000 cows or more, accounting for 34.6 percent of the nation's milk production.[6]

In 2014, the largest dairy operation in Wisconsin was Milk Source, with milk cows housed in four locations: Rosendale (8,400 cows), Kaukauna (6,800 cows), Omro (2,700 cows), and Grand Marsh (8,400 cows), plus a 50-cow show herd of elite Red & White and Black & White Holsteins.[7] In 2014, Milk Source employed about four hundred workers. The International Dairy Foods Association selected Milk Source for its prestigious Innovative Dairy Farmer of the Year award in 2014.[8]

A challenge for large dairy producers today is finding sufficient labor for the milking, feeding, and care of these large herds of milk cows. A large number of hired laborers are Latinos. As writer Michael Penn has noted, "The most significant risk [Wisconsin dairy farmers face] comes from the shifting winds of US immigration policy and enforcement. When Wisconsin dairy farmers began hiring foreign workers in the 1990s, the US government generally regarded the possibility that those workers lacked proper documentation with a winking nonchalance." After the terrorist attacks of 2001, tougher border security and law enforcement began to change this.[9]

DAIRY COOPERATIVES

Wisconsin is known as a pioneer in the establishment of cooperatives, especially dairy cooperatives. (For more on cooperatives, see pages 95–97.) The tradition continues, as dairy cooperatives play a major role in the processing and marketing

of Wisconsin's dairy products today. Some of the oldest cooperatives in the state are cheese factory and creamery cooperatives.[10] Besides providing a market for their milk, dairy co-ops provide member farmers such benefits as health insurance, professional help in producing quality milk, financial protection in the case of loss of milk production due to fire or storms, and political representation at state and national levels.

In 2011, twenty-five dairy cooperatives had headquarters in Wisconsin; in addition, several out-of-state cooperatives had members in the state, including Land O'Lakes (Minnesota), Associated Milk Producers, Inc. (Minnesota), Swiss Valley Farms (Iowa), Woodstock Progressive Milk Producers (Illinois), and Mid-West Dairymen's Cooperative (Illinois). In 2011, twenty-six dairy cooperatives operated cheese plants in the state.[11] Many dairy cooperatives are members of the National Milk Producers Federation, which was organized by dairy cooperatives in 1916 to protect their interest in federal legislation.[12]

Brunkow Cheese Co-op of Darlington got its start in 1899. It still operates as a cooperative today and makes a variety of cheeses, including the juustolopeia shown here.
WOLFGANG HOFFMAN/ UW-MADISON CALS

DAIRY BUSINESS INNOVATION CENTER

In the early 2000s, Wisconsin's dairy industry faced a crossroads. The numbers of dairy cattle and dairy farms were in decline. Some cheese plants operated at 70 percent capacity because they couldn't obtain enough milk.[13] With a federal grant of $1 million, Dan Carter, a cheese industry leader working with the University of Wisconsin–Madison's Center for Dairy Research, created the Dairy Business Innovation Center in 2004 with the mission of helping dairy plants with marketing, packaging, and the development of new varieties of cheese. The office had no state funding or physical headquarters but received administrative support from the Wisconsin Department of Agriculture, Trade and Consumer Protection. Its team of twenty consultants assisted more than two hundred dairy entrepreneurs with everything from facility issues to packaging and labeling. In its eight years of operation, the center contributed to the opening of forty-three new dairy processing plants, assisted in the expansion of another ninety-two operations, and helped in the development of forty varieties of cheese. Wisconsin's production of specialty cheeses during those years increased from about 15 percent of the nation's total to nearly 25 percent. Lacking long-term funding, the center closed on September 30, 2012.[14]

THE NATION'S LEADER IN CHEESE

Say "cheese," and you've said "Wisconsin." Since 1910, when Wisconsin bested New York as the nation's top dairy producer, the state has held the lead in cheese production, producing 2.8 billion pounds of the tasty product in 2013. About 90 percent of Wisconsin's milk goes into cheese production.[15]

Several types of cheese originated in Wisconsin, including brick and Colby. John Jossi, a Swiss-born cheese maker who operated a cheese factory in Dodge County, developed brick cheese in 1875. In that year he opened the first brick cheese factory in the United States, about eight miles northeast of Watertown. Brick cheese is ivory to creamy yellow in color, with a smooth, open texture, and was named for its customary shape and because early cheese makers sometimes used bricks to press out moisture. Colby was named after the community where it was developed— Colby, Wisconsin, near where dairy farmers Ambrose and Susan Steinwand purchased 160 acres of land in 1877 and opened a small cheese factory in 1882.[16]

The most popular story of Colby cheese's beginning involves Ambrose's son, Joseph Steinwand, who was interested in developing a new kind of cheese. One day

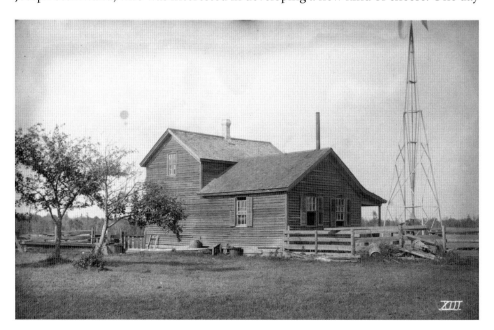

The Joseph Steinwand
Cheese Factory in Colby
(Clark County), circa 1895
WHI IMAGE ID 95179

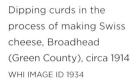

Dipping curds in the process of making Swiss cheese, Broadhead (Green County), circa 1914

WHI IMAGE ID 1934

in 1885, he was struggling with a batch of cheddar. Joseph tried adding an extra step to the process—he washed the curd with cold water and then drained it off, creating a cheese that was more moist and open-textured than cheddar.[17]

Swiss and Limburger cheeses helped thrust Green County into the cheese spotlight in the early 1900s. Rudolph Benkert, a Swiss immigrant, arrived in Green County in 1867 and began making small amounts of Limburger cheese that year. By 1925, Green County was producing 4.2 million pounds of Limburger, nearly all of the United States' Limburger production.[18] Limburger cheese has a unique "personality," having once been described by author John Luchsinger as "a premeditated outrage on the organs of smell." Baumgartner's Cheese Store and Tavern in downtown Monroe draws customers in with a one-of-a-kind sandwich: a slab of Limburger cheese on rye bread, plus onions and mustard. The owners warn, "Limburger: don't eat it with your nose."[19] In 2014, only one cheese factory in North America, the Chalet Cheese Cooperative near Monroe, produced Limburger cheese.

Swiss cheese, best known for its firm, ivory-colored appearance, nutty taste, and especially its holes, has a long history in Wisconsin. Nicholas Gerber is credited with starting the first Swiss cheese factory in Green County in 1869. Soon Green County became associated with Swiss cheese, with Monroe, the county seat, claiming the title "Swiss Cheese Capital of the World." In 1914, a group of Monroe merchants began what is now known as Green County Cheese Days. Held every even-numbered year, the festival brings thousands of people to Monroe to sample delicious food, enjoy good music, and learn about the Swiss and cheese making in Green County.

By 2014, Wisconsin cheese makers were working in 134 cheese plants and making more than 600 varieties of cheese. Mozzarella led the way with the largest production

An array of specialty cheeses made in Wisconsin
WOLFGANG HOFFMAN/
UW–MADISON CALS

(962 million pounds), followed by cheddar in second place (567 million pounds). Both mozzarella and cheddar, as well as several other cheese varieties, are sold in bulk wholesale lots. For instance, the Hennings cheese factory in Kiel sells cheddar in bulk sizes ranging from 12 pounds to 4,500 pounds. Bulk cheeses are sold primarily to retail cheese stores, food companies such as Kraft, and fast-food chains. Hennings also makes specialty cheeses.[20]

Wisconsin is a national leader in specialty cheese production. Specialty cheese is defined as "a value-added cheese product that is of high quality and limited quantity."[21] Specialty cheeses such as Gorgonzola, Gruyère, Asiago, feta, aged cheddar, Gouda, blue, and many others account for 46 percent of the total specialty cheese production in the United States.[22]

Smaller cheese factory cooperatives have proven valuable in the specialty cheese business. Because of the higher prices specialty cheeses command, cooperatives producing them can pay farmers a premium price for their milk and thus stay competitive. In the 1980s, the national cheese market was 80 percent wholesale bulk cheese—block and barrel cheddar, and mozzarella. Thus there was a need for the larger cheese cooperatives to meet the demands of the bulk cheese market (25 percent of the bulk cheese was used for pizza alone). Some of these larger cooperatives, however, also make specialty cheeses, as well as develop strong relationships with larger buyers of bulk cheese, such as pizza producers, by meeting unique custom orders.

Jointly sponsored by the University of Wisconsin Center for Dairy Research, the UW–Extension, and the Wisconsin Milk Marketing Board, the Wisconsin Master Cheesemaker program was established in 1993 as an advanced educational program for experienced cheese makers. To be accepted into the program, a cheese maker must currently be making cheese in a Wisconsin plant, have completed the Wisconsin Cheese Technology Short Course, and have held a Wisconsin cheese maker's license for a minimum of ten years. Upon completion of the three-year program and a

Cheese Masters

The number of specialty cheese makers in Wisconsin increases year by year. Three of the best known are all graduates of the Wisconsin Master Cheesemaker program.

Sid Cook, of Carr Valley Cheese, has won hundreds of awards for his cheeses. A fourth-generation cheese maker who early in his carrier began experimenting with new styles of cheese, Cook crafts eighty varieties. Half of those are his own creations, including his Cave Aged Marisa, a seasonal cheese made from pastured Wisconsin sheep milk that won first place at the 2012 World Championship Cheese Contest and the 2013 US Championship Cheese Contest.[1]

Bob Wills of Cedar Grove Cheese in Plain married into a cheese-making family at age thirty-five. Twenty years later, he makes award-winning specialty cheeses such as flavored Monterey Jack, Havarti, and Butterkase while also striving to make his cheese plant environmentally friendly. He created a greenhouse system for handling wastewater from his plant. In 2012, Wills opened Clock Shadow Creamery in Milwaukee, Wisconsin's first urban cheese factory.[2]

George, Charles, Tom, and Mark Crave began making Crave Brothers Farmstead Cheese in Waterloo in 2002. The brothers also manage a dairy farm where they milk a thousand cows and farm as many acres. Their cheese factory uses about 80 percent of the milk the farm produces. Crave Brothers Farmstead Cheese has won domestic and international awards for its Mascarpone Oaxaca, Farmer's Rope, fresh mozzarella, string cheese, and Les Frères, a washed-rind cheese of their own creation.[3]

Sid Cook, Carr Valley Cheese
WISCONSIN MILK MARKETING BOARD

NOTES

1. "Sid Cook, Carr Valley Cheese," Wisconsin Specialty Cheese Institute, www.wispecialtycheese.org/meet-the-cheesemaker/sid-cook-carr-valley-cheese; and Carr Valley Cheese, www.carrvalleycheese.com.

2. "Bob Wills, Cedar Grove Cheese," Wisconsin Specialty Cheese Institute, www.wispecialtycheese.org/meet-the-cheesemaker/bob-wills-cedar-grove-cheese.

3. Edward Janus, *Creating Dairyland* (Madison: Wisconsin Historical Society Press, 2011), pp. 79–93; "George Crave, Crave Brothers Farmstead Cheese," Wisconsin Specialty Cheese Institute, www.wispecialtycheese.org/meet-the-cheesemaker/george-crave-crave-brothers-farmstead-cheese.

Cheese maker Marieke Penterman makes award-winning Goudas in Thorp (Clark County).
COURTESY OF HOLLANDS FAMILY CHEESE

written examination, the master cheese maker is entitled to use the "Master's Mark" on products for which he or she is certified. The only program of its kind in the United States, the Master Cheesemaker program has provided a foundation for the massive growth of the state's specialty cheese business.[23]

The Wisconsin Specialty Cheese Institute, founded in 1994, is an organization of specialty cheese makers with the purpose of promoting and supporting "the robust, profitable specialty cheese industry in Wisconsin." The organization works closely with the Milk Marketing Board and, among other goals, seeks to "strengthen the position of Wisconsin specialty cheese companies by identifying new market opportunities and sharing cost-reduction strategies related to operations and distribution."[24]

Not only does Wisconsin produce an enormous quantity of cheese, the quality of its products is consistently high. The state's cheese makers consistently top the lists of national and world contest winners, claiming the top award at the (biennial) US Championship Cheese Contest in 2009, 2011, and 2013.[25] In the 2014 World Championship Cheese Contest, Wisconsin cheese makers took home 39 percent of the awards, including first-place honors in thirty-four of the ninety categories.[26]

DAIRY GOATS

Goats were one of the first animals to be domesticated and have provided food and drink for people for thousands of years. For people who are sensitive to cow's milk, goat's milk is a good alternative; it is easy to digest, low in cholesterol, and high in calcium, phosphorus, and vitamins A and B. Goats are not fussy eaters and will efficiently produce milk on marginal pasture and even brushy land that would not support dairy cows.[27]

By the 2000s, Wisconsin led the nation in the number of dairy goats. In 2012, Wisconsin had forty-six thousand milk goats on 994 farms, and nearly 13 percent of the milking goats in the United States were found in Wisconsin.[28]

LaClare Farms

At LaClare Farms near Chilton (Calumet County), owners Larry and Clara Hedrich milk 350 does. The Hedrichs bought their twenty-two-acre farm in 1978; with the property came two peacocks, a flock of laying hens, and two milking goats.

In 2005, the Hedrichs helped organize the Quality Dairy Goat Cooperative of Wisconsin. The cooperative, which includes six goat farms, sells goat milk to cheese plants both in Wisconsin and out of state. The milk is used for cheese, ice cream, and bottling. Larry manages the cooperative, and three of the Hedrichs' children work in the family business. The Hedrichs' daughter Katie, a licensed cheese maker, has won several awards for her goat cheese. The farm's signature cheese is LaClare Farm Evalon, which won Best of Show in the 2011 US Cheese Championship. At age twenty-five, Katie was the youngest cheese maker to win the prestigious award, beating out some 1,604 entries of cow, sheep, and goat products.[1]

In 2012, LaClare Farms broke ground for a thirty-five-thousand-square-foot farmstead dairy plant on State Highway 151, north of the village of Pipe. At the new facility, customers can see goats being milked; watch cheese, soap, and other goat milk products being made; and taste goat milk products in the restaurant.[2] The Hedrichs raise six breeds of dairy goats: Saanens, Alpines, Toggenburgs, Nubians, Lamanchas, and Oberhasli. Their average production is about six to eight pounds of milk per day, or about a gallon. (As a comparison, a dairy cow produces about sixty pounds of milk per day, or seven gallons.)[3]

NOTES

1. Personal correspondence from Clara Hedrich, June 26, 2012; Sharon Selz, "Their Cheese Stands Alone," *Country Woman,* May 2012, pp. 26–29.

2. "LaClare Farms Breaks Ground on New Wisconsin Farmstead Dairy Plant," *Wisconsin State Farmer,* December 14, 2012.

3. Personal correspondence from Clara Hedrich, June 26, 2012; Selz, "Their Cheese Stands Alone."

Scientists at the US Dairy Forage Research Center farm near Prairie du Sac seek solutions for dealing with large quantities of manure. Here they use an airtight chamber to measure cows' methane production.

SEVIE KENYON/UW-MADISON CALS

CONCENTRATED ANIMAL FEEDING OPERATIONS (CAFOS)

The Environmental Protection Agency (EPA) defines a CAFO as an agricultural enterprise where animals are kept and raised in a confined situation. Rather than being allowed to graze and find feed in pastures, animals have their feed brought to them. A CAFO is further defined as having more than 1,000 animal units, with each unit equivalent to 1,000 pounds live weight. This translates to 1,000 head of beef cattle, 700 dairy cows, 2,500 swine weighing more than 55 pounds each, 125,000 broiler chickens, or 82,000 laying hens or pullets confined on site for more than 45 days per year. CAFOs are regulated by the EPA under the Clean Water Act of 2003 and 2008.[29]

According to the 2012 agricultural census, by that year Wisconsin had 131 dairy herds with more than 1,000 cows, plus another 256 with 500–999 cows. According to the Clean Water Action Council of Northeast Wisconsin, 214 Wisconsin dairy herds fell within the CAFO classification, with 99 of them in northeastern Wisconsin.[30]

CAFOs are commonly referred to as factory farms and have engendered considerable controversy, especially as their numbers increase. The Clean Water Action Council of Northeast Wisconsin has identified six major drawbacks of dairy CAFOs: water pollution, threats to human health, severe odors, traffic and road damage, destruction of property values, and the driving out of family farms.[31]

Wisconsin's John Muir Chapter of the Sierra Club also raises serious questions about CAFOs, including the tradeoff between cheap food, which CAFOs can produce, and the cost to the environment. As one Sierra Club writer noted, "CAFOs' impact on public health and the environment diminishes their relative cost-effectiveness. If taxpayers have to shoulder the burden of cleaning up contaminated drinking water and treating diseases caused by CAFO byproducts, the additional costs negate the low cost of CAFO-produced food."[32]

Animal abuse charges have also been leveled against several dairy CAFOs. At a Birnamwood, Wisconsin, dairy farm, the animal rights group Mercy for Animals filmed an undercover video in 2014 of farm employees abusing cows. In the wake of the news story, the farm saw a public backlash and lost milk sales. The farm owners

Manure Digesters

In 2014, Wisconsin had thirty-four manure digesters, the most of any state. A manure digester uses an anaerobic process to break down the materials in manure. One of the by-products of the process is biogas, a mixture of methane and carbon dioxide, which can be used to produce heat, electricity, and fuel. Other by-products of manure digestion can be used as fertilizer and animal bedding.[1]

Digesters remove as much as 60 percent of the phosphorus from the processed manure. While it is often too expensive for one farmer—especially one of average size (117 cows)—to install a manure digester, community digesters are a good alternative. A community manure digester near Waunakee processes manure from three large farms.

At the Crave Brothers Farmstead Cheese farm in Waterloo, an onsite manure digester converts the manure from more than one thousand dairy cows into biogas that is used to generate enough electricity to power their farm, their cheese factory, and three hundred area homes. The digester is owned and installed by Clear Horizons, a Wisconsin firm specializing in organic waste management.[2]

To handle some of the manure produced by their 8,400 milk cows, Milk Source has formed a partnership with the University of Wisconsin–Oshkosh to build a $10 million biogas plant near its Rosendale Dairy facility. The plan is for the plant to generate 7.5 megawatts of electricity that will be returned to the grid.[3]

As technology improves and costs come down, more dairy farms will likely use manure digesters, helping to solve one major problem the industry faces: handling copious amounts of manure in an environmentally friendly and sustainable way.

NOTES

1. "Biogas and Anaerobic Digesters," Clean Wisconsin, www.cleanwisconsin.org/index.php?module=cms&page=756.

2. "Sustainable Story," Crave Brothers Farmstead Cheese, www.cravecheese.com/dairy-farm.php?Sustainable-Story-3.

3. "The Milk Source Way," AgWeb, www.agweb.com/article/the_milk_source_way_NAA_Jim_Dickrell.

have since put in place several precautions intended to prevent such abuse in the future, including increased supervision of animal care.[33]

To be sure, the dairy industry has its critics. As mega dairy farms replace the smaller dairy herds that once dotted the state, vocal critics have challenged the industry, ranging from animal welfare groups concerned about inhumane treatment of animals to environmental organizations worried about the effects of improper disposal of animal waste, air quality issues, creation of greenhouse gases, increased nitrogen levels in soil, contamination of groundwater and local wells, and lake and stream pollution. According to experts, agriculture "accounts for roughly 70 percent of the phosphorus runoff in watersheds across the state."[34]

The development of manure digesters that transform cow manure into methane for the production of electricity has quelled some of the environmental concerns about the environmental problems posed by dairy cattle manure.

As dairy farmers look to the future, challenges will continue. A major one is age. The average age of a Wisconsin farmer is nearing sixty years, and only 9 percent of Wisconsin farm operators are thirty-four or younger, according to the 2012 agricultural census. In addition, marketing, milk prices, and feed costs continue to challenge the dairy industry. And one of the biggest unanswered questions is how climate change will affect dairy farming—especially how the steady increase in temperatures will affect the production of crops necessary for sustaining a substantial dairy industry. (For more on climate change, see page 267.) It seems change is the one constant in Wisconsin's agriculture history, from earliest times to the new age.

A NEW AGE OF AG

The early years of the twenty-first century saw continued revolutionary changes in Wisconsin's agriculture. For example, the first ethanol plant in Wisconsin was built in 2001; by 2014 the state's annual ethanol production reached 470 million gallons, making the state the ninth-largest producer of ethanol in the country.[1] (See page 252 for corn acreage statistics.)

Export demand for Wisconsin agricultural products increased for the third quarter of 2014 by 17 percent over 2013. Wisconsin farms and agribusinesses exported nearly $2.8 billion in agricultural products to 138 countries, making Wisconsin number twelve in the nation for agricultural exports. Wisconsin's exports of dairy products were valued at $382 million, third in the United States for this category. The export of dairy products to Mexico increased by 29 percent over 2013, and exports to China increased by a dramatic 77 percent in the same period. The dairy products in most demand were milk concentrate, whey protein, cheese, butter, and buttermilk. Wisconsin ranked first in bovine genetics, whey, ginseng, processed sweet corn, mink fur skins, and processed cranberries and second nationally in cheese exports.[2]

The secretary of Wisconsin's Department of Agriculture, Trade and Consumer Protection, Ben Brancel, said, "When these [agricultural] companies move into new markets, they strengthen their businesses, strengthen Wisconsin's economy and help feed the world."[3]

A 2012 report by the University of Wisconsin Department of Agricultural and Applied Economics noted that "Wisconsin farmers as a whole earned a record high income of $2.4 billion in 2011. This was up about $350 million from 2010 and three

A worker at the University of Wisconsin–Extension's Arlington Research Station applied nitrogen fertilizer to a field in mid-April.

SEVIE KENYON/UW-MADISON CALS

times the very depressed level of $800 million in 2009. The new record in net farm income reflects record high prices for milk, cattle, hogs, corn and soybeans."[4]

In 2010, the top five Wisconsin agricultural commodities were dairy products ($4.15 million), corn ($1.12 million), cattle and calves ($.86 million), soybeans ($.70 million), and greenhouse/nursery ($.24 million), for a total of $7.07 million. The top five commodities made up 79.5 percent of total agricultural receipts. The remaining 20.5 percent included income from a variety of enterprises, including canning crops, cranberries, mink pelts, ginseng, and others.[5]

Wisconsin's more than one-hundred-year-old dairy industry remains strong and vibrant—especially thanks to the strength of exports and the development of specialty cheeses to enhance the overall cheese market. Continued genetic research has resulted in greater milk yields per cow. Although climate and weather will continue to challenge farmers in the twenty-first century—as they always have—agriculture seems well positioned to remain a major economic force in Wisconsin.

POULTRY AND LIVESTOCK

In 1945, Wisconsin farmers reported 18 million "chickens on farms." By 1997, this number had plummeted to 5.03 million.[6] In 2010, Wisconsin ranked eighteenth among the states in egg production, with Iowa the leading egg producer.[7]

By the 2000s, Wisconsin was not a major livestock-raising state. In 2010, the state had 340,000 hogs and pigs, 90,000 sheep, and about 250,000 beef cattle on feed, compared to 1.27 million milk cows.[8]

Hog numbers declined in the 2000s, but the number of hog farmers in the state increased. From 2002 to 2007, hog numbers decreased from 535,393 to 436,814, while the number of hog farmers increased from 2,993 to 3,268.[9]

The number of beef farmers increased over the same period, and in 2012 there were more beef producers (14,800) than dairy producers (12,100) in the state. But the average-size beef herd was about 18 cows and the average-size dairy herd was about 110 milk cows. So while Wisconsin had 265,000 beef cows recorded in Wisconsin in 2011, it had 1.27 million dairy cows.[10]

The beef industry in Wisconsin, although considerably smaller than that of several western states, continues to grow. Most beef operations, some of them organic, are small, family-owned farms where raising beef is usually not the sole source of income. The leading Wisconsin beef-producing counties in 2011 were Grant, Iowa, Lafayette, Vernon, and Monroe.[11]

A modern dairy barn in Dane County
STEVE APPS

FIELD CROPS

Wisconsin farmers continue to grow field crops as they have done since pioneer days. During the 2000s, the dairy industry demanded much of Wisconsin's farmers' field crops, but the export market also influenced the production of corn and soybeans beyond the needs of the livestock and dairy industry in the state.

In 2012, Wisconsin farmers harvested 4.35 million acres of corn, 1.70 million acres of soybeans, 245,000 acres of winter wheat, 130,000 acres of oats, 15,000 acres of barley, and 1.5 million acres of dry hay. Of the 4.35 million acres of corn, about 3.30 million acres was harvested for grain; much of the remainder went for the production of ethanol. In 2006, Wisconsin farmers harvested 2.8 million acres of corn; by 2012 the acreage had increased by 1.55 million acres. Corn silage continues to be the main feed source for dairy cattle, and even as it meets the ethanol industry's demand for corn, Wisconsin remains the nation's number-one producer of corn for silage.[12]

VEGETABLE AND FRUIT CROPS

In 2012, Wisconsin was second in the nation for growing vegetables for processing, exceeded only by California. In that year, Wisconsin ranked number one in the

Harvesting cranberries at dawn

© ANDY MANIS/WISCONSIN STATE CRANBERRY GROWERS ASSOCIATION

nation for the production of processing snap beans, third in processing sweet corn, third in green pea production, fifth in cucumbers for pickles, and first in carrots for processing. The state also grew a substantial acreage of fresh market sweet corn, fresh market cabbage, and onions.[13]

The vegetable canning industry also remains strong in the state. In 2012, 104 licensed vegetable processing plants operated in Wisconsin.[14]

Cranberries continue to be the shining light for Wisconsin fruit production. In 2012, Wisconsin produced nearly 60 percent of all the cranberries grown in the United States (4.5 million barrels compared to number-two producer Massachusetts with 2.1 million barrels). The state also grows substantial acreages of cherries (number five in the nation), strawberries, and apples.[15]

Award-winning wines produced in Door County
TRAVELWISCONSIN.COM, COURTESY OF THE WISCONSIN DEPARTMENT OF TOURISM

GRAPES AND WINE

Although grape growing and winemaking don't come immediately to mind when you mention Wisconsin, the state is becoming important in the grape and wine business. California produces about 90 percent of the wine in the United States and grows the most grapes; in 2010, California had 3,364 wineries.[16] Today Wisconsin has 73.[17]

Wineries are found in five regions in the state: Door County, the glacial hills region (north of Milwaukee in the Kettle Moraine area), the Driftless region (south-western Wisconsin), the Fox Valley (From Lake Winnebago to Green Bay), and the North Woods. New wineries are popping up nearly every month.

Vernon County, once known for growing tobacco as a cash crop, has shifted from tobacco to grapes. With the leadership of Tim Rehbein, former Vernon County agricultural agent, former tobacco growers began planting grapevines in the spring of 2001. Twenty-one growers planted about ten acres of grapes in total. By 2012, the average vineyard in Vernon County was three acres. With varieties chosen carefully for winter hardiness and other factors, a vineyard in this region can produce about three tons of grapes per acre. "In 2012, a ton of grapes sold for about $1,500 and thus a farmer can earn about $4,500 per acre," said Rehbein.[18]

In addition to growing grapes for the winemaking industry, a few growers in Vernon County are growing table grapes, which they sell at local farmers' markets.

HOPS

In recent years, Wisconsin has seen a resurging interest in small breweries. By 2012, Wisconsin had more than one hundred breweries, most of them falling into the microbrewery or pub brewery category, meaning their production was limited. Rather than quantity, these small breweries focus on quality and flavor.

Along with the development of small breweries has come new interest in growing hops, as the small craft breweries provide a ready market. Gorst Valley Hops in Mazomanie began hops production in 2011; that year the company earned its food processing license from the Wisconsin Department of Agriculture, Trade and Consumer Protection, giving it the legal right to manufacture and sell hops. The company has a charter grower program and helps small-scale hops growers in the production of hops that are then delivered to Gorst Valley for processing.[19]

The Wisconsin Hop Exchange cooperative was organized in 2009 to provide a place for hop growers to meet, share their knowledge and experience, and have their hops crop processed and marketed to local craft breweries. All Wisconsin Hop Exchange products are grown in the state. In 2013, the cooperative handled thirteen varieties of hops from seventeen different farms. The total harvest equaled 7,500 pounds, all of which was pelletized and made ready to ship.[20]

AQUACULTURE AND AQUAPONICS

Aquaculture (often called fish farming) has grown in popularity along with the increased emphasis on healthy eating and the decrease in availability of wild fish. In Wisconsin, all fish farms must be registered with the Department of Agriculture, Trade and Consumer Protection. In 2011, Wisconsin had 2,500 registered fish farms, but only about 350 of them met the requirements of raising and selling fish for food, or for use as bait or related commercial purposes. The remaining registered fish farms were privately owned ponds where the owners stock fish for their own use.[21]

Commonly grown fish farm species are bluegills, perch, and rainbow trout. In 2012, Wisconsin ranked ninth in the nation in the production of farm-raised trout. The Wisconsin legislature passed a law in 2012 that relaxed some of the regulations that restricted the expansion of fish farms. According to Ron Johnson, an aquaculture specialist with the University of Wisconsin–Extension, the new legislation would reduce regulations without harming either the environment or human health. Thus the industry seems to be on the brink of rapid expansion.[22]

Aquaponics brings together aquaculture (the raising of fish) and hydroponics (the raising of plants in water). Fish and plants are grown in the same system. The waste from the fish provides an organic food source for the plants, and the plants provide a nature filter for the water the fish live in.[23] Some aquaponics operations are examples of urban farming, carried out in underused or deserted urban buildings.

URBAN FARMING

An old idea has returned to many of Wisconsin's cities and small towns—that of citizens growing their own food. What's new are the methods for doing it.

Growing Power

The Milwaukee-based organization Growing Power has earned a national reputation for its work in advancing urban farming. Founded in 1993 by Will Allen, a former pro basketball player and the son of South Carolina sharecroppers, the nonprofit Growing Power has evolved from a community food center to an international model of innovation in urban farming and food policy. Vegetables grown on Growing Power's twenty farms and in year-round urban hoop houses end up in a hundred thousand households in southeastern Wisconsin, along with regional school districts' lunch programs. The organization also runs a large-scale composting program, collecting eighty thousand pounds of food waste each week and composting it into rich soil.[1] Referred to as "the go-to expert on urban farming" by the *New York Times,* Will Allen offers Growing Power workshops on myriad topics from worm composting to aquaponics. He has won a number of grants to support urban ag initiatives, including a MacArthur Foundation Genius Grant in 2008.[2]

NOTES

1. Karen Herzog, JS Online, "Milwaukee Recognized for Urban Farms, Aquaponics," www.jsonline.com/news/milwaukee/130096388.html; and Growing Power, "History," www.growingpower.org/our_history.htm.

2. Elizabeth Royte, "Street Farmer," *New York Times,* July 1, 2009.

Will Allen, founder of Growing Power
COURTESY OF GROWING POWER

In the 1800s, when cities and small towns in Wisconsin were being organized, growing a garden in town was not only accepted but expected. During World War I, the federal government encouraged everyone, no matter where they lived, to grow a garden. The Depression years of the 1930s forced many people to grow their own food, and growing a victory garden was again an important part of the home-front war efforts during World War II.

Today's urbanites are learning that they can grow a considerable amount of food in a small space. Only a few square feet are necessary to produce tomatoes, lettuce, green beans, and other vegetables for the table.

Growing crops in confined areas is not a new idea, and many crops, such as hothouse tomatoes, have been produced hydroponically (in a water solution) for many years. Vertical farming—growing crops in tall city buildings—takes the concept a step further. Proponents of vertical farming cite many advantages, including year-round crop production, no weather-related crop failures, reduction in fossil fuel use (no tractors; no trucks for transportation of crops), and freeing up present-day farmland so it can return to its natural state.[24]

In many urban neighborhoods, people are also investing in a few laying hens to provide a ready source of fresh eggs for their family. Others have installed beehives to produce honey and pollinate plants. In most urban areas, a permit for raising backyard chickens or bees is required, and there are restrictions on the number of chickens and beehives that any single homeowner can have. In most cities roosters are not allowed—their early-morning crowing is usually not appreciated by neighbors. Other regulations having to do with the size, type, and location of enclosures and hives are common.

GRAZING

In the majority of large-scale animal and poultry operations, the animals are never allowed outside a building. The grazing movement—really, a return to how farm animals were managed until relatively recently—means allowing hogs, beef cattle, dairy cows, and poultry access to pasture for their feed during the growing season, usually from about May to late September in Wisconsin. During the winter months, these animals are fed stored hay, silage, or grain, depending on their species. Animals given the opportunity to graze on pasture are marketed with such terms as "free-range chickens," "grass-fed beef," and "pasture-raised pork."

Some farmers use grazing techniques because they believe it is beneficial for animals to have regular access to the out-of-doors with fresh air and sunshine and

Bob and Beth Van De Boom raise grass-fed beef steers at V D B Organic Farms near Delevan (Walworth County).
SEVIE KENYON/UW–MADISON CALS

to eat naturally growing, unharvested crops for several months of the year. There is also the very practical benefit that during the time that these animals are not confined, they are naturally spreading their waste on the fields where they graze. And there are the obvious cost savings when animals find their own feed and naturally dispose of their waste.

Research also suggests that pasture-fed cows, for example, produce higher-quality milk. A UW research project started in 2009 showed that the milk from cows fed on pasture-produced dairy products that are "more golden in color . . . creamier in texture . . . and the flavor and aroma are different. Some describe flavors and aromas from pasture-fed products 'more complex' while others note 'earthy, grassy' flavors."[25] Anecdotal evidence suggests that the meat from free-range poultry and pasture-fed beef has different flavors than meat from animals raised in confined CAFOs. (For more about CAFOs, see page 246.)

AGRITOURISM

Agritourism has been part of Wisconsin's agricultural fabric since the first farmer set up a roadside stand to sell vegetables, planted a few extra rows of strawberries and invited people to pick their own, or invited urban friends and relatives to vacation at their farms.

As increasing numbers of people have little or no connection to farming, many having never even set foot on a farm, agricultural tourism has become an increasingly important way to introduce urban people to farm life. The Wisconsin Agricultural Tourism Association (WATA) maintains a list of farms that provide tourism opportunities ranging from bed-and-breakfast experiences to U-pick orchards to opportunities to milk a goat or pet a lamb or wander through a living maze cut into a cornfield. While they bring people closer to the state's farming heritage, these enterprises also add to the farmers' income—contemporary examples of the diversified farming that took hold in the late nineteenth century.

Looking for ways to add income to their small farming operation near Sparta in Monroe County, Don and Donna Justin opened the farm to visitors in 1985. "It's been an interesting time trying to find out what people are looking for," Donna said. Visitors seeking a quiet, rural experience can relax, hike miles of trails, and ski while they spend time in a log cabin or the farmhouse.[26]

The Strawberry Festival held every June in Cedarburg (Ozaukee County) draws more than 100,000 people.
DONALD S. ABRAMS, COURTESY OF THE WISCONSIN DEPARTMENT OF TOURISM

Draft horses pulled a one-bottom walking plow at Wade House historic site in Greenbush.
WADE HOUSE HISTORIC SITE/WISCONSIN HISTORICAL SOCIETY

The income farmers receive from opening their farms to visitors is modest, but for small farmers, every bit of extra income helps. Beyond the economic rewards, these farmers are happy to provide urban visitors the opportunity to learn about rural life. As Joel Swanson, owner of Trillium Farm near La Farge, noted, "The goal is to keep people in contact with where their food comes from."[27]

Wisconsin people embrace any opportunity to get together and have a good time, and the state's agricultural endeavors are proudly celebrated at food and cultural festivals throughout the year. From June Dairy Month breakfasts on farms throughout the dairy regions to Osceola Rhubarb Days, Cranberry Blossom Festival in Wisconsin

Rapids, Strawberry Fest in Waupaca, Cherry Festival in Jacksonport, Sun Prairie's Sweet Corn Festival, Watermelon Festival in Pardeeville, and the Gays Mills Apple Festival, urban and rural people alike visit new places and old stomping grounds to sample the many flavors of the state.

For those interested in learning more about the farming practices, buildings, animals, and equipment of earlier days, many local historical museums provide a window into the past through exhibits and programming. Several Wisconsin Historic Sites, including Old World Wisconsin (near Eagle), Stonefield Village (Cassville), and Wade House (Greenbush) also allow visitors to experience the sights and sounds of life in an early agricultural community.

FARMERS' MARKETS

Since the late 1900s, farmers' markets have helped farmers to sell their produce directly to customers. The first farmers' market in what became the United States opened in Boston in 1634. As the "eat local" movement has grown in recent years, the number of farmers' markets nationwide has exploded, nearly doubling from 4,600 to 8,100 in the years 2008–13, according to the US Department of Agriculture.[28]

One of the largest and best known is the Dane County Farmers' Market, which was started in 1972 when Mayor William Dyke contacted the Dane County

Even though harvest is many weeks away, spring visitors to the Dane County Farmers' Market will find plenty of items for sale.

STEVE APPS

UW–Extension office and the Central Madison Chamber of Commerce to organize a farmers' market around the Capitol Square in downtown Madison on Saturday mornings. Market managers insist that all products sold must be produced in Wisconsin. About 300 market vendors sell throughout the year, with about 160 selling on any given Saturday.[29]

COMMUNITY-SUPPORTED AGRICULTURE

The first community-supported agriculture (CSA) programs in the United States were started in the 1980s. With a CSA membership, an individual or family purchases a number of shares directly from the farmer. Depending on the membership agreement, the farmer delivers farm shares—boxes or bags of produce, often organic—weekly or biweekly throughout the growing season. A typical share can include vegetables, fruits, cheeses, eggs, flowers, meats, and even preserves. The contents of the box vary as the season progresses; early-season shares might contain spinach, lettuce, and radishes, while later deliveries might include sweet corn, tomatoes, potatoes, and winter squash. CSA shares often include recipes for the enclosed foods and newsletters about the farm's various activities and opportunities for involvement on the farm.

For CSA farmers, the arrangement means they will receive payment early in the season, which helps their cash flow. Then, throughout the growing season, the farmer and the customer share the risk. If drought, hail, frost, or flood should strike, the grower and the member share the burden of a smaller crop. If the fields produce a bumper crop, both farmer and member benefit. CSA farmers enjoy the chance to get to know their customers, and members enjoy all the benefits of ultra-fresh food. Occasionally, members are introduced to unfamiliar vegetables that become new favorites. And in most cases, families get to visit "their" farm at least once a season, providing a great opportunity to teach children—and people of all ages—where their food comes from.

The Madison-based FairShare CSA Coalition, a nonprofit organization, supports CSA farmers across southern Wisconsin and helps them make connections with consumers. Some fifty CSA farmers were members of the coalition in 2012.[30]

BUY LOCAL, EAT LOCAL

Beginning in the early 2000s, the "buy local, eat local" movement has grown rapidly. Madison's Willy Street Cooperative is one of many organizations to promote the idea of buying locally produced foods. Willy Street Cooperative defines *local* as within 150 miles of one's home. In an article advocating an "Eat Local Month," a representative of the cooperative wrote this answer to the question, "Why eat local?": "Local foods tend to be fresher than those shipped across the country or farther away, and fresh food has more nutrients. Transporting food long distances requires more fossil fuels and packaging than those grown and prepared closer to home. You're also supporting your local farmers and keeping the agricultural viability of their communities alive."[31]

REAP Food Group

The Dane County Research, Education, Action and Policy on Food Group was founded in 1997 by academics, elected officials, and citizens who were

REAP hosts the annual Food for Thought Festival on Madison's Capitol Square. TERESE ALLEN

interested in food issues. Later renamed REAP Food Group, the organization hosted its first Food for Thought Festival in Madison in 1999, bringing together people concerned about building a sustainable food system. In 2004, the group became a 501(c)3 nonprofit organization, which made it eligible to receive donations, apply for grants, and hire staff. In 2002, the organization published its first *Farm Fresh Atlas* in cooperation with the University of Wisconsin Center for Integrated Agricultural Systems (CIAS) and the Dane County Farmers' Market. Also in 2002, REAP volunteers and CIAS launched the Wisconsin Homegrown Lunch program, designed to bring more local foods into the schools.

In 2014, REAP had a staff of six, plus four half-time Farm to School AmeriCorps members. The group continues its mission to "provide a voice for the movement working to grow a healthy, socially just food system that is environmentally and economically sustainable."

NOTES

Reap Food Group, www.reapfoodgroup.org.

A growing number of Wisconsin restaurants feature locally grown food. Columnist Mary Bergin discovered that several of them are located on Wisconsin farms. Near Hayward, Bergin visited North Star Homestead Farms, where the restaurant's key ingredients come from the farm's greenhouse and sheep. The Trout House at Rushing Waters, near Palmyra, features fresh-caught trout that live in spring-fed water on the farm. Blind Horse Restaurant and Winery in Kohler, in a 130-year-old farmhouse, serves wine made on-site.[32]

Other restaurants are known for purchasing ingredients from local growers. One of the best known in southern Wisconsin is Madison's L'Etoile, which has featured locally grown ingredients for more than thirty years. Chef Tory Miller develops seasonal menus and purchases directly from local farmers and the Dane County Farmers' Market. The REAP Food Group's annual *Farm Fresh Atlas* includes a list of restaurants in southern Wisconsin that feature locally sourced foods.[33]

FARM TO SCHOOL

A middle school student showed off produce in her school's summer vegetable garden.

PHOTO BY BILL LUBING

The USDA's Farm to School program, with roots in several pilot programs started in the 1990s, is designed to bring fresh foods to school lunch programs. Some schools in turn have begun growing their own vegetable gardens, an activity that not only provides fresh foods to the school lunch table, but also helps teach children valuable lessons about growing food and understanding where food comes from. Organizations such as REAP Food Group have assisted in both promoting and implementing these efforts. The Department of Agriculture, Trade and Consumer Protection promotes statewide Wisconsin Farm to School programs, working with the University of Wisconsin–Madison Center for Integrated Agricultural Systems, the University of Wisconsin–Extension, the Department of Public Instruction, and the Department of Health to encourage and assist schools interested in the program. Goals of the Wisconsin Farm to School program include expanding markets for Wisconsin farmers, promoting children's health by providing fresh foods, and increasing children's knowledge about agriculture and food.[34]

THE FUTURE OF FARMING AND RURAL LIFE

Winston Churchill said, "It is always wise to look ahead, but difficult to look further than you can see." The most sensible thing that can be said about the future of agriculture is that it will continue to change. As we look to the future, some of the most compelling questions are: What is the minimum number of farmers necessary to provide food and fiber for the growing US and world populations? What should the nature of those farming operations be? The current state of agriculture provides some clues to what we can expect in the years ahead.

DECLINING FAMILY FARM NUMBERS

In 2012, less than 1 percent of the total US population of about 285 million claimed farming as an occupation. Approximately 2 percent of the population lived on farms.[1]

The number of Wisconsin farms declined dramatically from a high of 199,977 in 1935 to 76,800 in 2012. Many farms consolidated as farmers bought out their neighbors and became larger enterprises. The average size of a farm in 1935 was 117 acres; in 2012 it was 195 acres.[2]

Around the major metro areas like Milwaukee, Madison, and Green Bay, hundreds of farms have succumbed to urban development as the cities marched out into the countryside. Some farms have become golf courses. Other farmland has been converted to use for homes, condos, and shopping centers.

The small family farm of 80 or 160 acres that many people think of in the early days of Wisconsin's settlement, when husband, wife, and children worked together to make a living and a life, was mostly a memory by the 2000s—but not entirely. Of the 76,800 Wisconsin farms in 2012, 57,400 were 146 acres or less in size and grossed $100,000 or less.[3]

Wisconsin's Amish communities represent one group of these small family farms. In 2010, the state's Amish population was estimated at more than fifteen thousand, making Wisconsin's the fourth-largest Amish population in the nation (after Pennsylvania, Ohio, and Indiana). The majority of the Amish settlements in the state today are in central and western counties, with one of the largest concentrations of Amish in Vernon and Monroe Counties.[4] In Amish communities one can still see farming as it was when horses did the heavy work and there was no electricity.

Of course, many of the state's large farms, even those milking thousands of cows and tending hundreds of acres of crops, are still family owned and operated. While historically a "family farm" usually consisted of a husband and wife and their children, today's large family farms often include several related family members and their spouses and children, all working together to run the farm and the business, often along with some hired help. So the family farm has not disappeared, but in most instances it takes a vastly different form than it did in those early settlement days.

Henschel Family Farm

On their farm near Carlsville in Door County, four generations of the Henschel family have worked the land. Today Mike and Jamie Henschel follow in the footsteps of Mike's great-grandfather, Ed Henschel, a German immigrant who moved his family to Door County in 1902. Mike Henschel said, "I'm very proud of what we do. One son in each generation of my family has kept the farm going."

The Henschel farm is an example of a thriving modern-day diversified family farm. The Henschels have always raised dairy cattle. Mike's grandfather, Ray, planted a cherry orchard; Mike's father, Roger, added a sawmill and pigs to the farming operation. And Mike has gotten into the maple syrup business.

In 2014, the Henschels owned 410 acres and rented an additional 150 acres. The family milks fifty dairy cows, markets steers and pigs, and grows canning peas, winter wheat, oats, corn, alfalfa, soybeans, and cherries that they sell to northern Door County markets. The farm's sawmill cuts about two hundred thousand board feet of lumber a year. "Everything has a season," Jamie Henschel said. "It all fits together."

"We love what we do and want to be here for a very long time," Mike Henschel explained. "This is a dominant farm area, and we want that to continue."

NOTES

Patti Podgers, "Carrying on the Tradition," *Door County Magazine*, Fall 2004, p. 35.

Beginning Dairy and Livestock Farmers Program

In response to the declining number of young people entering farming, and to offer an alternative to confined animal agriculture, the University of Wisconsin–Madison has sponsored a Beginning Dairy and Livestock Farmers Program since 1995.

The program grew out of cooperation between UW–Madison's Farm and Industry Short Course and the Center for Integrated Agricultural systems, also on the Madison campus. The only program of its type in the nation, it focuses on pasture-based dairy and livestock operations and is designed to "educate, prepare and mentor entering and transitioning dairy and livestock farmers."

The curriculum includes "specialized training through traditional classroom activities, hands-on internships, and farm tours of pasture-based farms managed by successful graduates and mentors." The program emphasizes the business and financial planning necessary to operate a successful farm. Classroom instruction usually runs from the middle of November through March, with internships in April through July.

The program's distance-education option allows enrollees to work with a local facilitator who leads a seminar at one of seventeen sites across Wisconsin.

Dick Cates, director of the Beginning Dairy and Livestock Farmers Program at UW–Madison's College of Agricultural and Life Sciences, talked with a group of young farmers.
COURTESY OF GERHARD FISCHER

Since the start of the program, more than four hundred students have earned a certificate in grass-based dairying. About 75 percent of the program's graduates are actively engaged in dairy or livestock farming, and about half of these new farmers have started their own farm businesses.

NOTES

"Our Accomplishments," UW–Madison Center for Integrated Agriculture Systems, School for Beginning Dairy and Livestock Farmers, www.cias.wisc.edu/wsbdf/accomplishments.htm.

SUSTAINABLE AGRICULTURE

By the turn of the twenty-first century, many large-scale farming operations had emerged across the country, especially in dairy, meat livestock, and poultry production. In 2012, 4,300 Wisconsin farms were a thousand acres or more in size.[5]

The sustainable agriculture movement developed both as an alternative to these large-scale operations and as a response to the growing need for environmentally sound agricultural practices on farms of any size. The 1990 Farm Bill defined sustainable agriculture as

> an integrated system of plant and animal production having a site-specific application that will over the long term: satisfy human and food and fiber needs; enhance environmental quality and the natural resource base upon which the agricultural economy depends; make the most efficient use of nonrenewable resources and on-farm resources and integrate, where appropriate, natural biological cycles and controls; sustain the economic viability of farm operations; and enhance the quality of life for farmers and society as a whole.[6]

An iconic Wisconsin farmscape

SEVIE KENYON/UW–MADISON CALS

Center for Integrated Agricultural Systems

Celebrating its twenty-fifth anniversary in 2014, the University of Wisconsin Center for Integrated Agricultural Systems has as its mission "to build UW sustainable agriculture research programs that respond to farmer and citizen needs. . . . The goal of our work at CIAS is to learn how particular integrated farming systems can contribute to environmental, economic, social and intergenerational sustainability." The center works with a Citizens Advisory Council and a group of UW faculty associates to create education and training programs related to sustainable agriculture as well as multidisciplinary research projects.

The center's recent research and project activities have included:

- Providing mini-grants to support graduate students doing research in sustainable agriculture.

- Developing Farm to School toolkits to aid school nutrition programs and producers in creating successful farm to school programs.
- A research project designed to identify major nonpoint pollution sources on farms and offer solutions to preventing runoff.
- Research examining grassland cropping systems as an alternative source of biofuel.
- Development of the report *Status of Organic Agriculture in Wisconsin: 2014.*
- Sponsoring the F. H. King Students for Sustainable Agriculture organization.

NOTES

UW–Madison Center for Integrated Agriculture Systems, www.cias.wisc.edu.

UW College of Agricultural and Life Sciences agronomy professor and grasslands expert Randy Jackson co-leads a sustainability research group for the Great Lakes Bioenergy Research Center.

COURTESY OF BETH SKOGEN

Wisconsin farmers carry out sustainable agricultural practices in a variety of ways, including grazing, organic farming, and small-scale vegetable and animal farming.

CLIMATE CHANGE

In a study of climate records from 1950 to 2011, UW–Madison researchers discovered that Wisconsin's annual average temperature had risen over that time by 1.3 degrees Fahrenheit (2.5 degrees in winter). They also observed that more total precipitation, with more intense storms, is likely in many parts of the state.[7]

Warmer winters lead to increased manure runoff from Wisconsin fields.

COURTESY OF HERB GARN

Researchers at the US Dairy Forage Research Center farm conduct a study of the effect of cows' diet on greenhouse gases.

SEVIE KENYON/UW–MADISON CALS

A group of scientists assembled by the Wisconsin Initiative on Climate Change Impacts considered the ramifications of the report on the future of Wisconsin agriculture. The group concluded:

> In general, it seems that while warming temperatures in either of the shoulder seasons (spring, fall) would boost agricultural production by extending the growing season period across the state, increased warming during the core of the growing season (e.g. June through August) appears to have a negative impact on row crop production in our state. Thus, the bottom line is that climate has changed and agriculture has already been impacted in an adverse way in some cases.[8]

Unfortunately, global warming has become a contentious issue across the country, including in Wisconsin. Even with a growing body of well-researched knowledge and overwhelming agreement by the scientific community about the effects of climate change, many deniers loudly proclaim that global warming does not exist. Of course, ignoring scientific evidence is not new. Ron Seely, environmental writer for the *Wisconsin State Journal,* equates those who deny the existence of global warming with those who refused to accept the evidence that Rachel Carson, author of the seminal environmental work *Silent Spring,* presented more than fifty years ago about the side effects of the insecticide DDT.[9]

Researchers and educators face a difficult challenge as they work to teach Wisconsin people about climate change's impact on the state's agriculture (as well as cultural and economic effects). New crops and crop varieties and agriculture management strategies will be needed as the climate continues to change.[10]

FOOD SAFETY

Safe and healthful food has long been one of agriculture's primary goals. Yet occasionally illness results from food-borne organisms. In 2013, 550 people became ill from eating chicken contaminated with salmonella.[11] In 2014, a national beef-packing company recalled 1.8 million pounds of ground beef because of *E. coli* contamination.[12]

In Wisconsin in 2014, thirty-eight people associated with a high school football team became ill from drinking raw (unpasteurized) milk contaminated with harmful bacteria.[13] Had the milk been pasteurized, no illness would have occurred. Yet a sizable group of people, many of them in Wisconsin, believe that raw milk offers health and nutrition benefits not found in pasteurized milk, and that they should have a right to purchase and consume it. Under current Wisconsin law, it is illegal to sell or distribute unpasteurized milk. In October 2014, raw milk advocates in Walworth County and New Holstein and a dairy farmer in Loganville filed a petition with the Wisconsin Supreme Court claiming that it should be the right of consumers and food groups to buy raw milk directly from a farm. As of the end of 2014, a decision had not been rendered.[14]

Protecting the nation's food supply from disease-bearing organisms will continue to be a challenge, especially as population growth and climate change bring food security issues to the fore.

AGRICULTURAL POLICY

By the 2010s, with national budget deficits mounting, farm subsidies became increasingly controversial and highly politicized. For example, in a 2012 report, the US Government Accountability Office stated that crop insurance subsidies had increased from $951 million in 2000 to $7.3 billion in 2011. In response, Senator Tom Colburn of Oklahoma, a critic of the program, pointed out that "high premium subsidies have hurt small and beginning farmers because the subsidies themselves have distorted the market."[15]

At their eighty-first annual convention in January 2012, delegates of the Wisconsin Farmers Union discussed an array of policy issues, including agriculture programs and the family farm. In its newsletter later that winter, the Wisconsin Farmers Union reaffirmed "our position that federal governmental policies and programs are essential to protect family farmers against the hazards of the marketplace where almost everyone else, except the farmer, is protected. The power of public policy must be used to sustain the independent farmer in an economy that is otherwise strongly concentrated. Family farms must be protected against the economic sacrifices that may be necessary to balance our nation's trade and ensure world peace."[16]

The 2014 Farm Bill addressed complaints about direct payments to farm producers by eliminating them. However, the bill did continue crop insurance programs that protect farmers from drought, floods, and other crop-destroying events; and it provided $15 million to support rural business development. It also included $200 million for international market development, endowed $200 million for a foundation for agricultural research, and reauthorized $880 million for energy programs.[17]

Occasionally the federal government passes emergency support programs for specific crops. In 2014, Wisconsin cranberry growers faced an oversupply, largely due to a record crop in 2013. To prop up cranberry prices, in November the US Department of Agriculture agreed to purchase up to $55 million in cranberry products, which it would make available to low-income families through the federal government's Emergency Food Assistance Program and distributed by local agencies such as food pantries, school lunches, and soup kitchens.[18]

HISTORIC PRESERVATION

In the fall of 1993, a group met at the Wisconsin Historical Society headquarters in Madison to discuss whether there was interest in saving the state's historic barns. Barn preservation workshops have since been conducted across the state. Charles Law, director of the University of Wisconsin–Extension's Local Government Center and one of the founders of the Wisconsin Barn Preservation Program, has said, "The interest [in barn preservation] will continue at a high level with land use changes. For increasing numbers of people, old buildings are an asset to a piece of property. They keep the rural landscape alive."[19]

In Oconto County, the Chase Stone Barn Committee has successfully restored this barn built entirely of fieldstone. The barn was designed and built in 1903 by Daniel E. Krause; today it is listed on the National and State Registers of Historic Places.

STEVE APPS

The Division of Historic Preservation at the Wisconsin Historical Society administers the State Register of Historic Places, a program that promotes the preservation, protection, and use of Wisconsin's prehistoric and historic properties, including barns. Through efforts such as these, an important piece of Wisconsin history is being preserved. It is one thing to read history, but history comes alive when one can see it through an old building and the many stories it has to tell.

Wisconsin's agriculture has a rich history. With appropriate education, broad-based research, and a caring philosophy, we can ensure that it has an equally rich future.
SEVIE KENYON/UW-MADISON CALS

In the introduction to this book, I wrote about the intertwining threads that make up the story of Wisconsin agriculture. As we face the future of farming in this state, those threads will be ever more complex and more tightly woven.

Immense challenges to Wisconsin agriculture loom on the horizon. By 2020, the world's population is predicted to reach 7.6 billion people.[20] What will Wisconsin's role be in providing food for those people? The production of such enormous amounts of food will lead to ever-increasing concerns about farming's influence on the environment, the humane treatment of animals, and matters of public health, especially those related to food safety.

Agricultural research and education will play vital roles as we confront these challenges. More than ever, research must take an integrated approach, bringing together the best minds from the biological sciences, such as biotechnology, with those representing the social sciences, economics, and sociology, and embracing those from the humanities as well. Every problem researched has a history, and increasingly every problem also has an ethical dimension. Such broad-based research teams can identify the sorts of innovative solutions that are often not revealed by narrowly focused research.

Agricultural education—both in classrooms and that offered by the press and by farming organizations and trade groups—will play an increasingly crucial role in helping farmers become critical thinkers. Farming in the twenty-first century requires careful consideration not only of economic efficiencies, but also of ethical methods of production—incorporating concern for the land, the environment, and future generations. Educators must be prepared to assist farmers who will be constantly challenged to keep up to date with new technology, but ag education should include more than mere technology transfer. Educators must help farmers make decisions about which innovations to adapt and which to reject, which traditional farming practices to carry into the future and which to leave behind. Not all that is new is wonderful or beneficial; not all that is old is obsolete or worthless.

Agriculture has faced many challenges in the past; future challenges will be even greater and more formidable. But Wisconsin people have a legacy of meeting challenges—of adapting, innovating, and persevering. This resolve will keep Wisconsin's agriculture strong and vibrant in the years to come and help ensure that future generations continue to enjoy the bounty of the land.

Cranberry pickers near Wisconsin Rapids, circa 1950

WHI IMAGE ID 85459

NOTES

INTRODUCTION

1. Joseph Schafer, *A History of Agriculture in Wisconsin* (Madison: State Historical Society of Wisconsin, 1922), p. xii.

CHAPTER 1

1. David M. Mickelson, "Wisconsin Glacial Landscapes," in *Wisconsin Land and Life,* ed. Robert C. Ostergren and Thomas R. Vale (Madison: University of Wisconsin Press, 1997), pp. 35–48.
2. Ibid., p. 130.
3. Ibid.
4. Gwen Schultz, *Wisconsin's Foundations: A Review of the State's Geology and Its Influence on Geography and Human Activity* (Madison: University of Wisconsin Press, 2004), pp. 166–168.
5. Lawrence Martin, *The Physical Geography of Wisconsin* (Madison: University of Wisconsin Press, 1965), p. 326.
6. Mickelson, "Wisconsin Glacial Landscapes," p. 39.
7. Charles D. Stewart, "On a Moraine," *Atlantic Monthly,* September 1909, p. 316.
8. Martin, *Physical Geography of Wisconsin,* p. 83.
9. Edward Daniels, quoted in Martin, *Physical Geography of Wisconsin,* p. 84.
10. "Climate of Wisconsin," www.uwex.edu/sco/stateclimate.html.

CHAPTER 2

1. Robert C. Nesbit, *Wisconsin: A History,* 2nd ed. (Madison: University of Wisconsin Press, 1989), p. 10.
2. Jennifer R. Harvey (principal investigator), *Phase I: Archaeological Investigations of Areas of Meacham Family Trust Property, Village of Howard, Brown County Wisconsin* (Great Lakes Archaeological Research Center, 2013), p. 8, http://inwisconsin.com/content/uploads/2013/04/Howard_Archaeological-Historical-Report.pdf.
3. Ibid.
4. Patty Loew, *Indian Nations of Wisconsin: Histories of Endurance and Renewal,* 2nd ed. (Madison: Wisconsin Historical Society Press, 2013), pp. 4–5.
5. Harvey, *Phase I: Archaeological Investigations,* pp. 10–11.
6. Ibid., p. 12.
7. Loew, *Indian Nations of Wisconsin,* 2nd ed., p. 5.
8. Robert A. Birmingham and Leslie E. Eisenberg, *Indian Mounds of Wisconsin* (Madison: University of Wisconsin Press, 2000), pp. 166–167.

9. Robert A. Birmingham and Lynne G. Goldstein, *Aztalan: Mysteries of an Ancient Indian Town* (Madison: Wisconsin Historical Society Press, 2005), p. 77.

10. Birmingham and Eisenberg, *Indian Mounds of Wisconsin,* p. 101.

11. Erika Janik, "Crops of Yore," *Isthmus (Madison, WI),* August 17, 2007.

12. Nesbit, *Wisconsin: A History,* 2nd ed., pp. 10, 11.

13. Loew, *Indian Nations of Wisconsin,* 2nd ed., p. 12.

14. Ibid., p. 15.

CHAPTER 3

1. Alice E. Smith, *The History of Wisconsin,* vol. 1, *From Exploration to Statehood* (Madison: State Historical Society of Wisconsin, 1973), p. 513.

2. Reuben Gold Thwaites, *Stories of the Badger State* (New York: American Book Company, 1900), pp. 34–38.

3. Ibid., pp. 45–49.

4. "The Fur Trade Era: 1650s to 1850s," Wisconsin Historical Society, at wisconsinhistory.org.

5. Smith, *History of Wisconsin,* vol. 1, p. 164.

6. Ibid., p. 114.

7. "Narrative of Spoon Decorah," *Collections of the State Historical Society of Wisconsin* 13 (1895), p. 458.

8. Bobbie Malone and Kori Oberle, *Wisconsin: Our State, Our Story* (Madison: Wisconsin Historical Society Press, 2008), p. 86.

9. "Lead Mining in Southwestern Wisconsin," Wisconsin Historical Society, www.wisconsinhistory.org/turningpoints/tp-026.

10. Smith, *History of Wisconsin,* vol. 1, p. 183.

11. "Lead Mining in Southwestern Wisconsin."

12. Thwaites, *Stories of the Badger State,* pp. 122–123, 124.

13. Personal correspondence from James Mohr, December 11, 2011.

14. Kazimierz J. Zaniewski and Carol J. Rosen, *The Atlas of Ethnic Diversity in Wisconsin* (Madison: University of Wisconsin Press, 1998), 151.

15. Malone and Oberle, *Wisconsin: Our State, Our Story,* p. 86.

16. Robert Gough, *Farming the Cutover* (Lawrence: University Press of Kansas, 1997), pp. 12–13.

17. Malone and Oberle, *Wisconsin: Our State, Our Story,* p. 86.

18. Gough, *Farming the Cutover,* p. 18.

19. Lucile Kane, "Settling the Wisconsin Cutovers," *Wisconsin Magazine of History,* Winter 1956–1957, p. 91.

20. Robert C. Nesbit, *Wisconsin: A History,* 2nd ed., (Madison: University of Wisconsin Press, 1989), p. 309.

CHAPTER 4

1. Joseph Schafer, *A History of Agriculture in Wisconsin* (Madison: State Historical Society of Wisconsin, 1922), pp. 27–31.

2. Ibid.

3. Johannes Strohschank and William G. Thiel, *The Wisconsin Office of Emigration: 1852–1855* (Madison: Max Kade Institute for German-American Studies, University of Wisconsin–Madison, 2005), p. 1.

4. Reuben Gold Thwaites, *Stories of the Badger State* (New York: American Book Company, 1900), pp. 223–225.

5. Robert C. Nesbit, *Wisconsin: A History,* 2nd ed. (Madison: University of Wisconsin Press, 1989), p. 155.

6. Alice E. Smith, *The History of Wisconsin,* vol. 1, *From Exploration to Statehood* (Madison: State Historical Society of Wisconsin, 1973), p. 8.

7. Wisconsin Cartographers' Guild, *Wisconsin's Past and Present: A Historical Atlas* (Madison: University of Wisconsin Press, 1998), pp. 16–23.

8. Strohschank and Thiel, *The Wisconsin Office of Emigration,* pp. 5, 9, 12.

9. Gunleik Asmundson Bondal, *Letter, 1854,* University of Wisconsin Digital Collections/State of Wisconsin Collection, http://digicoll.library.wisc.edu/cgibin/WI/WIidx?type=div&did=WI.Bondal2m.i0002&isize=M.

10. Richard J. Fapso, *Norwegians in Wisconsin,* rev. ed. (Madison: Wisconsin Historical Society Press, 2001), p. 56.

11. Smith, *History of Wisconsin,* vol. 1, p. 475.

12. Zachary Cooper, *Black Settlers in Rural Wisconsin* (Madison: State Historical Society of Wisconsin, 1994), pp. 5–6.

13. Ibid., pp. 21–26.

14. Schafer, *A History of Agriculture in Wisconsin,* p. 38.

15. Thwaites, *Stories of the Badger State,* p. 173.

16. R. Carlyle Buley, *The Old Northwest: Pioneer Period, 1815–1840* (Bloomington: Indiana University Press, 1951), p. 159.

17. "Early Pioneer Life," *Elkhorn Independent,* April 29, 1909.

18. "Came to Cicero When Oxen Trod Forest Trail," *Appleton Post-Crescent,* February 9, 1924.

19. Benjamin Horace Hibbard, *The History of Agriculture in Dane County, Wisconsin* (Madison: Bulletin of the University of Wisconsin no. 101, 1904), p. 115.

20. "Buck and Bright, Faithful Oxen, Helped Pioneer Carve Out Farms," *Antigo Daily Journal,* April 2, 1930.

21. "Intimate Incidents of Pioneer Life in Richland County," parts 1–5, *Richland Center Democrat,* March 1924.

22. "Fascinating Tales of Pioneer Days: Madame de Nevue Gives Some of Her Personal Recollections of the Long Ago," *Fond du Lac Commonwealth,* June 12, 1905.

23. Mark Wyman, *The Wisconsin Frontier* (Bloomington: Indiana University Press, 1998), pp. 180–181.

24. Smith, *History of Wisconsin,* vol. 1, p. 494.

25. Ibid., p. 495.

26. "Milwaukee's First Telegraph Line," *Milwaukee Sentinel,* September 10, 1899.

27. I. O. Schaub, *Agricultural Extension Work: A Brief History,* Extension Circular no. 377 (Raleigh: North Carolina Agricultural Extension Service, November 1953).

CHAPTER 5

1. Joseph Schafer, *A History of Agriculture in Wisconsin* (Madison: State Historical Society of Wisconsin, 1922), p. 84.

2. Alice E. Smith, *The History of Wisconsin,* vol. 1, *From Exploration to Statehood* (Madison: State Historical Society of Wisconsin, 1973), pp. 520–521.

3. "Tells of Farming in 'Wiskonsan' in 1842," *Wisconsin State Journal,* March 7, 1935.

4. "Letter Written 85 years Ago by Waupun Man Tells the East about Early Farming Methods in Wisconsin," *Leader News (Waupun, WI),* July 18, 1935.

5. Schafer, *A History of Agriculture in Wisconsin,* p. 87.

6. Jerry Apps, *Barns of Wisconsin,* 3rd ed. (Madison: Wisconsin Historical Society Press, 2010), pp. 23–24.

7. Jerry Apps, *Horse-Drawn Days: A Century of Farming with Horses* (Madison: Wisconsin Historical Society Press, 2010), p. 24.

8. *Dictionary of Wisconsin Biography* (Madison: State Historical Society of Wisconsin, 1960), pp. 120–121.

9. Ibid., p. 13–14.

10. Apps, *Horse-Drawn Days,* pp. 144–145.

11. Schafer, *A History of Agriculture in Wisconsin,* p. 89.

12. Apps, *Horse-Drawn Days,* p. 89.

13. Smith, *History of Wisconsin,* vol. 1, p. 522.

14. Robert C. Nesbit, *Wisconsin: A History,* 2nd ed. (Madison: University of Wisconsin Press, 1989), p. 273.

15. *Seventh Census of the United States, 1850* (Washington, DC: US Census Bureau, 1853), pp. 917, 925.

16. Ibid., pp. 931–933.

17. Frederick Merk, *Economic History of Wisconsin during the Civil War Decade* (Madison: State Historical Society of Wisconsin, 1916), pp. 15–16.

18. Ibid., p. 129.

19. Jerry Apps, *Mills of Wisconsin and the Midwest* (Madison, WI: Tamarack Press, 1980), pp. 36–42.

20. Merk, *Economic History of Wisconsin,* pp. 129–134.

21. Wisconsin Crop and Livestock Reporting Service, *Wisconsin Agriculture in Mid-Century* (Madison: Wisconsin State Department of Agriculture Bulletin no. 325, 1953), p. 75.

22. Nesbit, *Wisconsin: A History,* 2nd ed., pp. 281–282.

23. Schafer, *A History of Agriculture in Wisconsin,* p. 94.

CHAPTER 6

1. Joseph Schafer, *A History of Agriculture in Wisconsin* (Madison: State Historical Society of Wisconsin, 1922), p. 97.

2. Frederick Merk, *Economic History of Wisconsin during the Civil War Decade* (Madison: State Historical Society of Wisconsin, 1916), pp. 20–21.

3. "Productions of Agriculture," *Ninth Census of the United States, 1870* (Washington, DC: US Census Bureau, 1870), p. 82.

4. Wisconsin Crop and Livestock Reporting Service, *Wisconsin Agriculture in Mid-Century* (Madison: Wisconsin State Department of Agriculture Bulletin no. 325, 1953), p. 75.

5. Jerry Apps, *Breweries of Wisconsin,* 2nd ed. (Madison: University of Wisconsin Press, 2005), pp. 24–30.

6. Fred L. Holmes, "Craze for Hops Held Wisconsin. . . ." *Capital Times (Madison),* February 14, 1921.

7. Laura Paine, "The Hops Era: Wisconsin's Agricultural Gold Rush," *Wisconsin Academy Review* (June 1990), p. 27.

8. Bernard W. Schwartz, "A History of Hops in America," *Steiner's Guide to American Hops* (n.p.: S. S. Steiner, 1973), p. 46.

9. Paine, "The Hops Era," p. 23.

10. Apps, *Breweries of Wisconsin,* 2nd ed., p. 29.

11. "John Rooney," *Baraboo News,* October 26, 1911.

12. *Seventh Census of the United States, 1850* (Washington, DC: US Census Bureau, 1853), p. 932.

13. "Productions of Agriculture," p. 88.

14. Merk, *Economic History of Wisconsin,* p. 37.

15. Wisconsin Crop and Livestock Reporting Service, *Wisconsin Agriculture in Mid-Century,* p. 68.

16. Merk, *Economic History of Wisconsin,* p. 37.

17. Wisconsin Crop and Livestock Reporting Service, *Wisconsin Agriculture in Mid-Century,* p. 68.

18. "Bekkedal Tobacco Warehouse," Wisconsin Historical Society, www.wisconsinhistory.org/turningpoints/search.asp?id=1468.

19. "Pool Buys Warehouse," *Tobacco: A Weekly Trade Review,* October 26, 1922, p. 4.

20. Schafer, *A History of Agriculture in Wisconsin,* p. 109.

21. Merk, *Economic History of Wisconsin,* pp. 31–32, 109.

22. *Fond du Lac Journal,* September 2, 1869.

23. Merk, *Economic History of Wisconsin,* p. 33.

24. W. A. Titus, "A Pioneer Beet Sugar Refinery," *Wisconsin Magazine of History,* December 1945, pp. 191–194; and Henry H. Bakken and George Max Beal, "The Cost of Manufacturing and Marketing Sugar in Wisconsin," University of Wisconsin Digital Collections/State of Wisconsin Collection, http://digicoll.library.wisc.edu/cgi-bin/WI/WI-idx?id=WI.CostSugar.

25. Merk, *Economic History of Wisconsin,* p. 38.

26. Bakken and Beal, "The Cost of Manufacturing and Marketing Sugar."

27. Merk, *Economic History of Wisconsin,* p. 35.

28. *Third Biennial Report of Labor and Industrial Statistics, Wisconsin 1887–1888* (Madison, Wisconsin: Bureau of Labor and Industrial Statistics, 1888), p. 238; *Ninth Biennial Report of Labor and Industrial Statistics, Wisconsin, 1898–1899* (Madison, Wisconsin: Bureau of Labor and Industrial Statistics, 1899), p. 103.

29. Wisconsin Crop and Livestock Reporting Service, *Wisconsin Agriculture in Mid-Century,* p. 75.

30. Benjamin Horace Hibbard, *The History of Agriculture in Dane County, Wisconsin* (Madison: Bulletin of the University of Wisconsin no. 101, 1904), p. 147.

31. Wisconsin Crop and Livestock Reporting Service, *Wisconsin Agriculture in Mid-Century,* pp. 67, 74; and *Wisconsin 2011 Agricultural Statistics* (Madison: Wisconsin State Department of Agriculture), p. 33.

32. Quoted in Emory A. Odell, "Swiss Cheese Industry," *Monroe Evening Times,* 1936, p. 6.

CHAPTER 7

1. Frederick Merk, *Economic History of Wisconsin during the Civil War Decade* (Madison: State Historical Society of Wisconsin, 1916), p. 23.

2. Eric Lampard, *The Rise of the Dairy Industry in Wisconsin: A Study in Agricultural Change, 1820–1920* (Madison: State Historical Society of Wisconsin, 1963), p. 71.

3. J. G. Pickett, "Pioneer Dairying in Wisconsin," in D. W. Curtis, Sec., *Sixth Annual Report of the Wisconsin Dairymen's Association* (Madison: Wisconsin Dairymen's Association, 1878), pp. 96–97.

4. Gustave William Buchen, *Historic Sheboygan County* (Sheboygan, WI: Sheboygan County Historical Society, 1944), pp. 275–276.

5. Ibid.

6. Ibid.

7. "Hazen Ventures Are Recalled by Descendent," *Brandon Times,* June 11, 1927.

8. Loren H. Osman, *W. D. Hoard: A Man for His Time* (Fort Atkinson, WI: W. D. Hoard and Sons Company, 1985), p. 55.

9. Ibid.

10. "An Editor Whose Cow Philosophy Made Wisconsin the Leading Dairy State," *Milwaukee Journal,* February 7, 1935; and "Generations of Leadership," www.hoards.com/biographies.

11. Joseph Schafer, *A History of Agriculture in Wisconsin* (Madison: State Historical Society of Wisconsin, 1922), p. 155.

12. "An Editor Whose Cow Philosophy . . ."

13. Lampard, *The Rise of the Dairy Industry,* pp. 170–177.

14. Loyal Durand, "The Cheese Manufacturing Regions of Wisconsin, 1850–1950," *Transactions of the Wisconsin Academy of Sciences, Arts and Letters* 42 (1953): 113–115.

15. *Third Annual Report of the Wisconsin Dairymen's Association* (Fort Atkinson, WI: W. D. Hoard Printer, 1875), pp. 17–18.

16. Jerry Apps, *Cheese: The Making of a Wisconsin Tradition* (Amherst, WI: Amherst Press, 1998), p. 29.

17. Ed Janus, *Creating Dairyland* (Madison: Wisconsin Historical Society Press, 2011), p. 13.

CHAPTER 8

1. Joseph Schafer, *A History of Agriculture in Wisconsin* (Madison: State Historical Society of Wisconsin, 1922), p. 104.

2. J. W. Hoyt, *Transactions of the Wisconsin State Agricultural Society,* vol. 7 (Madison: Wisconsin State Agricultural Society, 1868), pp. 66–67.

3. Rufus King, *Transactions of the Wisconsin State Agricultural Society* (Madison, WI: Beriah Brown, State Printer, 1852), pp. 13–16.

4. "Lincoln's Milwaukee Speech," USDA National Agricultural Library, www.nal.usda .gov/lincolns-milwaukee-speech.

5. "WI: History of State Fairs," no date; unpublished material from Robert Williams, Wisconsin Department of Agriculture, Trade and Consumer Protection.

6. Christine Bold, *The Oxford History of Popular Print Culture,* vol. 6: *US Popular Print Culture 1860–1920* (New York: Oxford University Press, 2012), p. 127.

7. Richard N. Current, *The History of Wisconsin,* vol. 2, *The Civil War Era, 1848–1873* (Madison: State Historical Society of Wisconsin, 1976), pp. 92–93.

8. "A Brief History of *Wisconsin Agriculturist,*" special issue, *Wisconsin Agriculturist,* 1978.

9. "An Editor Whose Cow Philosophy Made Wisconsin the Leading Dairy State," *Milwaukee Journal,* February 7, 1935.

10. Jerry Apps, *The People Came First: A History of Wisconsin Cooperative Extension* (Madison: University of Wisconsin–Extension, 2002), p. 16.

11. John W. Jenkins, *A Centennial History: A History of the College of Agricultural and Life Sciences* (Madison: University of Wisconsin–Madison College of Agricultural and Life Sciences, 1991), p. 4.

12. Apps, *The People Came First,* p. 16.

13. Robert Nesbit, *Wisconsin: A History* (Madison: University of Wisconsin Press, 1973), p. 289.

14. Jenkins, *A Centennial History,* p. 6.

15. Vernon Carstensen, "The Birth of an Agricultural Experiment Station," in *The Growth of Agricultural Research in Wisconsin: A Lecture Series Commemorating the 75th Anniversary of the Wisconsin Experiment Station, 1883–1958* (Madison: University of Wisconsin, 1958), p. 7.

16. Apps, *The People Came First,* pp. 17–18.

17. W. H. Morrison and John Gould, eds., *Wisconsin Farmers' Institutes: Sessions: 1886–1887* (Milwaukee: Cramer, Aikens & Cramer, 1887), p. 1.

18. Geo. McKerrow, ed., *Farmers' Institutes: A Handbook of Agriculture, Bulletin no. 27* (Madison, WI: Democrat Printing Company, 1913), pp. 14–15, 260–291.

19. William A. Henry, "The Agricultural College," University of Wisconsin Digital Collections/State of Wisconsin Collection, http://digicoll.library.wisc.edu/WIReader/WER0657-1.html.

20. *First Annual Report of the Agricultural Experiment Station: University of Wisconsin for the Year 1883* (Madison, WI: Democrat Printing Co., State Printers), 1884.

21. Apps, *The People Came First,* pp. 18–19.

22. W. A. Henry, *The Wisconsin Dairy School and Its Work,* Biennial Report of the Dairy and Food Commissioner of Wisconsin for 1899–1900 (Madison, WI: Office of the Dairy Commissioners, 1901), p. 74.

23. Nesbit, *Wisconsin: A History,* p. 290.

24. Jenkins, *A Centennial History,* pp. 57–63, p. 112; www.bact.wisc.edu/history.php; http://foodsci.wisc.edu/about/history.php; www.plantpath.wisc.edu/geninfo-history; and www.cals.wisc.edu/about-cals/history/cals-firsts.

25. Nesbit, *Wisconsin: A History,* p. 290.

26. *Farmers' Course in Agriculture* (Madison: University of Wisconsin Bulletin no. 105, December 1904), p. 3.

27. Ibid.

28. Edith L. Clift, ed., *Wisconsin Farmers' Institute Cookbook No. 1* (Madison, WI: Office of Farmers' Institutes, 1908), p. 1.

29. *Farmers' Course in Agriculture*, p. 3.

30. "Wisconsin Agricultural Schools," Wisconsin Historical Society, at www.wisconsinhistory.org.

31. Ibid.

32. *Farmer's Voice (Chicago)*, August 29, 1903.

CHAPTER 9

1. Wisconsin Crop and Livestock Reporting Service, *Wisconsin Agriculture in Mid-Century* (Madison: Wisconsin State Department of Agriculture Bulletin no. 325, 1953), p. 82; and USDA National Agricultural Statistics Service, www.nass.usda.gov/Statistics_by_State/Wisconsin/Publications/Dairy/milkcowno.pdf.

2. "Wisconsin Dairy Herds Decline, Number of Cows Increase," *AgriMarketing*, February 5, 2013, www.agrimarketing.com/s/80219; Wisconsin Crop and Livestock Reporting Service, *Wisconsin Agriculture in Mid-Century*; and USDA National Agricultural Statistics Service.

3. Ed Janus, *Creating Dairyland* (Madison: Wisconsin Historical Society Press, 2011), p. 35.

4. United States Department of Agriculture (USDA), *Farmers in a Changing World: Yearbook of Agriculture, 1940* (Washington, DC: United States Government Printing Office, 1940), p. 258.

5. Ibid., p. 258.

6. Frederick Merk, *Economic History of Wisconsin during the Civil War Decade* (Madison: State Historical Society of Wisconsin, 1916), p. 26.

7. Ibid.

8. Jerry Apps, *Cheese: The Making of a Wisconsin Tradition* (Amherst, WI: Amherst Press, 1998), p. 22.

9. "Convention of the Dairymen of Wisconsin," *Jefferson County Union*, February 23, 1872.

10. Robert C. Nesbit, *The History of Wisconsin*, vol. 3, *Urbanization and Industrialization, 1873–1893* (Madison: State Historical Society of Wisconsin, 1985), p. 18.

11. *Third Annual Report of the Wisconsin Dairymen's Association* (Fort Atkinson, WI: W. D. Hoard Printer, 1875), pp. 11–14.

12. Eric Lampard, *The Rise of the Dairy Industry in Wisconsin: A Study in Agricultural Change, 1820–1920* (Madison: State Historical Society of Wisconsin, 1963), p. 103.

13. Bob Cropp and Truman Graff, *The History and Role of Dairy Cooperatives* (Madison: College of Agriculture and Life Sciences, University of Wisconsin–Madison, 2001), pp. 4–5.

14. USDA, *Farmers in a Changing World,* p. 259; and LaVerne H. Marquart, *Wisconsin's Agricultural Heritage: 1871–1971* (Lake Mills, WI: Rural Life Publishing, 1972), pp. 1–3.

15. USDA, *Farmers in a Changing World,* p. 259.

16. Marquart, *Wisconsin's Agricultural Heritage,* p. 8.

17. Ibid., pp. 6, 9.

18. Ibid., p. 38.

19. "Rural Free Delivery," United States Postal Service, https://about.usps.com/who-we-are/postal-history/rural-free-delivery.pdf.

20. USDA, *Farmers in a Changing World,* p. 260.

21. Frank Smoot, *Farm Life: A Century of Change for Farm Families and Their Neighbors* (Eau Claire, WI: Chippewa Valley Museum, 2004), p. 82.

22. H. C. Thom, *First Annual Report of the State Dairy and Food Commissioner* (Madison, WI: Office of State Dairy and Food Commissioner, 1890), pp. 18–19.

23. H. C. Adams, *Biennial Report of the Dairy and Food Commissioner of Wisconsin, 1895–1896* (Madison, WI: Office of the Dairy and Food Commissioner, 1896).

24. Loyal Durand, "The Cheese Manufacturing Regions of Wisconsin, 1850–1950," *Transactions of the Wisconsin Academy of Sciences, Arts and Letters* 42 (1953): 121.

25. H. L. Russell, *Report of the Director: Agricultural Experiment Station for 1911–1912* (Madison, WI: College of Agriculture, 1913), p. 67.

26. Ibid.

27. H. L. Russell, *Twenty-Fifth and Twenty-Sixth Annual Reports of the Agricultural Experiment Station* (Madison, WI: College of Agriculture, 1910), pp. 44–45.

28. Ibid., pp. 26–45.

29. Russell, *Report of the Director,* p. 64.

30. Jerry Apps, *The People Came First: A History of Cooperative Extension* (Madison: University of Wisconsin Extension, 2002), pp. 32–41.

31. Clarence Beaman Smith and Meridith Chester Wilson, *The Agricultural Extension System of the United States* (New York: John Wiley and Sons, 1930), p. 365.

32. Elmer Verner McCollum, *From Kansas Farm Boy to Scientist* (Lawrence: University of Kansas Press, 1964), pp. 118–124.

33. John W. Jenkins, *A Centennial History: A History of the College of Agricultural and Life Sciences* (Madison, WI: College of Agricultural and Life Sciences, 1991), p. 58.

34. Henry Charles Taylor, *A Farm Economist in Washington 1919–1925* (Madison: University of Wisconsin–Madison Department of Agricultural Economics, 1992), p. 5.

35. Jenkins, *A Centennial History,* p. 57.

36. Charles Josiah Galpin, *Rural Life* (New York: The Century Company, 1918).

CHAPTER 10

1. Lucile Kane, "Settling the Wisconsin Cutovers," *Wisconsin Magazine of History,* Winter 1956–1957, p. 91.

2. William A. Henry, *Northern WI: A Hand-Book for the Homeseeker* (Madison, WI: Democrat Printing Company, 1896), p. 7.

3. Kane, "Settling the Wisconsin Cutovers," p. 92.

4. Robert Gough, *Farming the Cutover* (Lawrence: University Press of Kansas, 1997), p. 1.

5. *Getting Rid of Stumps* (Madison: University of Wisconsin Agricultural Experiment Station Bulletin no. 295, 1918), p. 23.

6. Ray Stannard Baker, quoted in Mark Davis, "Getting Rid of the Stumps: Wisconsin's Land-Clearing Program—The Experience of the Northern Lake Country, 1900–1925," *Transactions of the Wisconsin Academy of Sciences, Arts and Letters* 84 (1996): 12.

7. Davis, "Getting Rid of the Stumps," pp. 15–16.

8. Personal correspondence from Nancy Maier, August 13, 2011. Andy Machmueller is her father.

9. Ibid.

10. Jerry Apps, *Barns of Wisconsin,* 3rd ed. (Madison: Wisconsin Historical Society Press, 2010), p. 34.

11. Ibid., pp. 33 50.

12. Ibid., pp. 54–60.

13. Peggy Lee Beedle, *Silos: An Agricultural Success Story* (Madison: University of Wisconsin–Extension, 2001), p. 6.

14. N. S. Fish, "The History of the Silo in Wisconsin," *Wisconsin Magazine of History,* Winter 1924–1925, p. 9.

15. Beedle, *Silos,* p. 6.

16. Fish, "The History of the Silo in Wisconsin," p. 9.

17. Wisconsin Crop and Livestock Reporting Service, *Wisconsin Agriculture in Mid-Century* (Madison: Wisconsin State Department of Agriculture Bulletin no. 325, 1953), p. 69.

18. Ibid., pp. 66, 68.

19. Charles Galpin, *Rural Life* (New York: Century Company, 1919), p. 23.

20. Paul H. Landis, *Rural Life in Process* (New York: McGraw-Hill, 1940), p. 175.

21. Harry Barsantee, "The History and Development of the Telephone in Wisconsin," *Wisconsin Magazine of History,* December 1926, pp. 150–163.

22. Wisconsin Crop and Livestock Reporting Service, *Wisconsin Agriculture in Mid-Century,* p. 22.

CHAPTER 11

1. Terese Allen, *Hometown Flavor* (Madison, WI: Prairie Oak Press, 1998), pp. 46–48.

2. Wisconsin Meat Industry Hall of Fame, "John Plankinton," www.ansci.wisc.edu/meat_hof/1995/plankinton.htm.

3. Paul E. Geib, "'Everything But the Squeal': The Meat-Packing Industry, 1840–1930," *Wisconsin Magazine of History,* Autumn 1994, p. 4.

4. Ibid., p. 4.

5. Ibid., p. 9.

6. Ibid., p. 15

7. Sarah Blondich, "The Milwaukee Packers: Sweet Smell of the Stockyards," *Express Milwaukee,* January 26, 2010.

8. Geib, "Everything But the Squeal," pp. 15–16.

9. Wisconsin Crop and Livestock Reporting Service, *Wisconsin Agriculture in Mid-Century* (Madison: Wisconsin State Department of Agriculture Bulletin no. 325, 1953), p. 68.

10. *1998 Wisconsin Agricultural Statistics* (Madison: Wisconsin Agricultural Statistics Service, 1998), p. 77.

11. Geib, "Everything But the Squeal," pp. 16–17.

12. Ibid., p. 15; and "Plankinton, John," Wisconsin Historical Society, http://wihist.org/1Jexodu.

13. Geib, "Everything But the Squeal," p. 20.

14. "Milton Peck," Wisconsin Meat Industry Hall of Fame, www.ansci.wisc.edu/Meat_HOF/index.htm.

15. "Oscar Mayer Foods Corp. History," www.fundinguniverse.com/company-histories/oscar-mayer-foods-corp-history; and "Oscar G. Mayer," Wisconsin Meat Industry Hall of Fame, www.ansci.wisc.edu/Meat_HOF/index.htm.

16. Ibid.

17. "Oscar Mayer Foods Corp. History."

18. "Robert Bray," Wisconsin Meat Industry Hall of Fame, www.ansci.wisc.edu/Meat_HOF/index.htm.

19. See Robert G. Kauffman, "An 85-Year History of the Meat and Science and Muscle Biology Program," unpublished manuscript (available from Kauffman), May 1, 2012, for a more complete story of the UW–Madison's contributions to the meatpacking industry.

CHAPTER 12

1. Harva Hachten and Terese Allen, *The Flavor of Wisconsin,* rev. ed. (Madison: Wisconsin Historical Society Press, 2009), p. 105.

2. "History of Cranberries," Cape Cod Cranberry Growers, www.cranberries.org/cranberries/history.html.

3. Ibid.

4. Ibid.

5. "Cranberry Culture," Wisconsin Historic Marker erected 1958, Highway 54, five miles west of Port Edwards, Wood County.

6. Neil E. Stevens and Jean Nash, "The Development of Cranberry Growing in Wisconsin," *Wisconsin Magazine of History,* March 1944, p. 277.

7. Ibid.

8. "Cranberries: A Description of Great Marshes," *Commercial Times* (*Milwaukee*), April 12, 1875.

9. Stevens and Nash, "The Development of Cranberry Growing in Wisconsin," p. 282.

10. "Cranberries: A Description of Great Marshes."

11. Stevens and Nash, p. 293.

12. Ibid., pp. 292–293.

13. Ibid., p. 281.

14. Breann Schossow, "Wisconsin Continues to Lead Nation as Top Cranberry Producer," Wisconsin Public Radio, www.wpr.org/wisconsin-continues-lead-nation-top-cranberry-producer.

CHAPTER 13

1. *1998 Wisconsin Agricultural Statistics* (Madison: Wisconsin Agricultural Statistics Service, 1998), p. 78.

2. Fred Stare, "Wisconsin's Canning Industry, Past and Present," *Wisconsin Magazine of History,* Autumn 1952, p. 35.

3. Ibid.

4. Ibid.

5. Ibid.

6. "About," Lakeside Foods, www.lakesidefoods.com/company/Profile/history.htm.

7. Stare, "Wisconsin's Canning Industry," p. 35.

8. *Green Bay Press Gazette,* "Let's Not Make the Same Mistake with Downtown Green Bay," www.greenbaypressgazette.com/story/opinion/columnists/2014/07/06/make-mistake-downtown-green-bay/12277021; and "Veg-all," Sager Creek Veggies, www.sagercreekveggies.com/brands/veg-all.

9. Midwest Food Processors Association, www.mwfpa.org.

10. "Commercial Vegetable Processing," Wisconsin Cultural Resources Study, Wisconsin Historical Society, http://wihist.org/1JewV9B.

11. Personal correspondence from John Schoenemann, emeritus professor, University of Wisconsin–Madison Department of Horticulture, September 11, 2012.

CHAPTER 14

1. Personal correspondence from John Schoenemann, emeritus professor, University of Wisconsin–Madison Department of Horticulture, April 4, 2012.

2. Interview with Robert Williams, January 17, 2012.

3. Personal correspondence from John Schoenemann, April 4, 2012.

4. See WI Statute 30.18 (1935) with 1959 amendment to regulate use of surface water for irrigation purposes.

5. Chishom-Ryder patent applications, www.google.com/patents/US3142949.

6. Interview with John Schoenemann, October 1, 2012.

7. Donald Last, "Potential versus Actual Development of Irrigated Agriculture in Central Wisconsin," *Transactions of the Wisconsin Academy of Sciences, Arts and Letters* 71, pt 2 (1983): 51.

8. *Status of Wisconsin Agriculture, 2013* (Madison: University of Wisconsin–Madison and Cooperative Extension, Department of Agricultural and Applied Economics, 2013), p. 27.

CHAPTER 15

1. John Muir, *The Story of My Boyhood and Youth* (Madison: University of Wisconsin Press, 1965), pp. 99–100.

2. "Wisconsin Apple Orchards," *Apple Journal,* www.applejournal.com/wi01.htm.

3. Jerry Apps, *The People Came First: A History of Cooperative Extension* (Madison: University of Wisconsin–Extension, 2002), p. 10.

4. Cortney Cain, "The Development of Apple Horticulture in Wisconsin," www.waga.org/images/WIAppleHistory.pdf.

5. Ibid.

6. Frederic Cranefield, *Commercial Fruit Growing in Wisconsin: A Report of the Twenty-Fourth Annual Farmers' Institute* (Madison: Wisconsin Farmers' Institutes Bulletin no. 24, 1910), p. 56.

7. Ibid., p. 57.

8. Ibid.

9. Ibid., p. 64.

10. Cain, "The Development of Apple Horticulture in Wisconsin."

11. Wisconsin Crop and Livestock Reporting Service, *Wisconsin Agriculture in Mid-Century* (Madison: Wisconsin State Department of Agriculture Bulletin no. 325, 1953), p. 79.

12. Cain, "The Development of Apple Horticulture in Wisconsin."

13. *Wisconsin's Rank in National Agricultural Production, 2010* (Washington, DC: USDA National Agricultural Statistics Service, p. 3).

14. Hjalmar Rued Holand, *History of Door County* (Chicago: S. J. Clarke, 1917), pp. 165–166.

15. Wisconsin Cherry Growers, "History of the Door County Cherry Industry," www.wisconsincherries.org/history.html.

16. Ibid.

17. "Door County Cherries Hit by $250,000 Frost," *Ludington (Michigan) Daily News,* May 27, 1930, p. 1.

18. Wisconsin Crop and Livestock Reporting Service, *Wisconsin Agriculture in Mid-Century,* p. 80.

19. *Wisconsin's Rank in National Agricultural Production, 2010,* p. 3.

20. Wisconsin Crop and Livestock Reporting Service, *Wisconsin Agriculture in Mid-Century,* p. 80.

21. *Wisconsin Strawberries–2012* (Washington, DC: USDA National Agricultural Statistics Service, 2013).

22. Harva Hachten and Terese Allen, *The Flavor of Wisconsin,* rev. ed. (Madison: Wisconsin Historical Society Press, 2009), p. 105; and Wollersheim Winery, www.wollersheim.com.

CHAPTER 16

1. A. H. Wright, *Wisconsin's Hemp Industry* (Madison: University of Wisconsin Agricultural Experiment Station Bulletin no. 293, May 1918), p. 3.

2. John Dvorak, "American's Harried Hemp Industry," www.hemphasis.net/History/harriedhemp.htm.

3. Jerry Apps, *Horse-Drawn Days: A Century of Farming with Horses* (Madison: Wisconsin Historical Society Press, 2010), pp. 139–141.

4. David P. West, "Hemp in Wisconsin," *Hemp World Magazine,* Winter 1998, pp. 2–4.

5. Ibid., p. 3.

6. Ibid., p. 5.

7. Wright, *Wisconsin's Hemp Industry,* p. 11.

8. Ibid., p. 12.

9. Ibid., p. 6.

10. Ibid., p. 14.

11. "Hemp for Victory," Global Hemp, www.globalhemp.com/1942/01/hemp-for-victory.html.

12. Personal correspondence from James G. Neu, October 28, 2011.

13. "Ginseng," *Alternative Field Crops Manual,* www.hort.purdue.edu/newcrop/afcm/ginseng.html.

14. Robert L. Beyfuss, "Ginseng Growing," New York State Department of Environmental Conservation, www.dec.ny.gov/animals/7472.html.

15. "Methods of Farming, Planting, Harvesting and Marketing the Crop," *Richland Center Democrat,* April 2, 1924.

16. Beyfuss, "Ginseng Growing."

17. Ibid.

18. Kathrene Sutherland Gedney Pinkerton, *Bright with Silver* (New York: W. Sloane Associates, 1947), p. 18.

19. "Fromm Family," Marathon County Historical Society, www.marathoncountyhistory.com/PeopleDetails.php?PeopleId=152.

20. "About Us," Ginseng Board of Wisconsin, www.ginsengboard.com/aboutus.cfm.

21. Katherine Esposito, "Bringing in Nature's Bounty," *Wisconsin Natural Resources,* April 2006, http://dnr.wi.gov/wnrmag/html/stories/2000/apr00/mossy.htm; and "Sphagnum Moss: Wisconsin's Invisible Industry," www.waymarking.com/waymarks/WM1K5P_Sphagnum_Moss_Wisconsins_Invisible_Industry_Historical_Marker.

22. "Long-Fibered Sphagnum Moss," Mosser Lee, www.mosserlee.com/page/What_Is_Sphagnum_Moss.aspx.

23. Esposito, "Bringing in Nature's Bounty."

24. James E. Landing, *American Essence: A History of the Peppermint and Spearmint Industry in the United States* (Kalamazoo, MI: Kalamazoo Public Museum, 1969), pp. 3–5.

25. Ibid., pp. 10–30.

26. K. A. Delahaut, "Crop Profile for Mint in Wisconsin," www.ipmcenters.org/cropprofiles/docs/wimint.pdf.

27. Christine Lindner, "Flavor Foods with Mint," *Chilton Times Journal,* January 21, 2011.

CHAPTER 17

1. Walter L. Gojmerac, *All about Bees, Beekeeping and Honey* (New York: Drake, 1977), pp. 7–8.

2. Ibid., p. 10.

3. Harva Hachten and Terese Allen, *The Flavor of Wisconsin,* rev. ed. (Madison: Wisconsin Historical Society Press, 2009), p. 105.

4. N. E. France, *Beekeeping in Wisconsin* (Madison, WI: Agricultural Experiment Station Bulletin no. 264, 1915), p. 6.

5. "Honey: Production and Value, Wisconsin 1993–97," *1998 Wisconsin Agricultural Statistics* (Madison: Wisconsin Agricultural Statistics Service, 1998), p. 74; and *Wisconsin—Honey Production* (Washington, DC: USDA National Agricultural Statistics Service, April 3, 2012), www.nass.usda.gov/Statistics_by_State/Wisconsin/Publications/Miscellaneous/honey.pdf.

6. Dan Hansen, "Honeybees Make Vital Contribution to Our Nation's Food Supply through Pollination," *Wisconsin State Farmer,* November 18, 2011.

7. Terese Allen and Bobbie Malone, *The Flavor of Wisconsin for Kids* (Madison: Wisconsin Historical Society Press, 2012), p. 16.

8. Lucy Eldersveld Murphy, *A Gathering of Rivers: Indians, Metis, and Mining in the Western Great Lakes 1737–1832* (Lincoln: University of Nebraska Press, 2000), p. 145.

9. Terese Allen, "Sweet: The History, Craft and Cookery of Maple Syrup," *Edible Madison,* Spring 2012, http://ediblemadison.com/articles/view/sweet.

10. "Came to Cicero When Oxen Trod Forest Trail," *Appleton Post-Crescent,* February 9, 1924.

11. Frederick Merk, *Economic History of Wisconsin during the Civil War Decade* (Madison: State Historical Society of Wisconsin, 1916), p. 47.

12. "Join Us," Wisconsin Maple Syrup Producers Association, http://wismaple.org/join-us.

13. *1998 Wisconsin Agricultural Statistics* (Madison: Wisconsin Agricultural Statistics Service, 1998), p. 78; and *2011 Wisconsin Agricultural Statistics* (Washington, DC: USDA National Agricultural Statistics Service), www.nass.usda.gov/Statistics_by_State/ Wisconsin/Publications/Annual_Statistical_Bulletin/bulletin2011_web.pdf.

14. "Wisconsin Maple Syrup Production Down Significantly From Last Year," USDA National Agricultural Statistics Service, June 18, 2012, www.wisbusiness.com/1008/ 120618_crop.pdf.

15. Karen Herzog, "Wisconsin Maple Producers Endure Worst Year in Memory," JSOnline, March 19, 2012.

16. "1954–2004: 50 Years Strong and Still Growing," Wisconsin Christmas Tree Producer's Association, anniversary album, Portage, WI, 2004, pp. 5–9.

17. Ibid.

18. *2007 Census of Agriculture—State Data, Wisconsin* (Washington, DC: USDA National Agricultural Statistics Service, 2007).

19. *2009 Census of Horticultural Specialties—Wisconsin* (Washington, DC: USDA National Agricultural Statistics Service, 2009).

20. Kathrene Sutherland Gedney Pinkerton, *Bright with Silver* (New York: W. Sloane Associates, 1947), pp. 114, 187.

20. "Business: Furs from Fromms," *Time,* February 24, 1936.

21. Personal correspondence from Glenn Lemmenes, December 19, 2011.

22. "Commercial Fur Farming in Wisconsin," Wisconsin Historical Society, http://wihist.org/1uzA15h; and *2014 Wisconsin Agricultural Statistics* (Washington, DC: USDA National Agricultural Statistics Service), http://www.nass.usda.gov/ Statistics_by_State/Wisconsin/Publications/Annual_Statistical_Bulletin/ bulletin2014_web.pdf; and *1998 Wisconsin Agricultural Statistics* (Washington, DC: USDA National Agricultural Statistics Service, p. 74).

23. Interview with Herb Magnuson, February 16, 2012.

24. Interview with Harry Erickson, February 23, 2012.

25. *Mink and Their Mink Pelts—Inventory and Number Sold: 2002 and 1997* (Washington, DC: USDA National Agricultural Statistics Service, 2002), www.agcensus.usda .gov/Publications/2002/Volume_1,_Chapter_2_County_Level/Wisconsin/ st55_2_020_020.pdf.

26. *Wisconsin—Mink* (Washington, DC: USDA National Agricultural Statistics Service, July 10, 2012), www.nass.usda.gov/Statistics_by_State/Wisconsin/Publications/ Livestock/mink.pdf.

CHAPTER 18

1. Paul W. Glad, *The History of Wisconsin,* vol. 5, *War, a New Era, and Depression, 1914–1946* (Madison: State Historical Society of Wisconsin, 1990), pp. 356–357.

2. Ibid., pp. 409–410, 419.

3. Wisconsin Crop and Livestock Reporting Service, *Wisconsin Agriculture in Mid-Century* (Madison: Wisconsin State Department of Agriculture Bulletin no. 325, 1953), p. 3.

4. "Farm Security Administration," Oklahoma Historical Society, http://digital.library .okstate.edu/encyclopedia/entries/F/FA015.html.

5. *History of Agricultural Price-Support and Adjustment Programs, 1933–84* (Washington, DC: USDA Economic Research Service, Agriculture Information Bulletin no. 485, December 1984), http://naldc.nal.usda.gov/download/CAT10842840/PDF.

6. Glad, *The History of Wisconsin,* vol. 5, p. 494.

7. "History of NRCS," USDA Natural Resources Conservation Service, www.nrcs.usda .gov/wps/portal/nrcs/main/national/about/history.

8. Neil M. Maher, *Nature's New Deal,* New York: Oxford University Press, 2008, pp. 122–123.

9. "Franklin D. Roosevelt," The American Presidency Project, www.presidency.ucsb.edu/ ws/?pid=15599.

10. Ibid.

11. Ed Jesse et al., "Rethinking Dairyland: Background for Decisions about Wisconsin's Dairy Industry," Marketing and Policy Briefing Paper no 78A, College of Agricultural and Life Sciences, University of Wisconsin–Madison, May 2002, p. 1.

12. "Records of the Rural Electrification Administration," National Archives Guide to Federal Records, www.archives.gov/research/guide-fed-records/groups/221. html#221.1.

13. John W. Jenkins, *A Centennial History: A History of the College of Agricultural and Life Sciences* (Madison: University of Wisconsin–Madison College of Agricultural and Life Sciences, 1991), p. 91.

14. Jennifer Smith, "The Culture of Ag," *Grow: Wisconsin's Magazine for the Life Sciences,* Summer 2012, p. 30.

15. Jenkins, *A Centennial History,* p. 112.

16. John Rector Barton, *Rural Artists of Wisconsin* (Madison: University of Wisconsin Press, 1948).

17. Robert E. Gard Foundation, "Robert E. Gard," www.gardfoundation.org/gard.html.

18. "Federal Writers' Project," US Library of Congress, www.loc.gov/rr/program/bib/newdeal/fwp.html.

CHAPTER 19

1. William F. Thompson, *The History of Wisconsin,* vol. 6, *Continuity and Change, 1940–1965* (Madison: State Historical Society of Wisconsin, 1988), pp. 66–67.

2. Ibid., p. 86.

3. Thompson, *History of Wisconsin,* vol. 6, pp. 86–87.

4. Betty Cowley, *Stalag WI: Inside WWII Prisoner-of-War Camps* (Oregon, WI: Badger Books, 2002), pp. 12–13.

5. Ibid., pp. 30–31, 188–193, 222–233.

6. Ibid., p. 13.

7. Thompson, *History of Wisconsin,* vol. 6, p. 91.

8. Ibid., p. 87.

9. "World War II Rationing on the US Homefront," Ames (Iowa) Historical Society, www.ameshistory.org/exhibits/events/rationing.htm.

10. Ibid.

11. Richard Haney, *"When Is Daddy Coming Home?"* (Madison: Wisconsin Historical Society Press, 2004), p. 60.

12. Wisconsin Crop and Livestock Reporting Service, *Wisconsin Agriculture in Mid-Century* (Madison: Wisconsin State Department of Agriculture Bulletin no. 325, 1953), pp. 43–45.

13. Ibid.

14. Ibid.

CHAPTER 20

1. William F. Thompson, *The History of Wisconsin,* vol. 6, *Continuity and Change, 1940–1965* (Madison: State Historical Society of Wisconsin, 1988), p. 1.

2. Jerry Apps, *The Quiet Season: Remembering Country Winters* (Madison: Wisconsin Historical Society Press, 2013), p. 137.

3. Wisconsin Crop and Livestock Reporting Service, *Wisconsin Agriculture in Mid-Century* (Madison: Wisconsin State Department of Agriculture Bulletin no. 325, 1953), p. 22.

4. Ibid., p. 3.

5. Jerry Apps, *One-Room Country Schools* (Amherst, WI: Amherst Press, 1996).

6. Wisconsin Crop and Livestock Reporting Service, *Wisconsin Agriculture in Mid-Century,* p. 13.

7. Ed Jesse et al., "Rethinking Dairyland: Background for Decisions about Wisconsin's Dairy Industry," Marketing and Policy Briefing Paper no 78A, College of Agricultural and Life Sciences, University of Wisconsin–Madison, May 2002, p. 1.

8. Wisconsin Crop and Livestock Reporting Service, *Wisconsin Agriculture in Mid-Century,* pp. 12–13.

9. Thompson, *The History of Wisconsin,* vol. 6, p. 138.

10. L. H. "Bud" Schultz, *History of the Dairy Science Department: University of Wisconsin–Madison* (Madison: University of Wisconsin–Madison Dairy Science Department, 2009), p. 29.

11. Ibid.

12. "History," Wisconsin Farm Technology Days, www.wifarmtechnologydays.com/history_highlights.php.

13. Ibid.

14. Wisconsin Crop and Livestock Reporting Service, *Wisconsin Agriculture in Mid-Century,* pp. 21–22.

15. Personal correspondence from David L. Shekoski, January 25, 2012.

16. *1998 Wisconsin Agricultural Statistics* (Madison: Wisconsin Agricultural Statistics Service, 1998), p. 76.

CHAPTER 21

1. *1998 Wisconsin Agricultural Statistics* (Madison: Wisconsin Agricultural Statistics Service, 1998), p. 76.

2. Douglas Jackson-Smith et al., *Farming in Wisconsin at the End of the Century: Results of the 1999 Wisconsin Farm Poll,* Wisconsin Farm Research Summary no. 4 (Madison: University of Wisconsin–Madison and University of Wisconsin–Extension Program on Agricultural Technology Studies, March 2000), p. 1.

3. *1998 Wisconsin Agricultural Statistics,* p. 76–77.

4. Interview with UW–Madison agricultural economist Ed Jesse, March 13, 2012.

5. Ibid.

6. Ibid.

7. Ed Jesse et al, "Rethinking Dairyland: Background for Decisions about Wisconsin's Dairy Industry," Marketing and Policy Briefing Paper no 78A, College of Agricultural and Life Sciences, University of Wisconsin–Madison, May 2002, pp. 3–4.

8. "History of the Crop Insurance Program," USDA Risk Management Agency, www.rma.usda.gov/aboutrma/what/history.html.

9. John N. Maclean, "Environmentalists Sound Battle Cry: Save the Soil," *Chicago Tribune,* March 21, 1985.

10. Lawrence K. Glaser, *Provisions of the Food Security Act of 1985* (Washington, DC: USDA Economic Research Service Agriculture Bulletin no. 498).

11. "Food Security Act of 1985," Center for Regulatory Effectiveness, www.thecre.com/fedlaw/legal14coast/food_security_act_of_1985_legal_matters.htm.

12. Wisconsin Agri-Business Association, http://wiagribusiness.org.

13. Wisconsin Agribusiness Council, www.wisagri.com.

14. "History of GPS," Mio, www.mio.com/technology-history-of-gps.htm.

15. Gloria Hafemeister, "Technology Invades Fields," *Wisconsin State Farmer,* November 24, 2014; "Official US Government Information about the Global Positioning System (GPS) and Related Topics," www.gps.gov/applications/agriculture.

16. *Wisconsin—June Acreage* (Washington, DC: USDA National Agricultural Statistics Service, July 3, 2012).

17. Felicia Wu, "An Analysis of Bt Corn's Benefits and Risks for National and Regional Policymakers Considering Bt Corn Adoption," *International Journal of Technology and Globalization* 2, nos. 1/2 (2006): 115–133.

18. Statement from World Health Organization in Christopher D. Cook, "Control over Your Food: Why Monsanto's GM Seeds Are Undemocratic," *Christian Science Monitor,* February 23, 2011.

19. Cook, "Control over Your Food."

20. Amy Harmon and Andrew Pollack, "Battle Brewing over Labeling of Genetically Modified Food," *New York Times,* May 24, 2012.

21. *Wisconsin—June Acreage.*

22. Sir Albert Howard, *An Agricultural Testament.* Oxford University Press: Oxford and New York, 1943.

23. Mary V. Gold, *Organic Production/Organic Food: Information Access Tools,* Alternative Farming Systems Information Center, USDA National Agricultural Library, June 2007.

24. Chris Carusi et al., "Organic Agriculture in Wisconsin: 2015 Status Report," UW–Madison Center for Integrated Agriculture Systems and the Wisconsin Department of Agriculture, Trade and Consumer Protection," February 2015, www.cias.wisc.edu.

25. Ibid.

CHAPTER 22

1. *2011 Wisconsin Agricultural Statistics* (Washington, DC: USDA National Agricultural Statistics Service), www.nass.usda.gov/Statistics_by_State/Wisconsin/Publications/Annual_Statistical_Bulletin/bulletin2011_web.pdf; and "Farm Statistics," Wisconsin Milk Marketing Board, http://media.eatwisconsincheese.com/dairyimpact/statistics/farmStatistics.

2. *Wisconsin Dairy Farm Trends, Percent of Wisconsin Dairy Farms by Herd Size* (Washington, DC: USDA National Agricultural Statistics Service, Wisconsin Census of Agriculture, 2007).

3. *Milk Cow Herd Size by Inventory and Sales: 2007* (Washington, DC: USDA National Agricultural Statistics Service, Wisconsin Census of Agriculture, 2007).

4. *Milk Cow Herd Size by Inventory and Sales: 2012* (Washington, DC: USDA National Agricultural Statistics Service, Wisconsin Census of Agriculture, 2012).

5. "2014 Dairy Data," Wisconsin Milk Marketing Board, www.wmmb.com/assets/ images/pdf/WisconsinDairyData.pdf.

6. *Farms, Land in Farms, and Livestock Operations, 2011 Summary* (Washington, DC: USDA National Agricultural Statistics Service, https://ofbf.org/uploads/ FarmLandIn-02–17–2012.pdf, p. 18).

7. "The Milk Source Way," www.agweb.com/article/the_milk_source_way_NAA_ Jim_Dickrell.

8. "Wisconsin's Milk Source Named 2014 Innovative Dairy Farmer of the Year," www.agweb.com/article/wisconsins_milk_source_named_2014_innovative_ dairy_farmer_of_the_year_NAA_Dairy_Today_Editors.

9. Michael Penn, "Invisible Hands," *Grow: Wisconsin's Magazine for the Life Sciences,* http://grow.cals.wisc.edu/agriculture/invisible-hands/3.

10. Florence C. Bell, *Farmer Co-ops in Wisconsin* (St. Paul, MN: St. Paul Bank for Cooperatives, 1941), pp. 2–5.

11. Personal correspondence from Robert Cropp, professor emeritus and dairy economist, University of Wisconsin–Madison, March 29, 2012.

12. Personal correspondence from Robert Cropp, September 8, 2012.

13. Karen Herzog, "Dairy Innovation Center to Shut Down," *Milwaukee Journal Sentinel,* September 13, 2012.

14. Heidi Clausen, "Dairy Business Innovation Center Closing," *The Country Today,* September 26, 2012.

15. "2014 Dairy Data," Wisconsin Milk Marketing Board.

16. Jerry Apps, *Cheese: The Making of a Wisconsin Tradition* (Amherst, WI: Amherst Press, 1998), pp. 133–134.

17. Ibid.

18. Emory Odell, "Swiss Cheese Industry," *Monroe Evening Leader Times,* 1936.

19. Helen O'Neill, Huffington Post, "Visit Monroe, Wisconsin—Home of Limburger, the World's Stinkiest Cheese," www.huffingtonpost.com/2013/05/08/visit-monroe-wisconsin-stinky-cheese-limburger_n_3239545.html.

20. Hennings Cheese, www.henningscheese.com.

21. Wisconsin Specialty Cheese Institute, www.wispecialtycheese.org.

22. "Did You Know?" Wisconsin Milk Marketing Board, Dairy Doing More, www.dairydoingmore.org/economicimpact/dairyfacts.

23. UW–Madison College of Agriculture and Life Sciences, Wisconsin Center for Dairy Research, www.cdr.wisc.edu/mastercheesemaker.

24. Wisconsin Specialty Cheese Institute.

25. "Did You Know?" Wisconsin Milk Marketing Board, Dairy Doing More.

26. Barry Adams, "Switzerland Wins Top Prize but Wisconsin Dominates World Championship Cheese Contest," *Wisconsin State Journal,* March 20, 2014.

27. Wisconsin Dairy Goat Association, www.wdga.org/about-goats.

28. *Wisconsin's Rank in the Nation's Agricultural Production,* USDA National Agricultural Statistics Service, www.nass.usda.gov/Statistics_by_State/Wisconsin/Publications/ Annual_Statistical_Bulletin/bulletin2013_web.pdf.

29. "Animal Feeding Operations," USDA Natural Resources Conservation Service, www.nrcs.usda.gov/wps/portal/nrcs/main/national/plantsanimals/livestock/afo.

30. "Factory Farming Impacts," Clean Water Action Council, www.cleanwateractioncouncil.org/issues/resource-issues/factory-farms.

31. Ibid.

32. "Facts about CAFOs," Sierra Club, Wisconsin John Muir Chapter, wisconsin .sierraclub.org/issues/greatlakes/articles/cafofacts.html.

33. B. C. Kowalski, *USA Today,* "Owner Vows to Curb Animal Abuse at Dairy Farm," www.usatoday.com/story/news/nation/2014/11/12/farm-owner-vows-to-curb-dairy-cow-abuse/18947029.

34. Jessica Vangeren, "Manure Digesters Seen as Best Hope for Curbing Lake Pollution, but Drawbacks Remain," *Capital Times (Madison),* April 30, 2014.

CHAPTER 23

1. "Ethanol," Wisconsin State Energy Office, www.stateenergyoffice.wi.gov/category.asp? linkcatid=2991&linkid=1462&locid=160.

2. "Wisconsin Agriculture Exports Up In 2014," *In Wisconsin,* http://inwisconsin.com/ news/wisconsin-agriculture-exports-up-in-2014.

3. Ibid.

4. Ed Jesse, *Status of Wisconsin Agriculture, 2012* (Madison: University of Wisconsin–Madison Department of Agricultural and Applied Economics, 2012), p. v.

5. "State Fact Sheets: Wisconsin," report, USDA Economic Research Service, May 2, 2012.

6. *1998 Wisconsin Agricultural Statistics* (Madison: Wisconsin Agricultural Statistics Service, 1998), p. 77.

7. *Wisconsin 2011 Agricultural Statistics* (Madison: Wisconsin State Department of Agriculture, 2011), p. 3.

8. Ibid.

9. *2007 Census of Agriculture—State Data, Wisconsin* (Washington, DC: USDA National Agricultural Statistics Service, 2007), p. 21; *2012 Census of Agriculture—State Data, Wisconsin,* www.nass.usda.gov/Statistics_by_State/Wisconsin/Publications/Annual_Statistical_Bulletin/page52.pdf.

11. "Where's the Beef in Wisconsin?" University of Wisconsin–Extension, http://fyi.uwex.edu/wbic/files/2010/01/Wheres-the-beef-2011.pdf.

12. *Wisconsin Crop Production: 2012 Growing Season Review* (Washington, DC: USDA National Agricultural Statistics Service, January 16, 2013).

13. *Wisconsin Vegetables 2012* (Washington, DC: USDA National Agricultural Statistics Service, February 4, 2013).

14. Personal correspondence from Sandra Cleveland, Program and Policy Analyst/Open Records Coordinator, Division of Food Safety, Wisconsin Department of Agriculture, Trade and Consumer Protection, September 18, 2012.

15. *Wisconsin's Rank in National Agricultural Production, 2010* (Washington, DC: USDA National Agricultural Statistics Service, p. 3).

16. "Number of California Wineries," Wine Institute, www.wineinstitute.org/resources/statistics/article124.

17. Becky Rochester, *Report of the Wisconsin Wineries Survey 2011,* Wisconsin Grape Growers Association, June 2011, p. 3.

18. Interview with Tim Rehbein, February 20, 2012.

19. "State of Wisconsin Licenses Madison-Area Hops Processor," *Agri-View,* October 6, 2011; and "About Gorst Valley Hops," Gorst Valley Hops, www.gorstvalleyhops.com/about.php.

20. "Wisconsin Hop Exchange Featured in Brewers Digest Magazine," Wisconsin Hop Exchange, http://coop.wisconsinhopexchange.com/uncategorized/wisconsin-hop-exchange-featured-in-brewers-digest-magazine.

21. "Fish Farms—Fish Farm Registration," Wisconsin Department of Trade, Agriculture, and Consumer Protection, http://datcp.wi.gov/Farms/Fish_Farms/Registration/index.aspx.

22. Rob Schultz, "Wisconsin Aquaculture: New Law Helps Turn the Tide for Fish Hatcheries," *Wisconsin State Journal,* July 15, 2012.

23. "What is Aquaponics?" The Aquaponics Source, http://theaquaponicsource.com/box/what-is-aquaponics.

24. The Vertical Farm, www.verticalfarm.com.

25. Jeanne Carpenter, Cheese Underground, "New Research Concludes Pasture Cheeses are "Quantifiably Different," February 9, 2013, cheeseunderground.blogspot.com.

26. Rob Schultz, "Agritourism Offers Vacationers a Taste of Country Life," *Wisconsin State Journal,* September 30, 2012.

27. Rob Schultz, "Trillium Farm," madison.com, http://host.madison.com/business/agritourism-offers-vacationers-a-taste-of-country-life/article_1935f104–0b04–11e2-b3b8–0019bb2963f4.html.

28. "Farmers Markets and Local Food Marketing," USDA Agricultural Marketing Services, www.ams.usda.gov/AMSv1.0/farmersmarkets.

29. "Dane County Farmers' Market History," Dane County Farmers' Market, http://dcfm.org/dcfm-history.

30. "About CSA," FairShare CSA Coaltion, www.csacoalition.org/our-farms/about-csa.

31. "Willy Street Co-op's Eat Local Month," Willy Street Co-op, www.willystreet.coop/eat-local-month.

32. Mary Bergin, "Pull Up a Seat at Wisconsin's Authentic Farm-to-table Gems," postcrescent.com, www.postcrescent.com/story/life/2014/10/18/pull-seat-wisconsins-authentic-farm-table-gems/17444151.

33. "Farm Fresh Atlas," Reap Food Group, www.reapfoodgroup.org/farm-fresh-atlas.

34. "Buy Local, Buy Wisconsin: Wisconsin Farm to School," Wisconsin Department of Trade, Agriculture, and Consumer Protection, http://datcp.wi.gov/Business/Buy_Local_Buy_Wisconsin/Farm_to_School_Program/index.aspx.

CHAPTER 24

1. "Demographics," US Environmental Protection Agency, www.epa.gov/oecaagct/ag101/demographics.html.

2. Wisconsin Crop and Livestock Reporting Service, *Wisconsin Agriculture in Mid-Century* (Madison: Wisconsin State Department of Agriculture Bulletin no. 325, 1953), p. 3; and *2012 Census of Agriculture—State Data* (Washington, DC: USDA National Agricultural Statistics Service), www.nass.usda.gov/Statistics_by_State/Wisconsin/Publications/Miscellaneous/fmnouswi.

3. *2012 Census of Agriculture—State Data*

4. "Amish Settlements in Wisconsin," University of Wisconsin–Eau Claire, www.uwec.edu/geography/Ivogeler/w188/utopian/amish-data2.htm; and "Wisconsin Amish," Amish America, http://amishamerica.com/wisconsin-amish.

5. *2012 Census of Agriculture—State Data.*

6. From the 1990 "Farm Bill," Food, Agriculture, Conservation, and Trade Act of 1990 (FACTA), Public Law 101–624, Title VI, Subtitle A., Section 1603.

7. "Report Assesses Climate Change Impacts, Adaptation Strategies," University of Wisconsin–Madison News, February 7, 2011, www.news.wisc.edu/18940.

8. Christopher J. Kucharik and Pete Nowak, *Agriculture Working Group Report,* Wisconsin Initiative on Climate Change Impact (Madison, WI: University of Wisconsin–Madison Nelson Institute for Environmental Studies, 2011), p. 6–8, www.wicci.wisc.edu/report/2011_WICCI-Report.pdf.

9. Ron Seely, "Climate Change Deniers Ignore Science, History," *Wisconsin State Journal,* June 29, 2012.

10. *Emerging Consensus Shows Climate Change Already Having Major Effects on Ecosystems and Species* (Washington, DC: US Geological Survey, December 18, 2012).

11. James Andrews, *Food Safety News,* "Is Zero Tolerance on Salmonella Feasible?" www.foodsafetynews.com/2014/02/is-zero-tolerance-on-salmonella-feasible/#.VHd02TFzQwA.

12. *Food Safety News,* "Update: Retail Locations Believed to Have Received Recalled Ground Beef Expands Again," www.foodsafetynews.com/2014/05/fsis-releases-list-of-retail-locations-likely-to-have-received-recalled-ground-beef/#.VHd13zFzQwA.

13. Rick Barrett, "Raw Milk Blamed as 38 at Durand High Football Potluck Are Sickened," JSOnline, November 16, 2014, www.jsonline.com/business/raw-milk-blamed-as-38-at-durand-high-football-potluck-are-sickened-b99390272z1–282848161.html.

14. Rick Barrett, "Raw-Milk Advocates Plan Appeal to State Supreme Court," JSOnline, October 6, 2014, www.jsonline.com/business/raw-milk-advocates-plan-appeal-to-state-supreme-court-b99365662z1–278244491.html.

15. Ron Nixon, "Report Says a Crop Subsidy Cap Could Save Billions," *New York Times,* April 11, 2012.

16. "Wisconsin Farmers Union News," *Wisconsin Farmers Union,* February/March 2012, pp. 7–10.

17. See www.usda.gov/documents/usda-2014-farm-bill-highlights.pdf for more information about the 2014 Farm Bill.

18. Madeline Behr, "A Happy Thanksgiving for Cranberry Caucus," greenbaypressgazette.com, November 26, 2014, www.greenbaypressgazette.com/story/money/2014/11/26/happy-thanksgiving-cranberry-caucus/19560197.

19. Jerry Apps, *Barns of Wisconsin,* 3rd ed. (Madison: Wisconsin Historical Society Press, 2010), p. 177.

20. US Census Bureau, "International Programs—World Population 1950–2050—US Census Bureau," www.census.gov/population/international/data/worldpop/table_population.php.

SELECTED BIBLIOGRAPHY

BOOKS

Allen, Terese, *Hometown Flavor.* Madison, WI: Prairie Oak Press, 1998.

Allen, Terese, and Bobbie Malone. *The Flavor of Wisconsin for Kids.* Madison: Wisconsin Historical Society Press, 2012.

Apps, Jerry. *Barns of Wisconsin.* 3rd ed. Madison: Wisconsin Historical Society Press, 2010.

———. *Breweries of Wisconsin.* 2nd ed. Madison: University of Wisconsin Press, 2005.

———. *Cheese: The Making of a Wisconsin Tradition.* Amherst, WI: Amherst Press, 1998.

———. *Horse-Drawn Days: A Century of Farming with Horses.* Madison: Wisconsin Historical Society Press, 2010.

———. *Mills of Wisconsin and the Midwest.* Madison, WI: Tamarack Press, 1980.

———. *Old Farm: A History.* Madison: Wisconsin Historical Society Press, 2008.

———. *One-Room Country Schools: History and Recollections.* Amherst, WI: Amherst Press, 1996.

———. *The People Came First: A History of Cooperative Extension.* Madison: University of Wisconsin Extension, 2002.

———. *Village of Roses.* Wild Rose, WI: Wild Rose Historical Society, 1973.

Barton, John Rector. *Rural Artists of Wisconsin.* Madison: University of Wisconsin Press, 1948.

Berry, Bill. *The Future of Farming and Rural Life in Wisconsin.* Madison: Wisconsin Academy of Sciences, Arts and Letters, 2007.

Birmingham, Robert A., and Leslie E. Eisenberg. *Indian Mounds of Wisconsin.* Madison: Wisconsin Historical Society Press, 2000.

Birmingham, Robert A., and Lynne G. Goldstein. *Aztalan: Mysteries of an Ancient Indian Town.* Madison: University of Wisconsin Press, 2005.

Bold, Christine. *The Oxford History of Popular Print Culture.* Vol. 6, *U.S. Popular Print Culture 1860–1920.* New York: Oxford University Press, 2012.

Brunner, Edmund deS., and E. Hesin Pao Yang. *Rural America and the Extension Service.* New York: Teachers College, Columbia University, 1949.

Buchen, Gustave William. *Historic Sheboygan County.* Sheboygan, WI: Sheboygan County Historical Society, 1944.

Buley, R. Carlyle, *The Old Northwest: Pioneer Period, 1815–1840.* Bloomington: Indiana University Press, 1951.

Cooper, Zachary. *Black Settlers in Rural Wisconsin.* Madison: Wisconsin Historical Society Press, 1994.

Cowley, Betty. *Stalag Wisconsin: Inside WWII Prisoner-of-War Camps.* Oregon, WI: Badger Books, 2002.

Current, Richard N. *The History of Wisconsin.* Vol. 2,*The Civil War Era, 1848–1873.* Madison: State Historical Society of Wisconsin, 1976.

Davidson, Randall. *9XM Talking: WHA Radio and the Wisconsin Idea.* Madison: University of Wisconsin Press, 2006.

Doering, Floyd J. *A History of Vocational Agriculture in Wisconsin, 1900–1976.* Madison: Wisconsin Department of Public Instruction, 1976.

Esterly, George. *Dictionary of Wisconsin Biography.* Madison: State Historical Society of Wisconsin, 1960.

Fapso, Richard J. *Norwegians in Wisconsin.* Rev. ed. Madison: Wisconsin Historical Society Press, 2001.

Galpin, Charles Josiah. *Rural Life.* New York: Century Company, 1919.

Gojmerac, Walter L. *All About Bees, Beekeeping and Honey.* New York: Drake, 1977.

Gough, Robert. *Farming the Cutover: A Social History of Northern Wisconsin, 1900–1940.* Lawrence: University Press of Kansas, 1997.

Gurda, John. *The Making of Milwaukee.* Milwaukee, WI: Milwaukee County Historical Society, 1999.

Haney, Richard. *"When Is Daddy Coming Home?" An American Family during World War II.* Madison: Wisconsin Historical Society Press, 2004.

Hachten, Harva, and Terese Allen. *The Flavor of Wisconsin: An Informal History of Food and Eating in the Badger State.* 2nd ed. Madison: Wisconsin Historical Society Press, 2009.

Holand, Hjalmar Rued. *History of Door County, Wisconsin: The County Beautiful.* Chicago: S. J. Clarke, 1917.

Janus, Edward. *Creating Dairyland: How Caring for Cows Saved Our Soil, Created Our Landscape, Brought Prosperity to Our State, and Still Shapes Our Way of Life in Wisconsin.* Madison: Wisconsin Historical Society Press, 2011.

Jenkins, John W. *A Centennial History: A History of the College of Agricultural and Life Sciences at the University of Wisconsin–Madison.* Madison, WI: College of Agricultural and Life Sciences, 1991.

Kaquatosh, Raymond C. *Little Hawk and the Lone Wolf: A Memoir.* Madison: Wisconsin Historical Society Press, 2014.

Lampard, Eric. *The Rise of the Dairy Industry in Wisconsin: A Study in Agricultural Change, 1820–1920.* Madison: State Historical Society of Wisconsin, 1963.

Landing, James E. *American Essence: A History of the Peppermint and Spearmint Industry in the United States.* Kalamazoo, MI: Kalamazoo Public Museum, 1969.

Landis, Paul, H. *Rural Life in Process.* New York: McGraw-Hill, 1940.

Lemanski, Lynn (Ed.), *State of Wisconsin 2011–2012 Blue Book.* Madison: Wisconsin Legislative Reference Bureau, 2011.

Loew, Patty. *Indian Nations of Wisconsin: Histories of Endurance and Renewal.* 2nd ed. Madison: Wisconsin Historical Society Press, 2013.

Maher, Neil M. *Nature's New Deal: The Civilian Conservation Corps and the Roots of the American Environmental Movement.* New York: Oxford University Press, 2008

Malone, Bobbie, and Kori Oberle. *Wisconsin: Our State, Our Story.* Madison: Wisconsin Historical Society Press, 2008.

Marquart, LaVerne H. *Wisconsin's Agricultural Heritage: 1871–1971.* Lake Mills, WI: Rural Life, 1972.

Martin, Lawrence. *The Physical Geography of Wisconsin.* Madison: University of Wisconsin Press, 1965.

McCollum, Elmer Verner. *From Kansas Farm Boy to Scientist: The Autobiography of Elmer Verner McCollum.* Lawrence: University of Kansas Press, 1964.

Merk, Frederick. *Economic History of Wisconsin during the Civil War Decade.* Madison: State Historical Society of Wisconsin, 1916.

Muir, John. *The Story of My Boyhood and Youth.* Madison: University of Wisconsin Press, 1965.

Murphy, Lucy Eldersveld. *A Gathering of Rivers: Indians, Metis, and Mining in the Western Great Lakes, 1737–1832.* Lincoln: University of Nebraska Press, 2000.

Nesbit, Robert C. *Wisconsin: A History.* 2nd ed. Madison: University of Wisconsin Press, 1989.

Osman, Loren, H. *W. D. Hoard: A Man for His Time.* Fort Atkinson, WI: W. D. Hoard and Sons, 1985.

Ostergren, Robert C., and Thomas R. Vale. *Wisconsin Land and Life.* Madison: University of Wisconsin Press, 1997.

Paris, Kathleen A. "Education for Employment: 70 Years of Vocational, Technical and Adult Education in Wisconsin." In *The State of Wisconsin 1981–1982 Blue Book,* edited by H. Rupert Theobald and Patricia V. Robbins. Madison: Wisconsin Legislative Research Bureau, 1981–1982.

Pinkerton, Kathrene Sutherland Gedney. *Bright with Silver.* New York: W. Sloane, 1947.

Povletich, William. *Green Bay Packers: Trials, Triumphs, and Tradition.* Madison: Wisconsin Historical Society Press, 2012.

Schafer, Joseph. *A History of Agriculture in Wisconsin.* Madison: State Historical Society of Wisconsin, 1922.

Schultz, Gwen. *Wisconsin's Foundations: A Review of the State's Geology and Its Influence on Geography and Human Activity.* Madison: University of Wisconsin Press, 2004.

Schultz, L. H. "Bud." *History of the Dairy Science Department: University of Wisconsin Madison.* Madison, WI: Dairy Science Department, 2009.

Schwartz, Bernard W. "A History of Hops in America." In *Steiner's Guide to American Hops.* New York: S. S. Steiner, 1973.

Smith, Alice E. *The History of Wisconsin.* Vol. 1, *From Exploration to Statehood.* Madison: State Historical Society of Wisconsin, 1973.

Smith, Clarence Beaman, and Meredith Chester Wilson. *The Agricultural Extension System of the United States.* New York: John Wiley and Sons, 1930.

Smoot, Frank. *Farm Life: A Century of Change for Farm Families and Their Neighbors.* Eau Claire, WI: Chippewa Valley Museum, 2004.

Strohschank, Johannes, and William G. Thiel. *The Wisconsin Office of Emigration: 1852–1855.* Madison: Max Kade Institute for German-American Studies, University of Wisconsin–Madison, 2005.

Thwaites, Reuben Gold. *Stories of the Badger State.* New York: American Book Company, 1900.

Thompson, William F. *The History of Wisconsin.* Vol. 6, *Continuity and Change: 1940–1965.* Madison: State Historical Society of Wisconsin, 1988.

United States Department of Agriculture. *Farmers in a Changing World: Yearbook of Agriculture, 1940.* Washington, DC: United States Government Printing Office, 1940.

University of Wisconsin Agronomy Department. *The First 100 Years: A Brief History of Agronomy at the University of Wisconsin–Madison from 1903 to 2002.* Madison: University of Wisconsin Agronomy Department, 2003.

Wisconsin Cartographers' Guild. *Wisconsin's Past and Present: A Historical Atlas.* Madison: University of Wisconsin Press, 1998.

Wyman, Mark. *The Wisconsin Frontier.* Bloomington: Indiana University Press, 1998.

Zaniewski, Kazimierz J., and Carol J. Rosen. *The Atlas of Ethnic Diversity in Wisconsin.* Madison: University of Wisconsin Press, 1998.

Zeitlin, Richard H. *Germans in Wisconsin.* Rev. ed. Madison: Wisconsin Historical Society Press, 2000.

PERIODICALS

Adams, Barry. "Switzerland Wins Top Prize but Wisconsin Dominates World Championship Cheese Contest." *Wisconsin State Journal,* March 20, 2014.

Barsantee, Harry. "The History and Development of the Telephone in Wisconsin." *Wisconsin Magazine of History,* December 1926, pp. 150–163.

Blondich, Sarah. "The Milwaukee Packers: Sweet Smell of the Stockyards." Express-Milwaukee.com, January 26, 2010.

"A Brief History of *Wisconsin Agriculturist.*" *Wisconsin Agriculturist* (1978).

Clark, Mary. "Rural Free Delivery." *Dane County Historical Society Newsletter,* Spring 2007.

Clausen, Heidi. "Dairy Business Innovation Center Closing." *The Country Today,* September 26, 2012.

Collisson, Charles F. "An Interview with Dr. Babcock." *De Laval Monthly,* February 1923.

Cook, Christopher D. "Control over Your Food: Why Monsanto's GM Seeds Are Undemocratic" *Christian Science Monitor,* February 23, 2011.

Davis, Mark. "Getting Rid of the Stumps, Wisconsin's Land-Clearing Program—the Experience of the Northern Lake Country, 1900–1925." *Transactions of the Wisconsin Academy of Sciences, Arts and Letters* 84 (1996): 11–22.

Durand, Loyal. "The Cheese Manufacturing Regions of Wisconsin, 1850–1950." *Transactions of the Wisconsin Academy of Sciences, Arts and Letters* 42 (1953): 109–130.

Esposito, Katherine. "Bringing in Nature's Bounty." *Wisconsin Natural Resources,* April 2006.

Fish, N. S. "The History of the Silo in Wisconsin" *Wisconsin Magazine of History,* December 1924, 160–170.

"The Function of Vitamin K: The Work of John W. Suttie." *Journal of Biological Chemistry* 283 (2008): pp. e9–e10.

Geib, Paul E. "'Everything But the Squeal': The Meat-Packing Industry, 1840–1930," *Wisconsin Magazine of History,* Autumn, 1994, pp. 2–23.

Hafemeister, Gloria. "Technology Invades Fields." *Wisconsin State Farmer,* November 24, 2014.

Hall, Clarence J. "From a Study of Inventory Maps There Came Wisconsin Cranberry Developments." *Cranberries: The National Cranberry Magazine,* May 1958.

Harmon, Amy, and Andrew Pollack. "Battle Brewing over Labeling of Genetically Modified Food." *New York Times,* May 24, 2012.

Holmes, Fred. L. "Craze for Hops Held Wisconsin." *Capital Times (Madison),* February 14, 1921.

Houlihan, Tamas. "Interview with Corey Kincaid." *Common'Tater,* May 2011.

Janik, Erika. "Crops of Yore." *Isthmus,* August 17, 2007.

Kane, Lucile. "Settling the Wisconsin Cutover." *Wisconsin Magazine of History,* Winter 1956–1967, pp. 91–98.

Last, Donald. "Potential versus Actual Development of Irrigated Agriculture in Central Wisconsin." *Transactions of the Wisconsin Academy of Sciences, Arts and Letters* 71, part 2 (1983): 51–56.

Lindner, Christine. "Flavor Foods with Mint." *Chilton Times Journal,* January 21, 2011.

Luther, E. L. "Farmers' Institutes in Wisconsin, 1885–1933," *Wisconsin Magazine of History,* September 1946, pp. 59–68.

Maclean, John N. "Environmentalists Sound Battle Cry: Save the Soil." *Chicago Tribune,* March 21, 1985.

Nixon, Ron. "Report Says a Crop Subsidy Cap Could Save Billions." *New York Times,* April 11, 2012.

Odell, Emory. "Swiss Cheese Industry." *Monroe Evening Leader Times,* 1936.

Paine, Laura. "The Hops Era: Wisconsin's Agricultural Gold Rush." *Wisconsin Academy Review,* June 1990, pp. 23–28.

Podgers, Patti. "Carrying on the Tradition." *Door County Magazine,* Fall 2004, p. 35.

Rees, Jonathon. "Caught in the Middle: The Seizure and Occupation of the Cudahy Brothers Company, 1944–1945," *Wisconsin Magazine of History,* Spring 1995, pp. 200–216.

Royte, Elizabeth. "Street Farmer." *New York Times,* July 1, 2009.

Schultz, Rob. "Wisconsin Aquaculture: New Law Helps Turn the Tide for Fish Hatcheries." *Wisconsin State Journal,* July 15, 2012.

———. "Agritourism Offers Vacationers a Taste of Country Life." *Wisconsin State Journal,* September 30, 2012.

Scott, Walter E., ed. "Emil Truog—Soil Scientist." *Wisconsin Academy Review,* Summer 1954, pp. 16–17.

Seely, Rob. "Climate Change Deniers Ignore Science, History." *Wisconsin State Journal,* June 29, 2012.

Smith, Jennifer. "The Culture of Ag." *Grow: Wisconsin's Magazine for the Life Sciences,* Summer 2012, pp. 28–33.

Stare, Fred. "Wisconsin's Canning Industry, Past and Present." *Wisconsin Magazine of History,* Autumn 1952, pp. 334–38.

Stevens, Neil E., and Jean Nash. "The Development of Cranberry Growing in Wisconsin." *Wisconsin Magazine of History,* March 1944, pp. 276–292.

Stewart, Charles D. "On a Moraine." *Atlantic Monthly,* September 1909.

Strey, Gerry. "The Oleo Wars: Wisconsin's Fight over the Demon Spread." *Wisconsin Magazine of History,* Autumn 2000, pp. 2–15.

Titus, W. A. "A Pioneer Beet Sugar Refinery." *Wisconsin Magazine of History,* December 1945, pp. 191–194.

"2011 Organic Production Survey: Wisconsin," USDA, National Agricultural Statistics Service, Madison, November 2012.

West, David P. "Hemp in Wisconsin." *Hemp World Magazine,* Winter 1998, pp. 1–19.

"Wisconsin Farmers Union News." *Wisconsin Farmers Union,* February/March 2012.

Wu, Felicia. "An Analysis of Bt Corn's Benefits and Risks for National and Regional Policymakers Considering Bt Corn Adoption." *International Journal of Technology and Globalization* 2, nos. 1/2 (2006): 115–133.

PAMPHLETS AND BULLETINS

Anniversary Album 1954–2004: 50 Years Strong and Still Growing. Wisconsin Christmas Tree Producer's Association, n.p., 2004.

Beedle, Peggy Lee. *Silos: An Agricultural Success Story.* Madison: University of Wisconsin–Extension, 2001.

Bell, Florence C. *Farmer Co-ops in Wisconsin.* St. Paul, MN: St. Paul Bank for Cooperatives, 1941.

Bussan, A. J. *Commercial Vegetable Production Wisconsin 2012.* Madison: University of Wisconsin–Extension, 2012.

Cheng, Len, and Paul D. Mitchell. *Status of the Wisconsin Ginseng Industry.* Madison: University of Wisconsin–Madison Department of Agricultural and Applied Economics, 2009.

Clift, Edith L., ed. *Wisconsin Farmers' Institute Cookbook No. 1.* Madison, WI: Office of Farmers' Institutes, 1908.

Cranefield, Frederic. *Commercial Fruit Growing in Wisconsin: A Report of the Twenty-Fourth Annual Farmers' Institute,* Bulletin no. 24. Madison: Wisconsin Farmers' Institutes, 1910.

Cropp, Bob, and Truman Graff. *The History and Role of Dairy Cooperatives.* Madison: University of Wisconsin–Madison College of Agriculture and Life Sciences, January 2001.

Farmers' Course in Agriculture. Bulletin of the University of Wisconsin, no. 105. December 1904.

France, N. E. *Beekeeping in Wisconsin.* Wisconsin Bulletin 264. Madison, WI: Agricultural Experiment Station, 1915.

Henry, William A. *Northern WI: A Hand-Book for the Homeseeker.* Madison, WI: Democrat Printing Company, 1896.

Hibbard, Benjamin Horace. *The History of Agriculture in Dane County, Wisconsin.* Bulletin of the University of Wisconsin no. 101. Madison: University of Wisconsin, 1904.

Jackson-Smith, Douglas, et al. *Farming in Wisconsin at the End of the Century: Results of the 1999 Wisconsin Farm Poll.* Wisconsin Farm Research Summary no. 4. Madison: University of Wisconsin–Madison and University of Wisconsin–Extension Program on Agricultural Technology Studies, March 2000.

Jesse, Ed. *Status of Wisconsin Agriculture, 2012.* Madison: University of Wisconsin–Madison Department of Agricultural and Applied Economics, 2012.

———et al. *Rethinking Dairyland: Background for Decisions about Wisconsin's Dairy Industry.* Marketing and Policy Briefing Paper no. 78A, College of Agricultural and Life Sciences, University of Wisconsin–Madison, May 2002.

Kucharik, Christopher J., and Pete Nowak. *Agriculture Working Group Report,* Wisconsin Initiative on Climate Change Impacts. Madison: University of Wisconsin–Madison Nelson Institute for Environmental Studies, 2011.

Lacy, Melvyn L., et al. *Mint Production in the Midwestern United States.* North Central Regional Extension Publication no. 155. East Lansing: Michigan Cooperative Extension Service, 1981.

McKerrow, Geo., ed. *Farmers' Institutes: A Handbook of Agriculture.* Bulletin no. 27. Madison, WI: Democrat Printing Company, 1913.

Nelson, Ray. *Verticillium Wilt of Peppermint.* East Lansing: Michigan State College Agricultural Experiment Station, 1950.

Ninth Census of the United States, 1870. Washington, DC: US Census Bureau, 1870.

Schaub, I. O. *Agricultural Extension Work: A Brief History.* Extension Circular no. 377. Raleigh: North Carolina Agricultural Extension Service, November 1953.

Seventh Census of the United States, 1850. Washington, DC: US Census Bureau, 1853.

Seventy-Five Years of Farm Bureau in Wisconsin. Madison: Wisconsin Farm Bureau Federation, 1994.

Taylor, Henry Charles. *A Farm Economist in Washington 1919–1925.* University of Wisconsin–Madison Department of Agricultural Economics, 1992.

USDA Economic Research Service, *History of Agricultural Price-Support and Adjustment Programs, 1933–84.* United States Department of Agriculture, Economic Research Service, Agriculture Information Bulletin no. 485, December 1984.

White, F. M. and E. R. Jones. *Getting Rid of Stumps,* Bulletin 295. Madison: University of Wisconsin Experiment Station, 1918.

Wisconsin Crop and Livestock Reporting Service, *Wisconsin Agriculture in Mid-Century,* Bulletin no. 325. Madison: Wisconsin State Department of Agriculture, 1953.

Wright, A. H. *Wisconsin's Hemp Industry,* Bulletin 293. Madison: University of Wisconsin Agricultural Experiment Station, May 1918.

REPORTS

Adams, H. C. *Biennial Report of the Dairy and Food Commissioner of Wisconsin, 1895–1896.* Madison, WI: Office of the Dairy and Food Commissioner, 1896.

Carstensen, Vernon. "The Birth of an Agricultural Experiment Station," in *The Growth of Agricultural Research in WI: A Lecture Series Commemorating the 75th Anniversary of the Wisconsin Experiment Station, 1883–1958.* Madison, WI: University of Wisconsin, 1958.

First Annual Report of the Agricultural Experiment Station: University of Wisconsin for the Year 1883. Madison, WI: Democrat Printing Company, State Printers, 1884.

Gilbert, William H. *Some Facts from Experience in Dairying.* Eighteenth Annual Report of the Wisconsin Dairymen's Association, 1890. Madison, WI: Democrat Printing Company, 1890.

Glaser, Lawrence K. *Provisions of the Food Security Act of 1985.* Agriculture Bulletin no. 498. United States Department of Agriculture, Economic Research Service.

Henry, W. A. *The Wisconsin Dairy School and Its Work.* Biennial Report of the Dairy and Food Commissioner of Wisconsin for 1899–1900. Madison, WI: Office of the Dairy Commissioners, 1901.

Henry, William A. *Fifteenth Annual Report of the Agricultural Experiment Station of the University of Wisconsin.* Madison, 1898.

Hoyt, J. W. *Transactions of the Wisconsin State Agricultural Society,* vol. 7. Madison: Wisconsin State Agricultural Society, 1868.

King, Rufus. *Transactions of the Wisconsin State Agricultural Society.* Madison, WI: Beriah Brown, State Printer, 1852.

Morrison, W. H., and John Gould, eds. *Wisconsin Farmers' Institutes: Sessions: 1886–1887.* Milwaukee: Cramer, Aikens & Cramer, 1887.

Pickett, J. G. "Pioneer Dairying in Wisconsin," in D. W. Curtis, Sec., *Sixth Annual Report of the Wisconsin Dairymen's Association.* Madison: Wisconsin Dairymen's Association, 1878.

Rochester, Becky. *Report of the Wisconsin Wineries Survey 2011.* Wisconsin Grape Growers Association, June 2011.

Russell, H. L. *Report of the Director: Agricultural Experiment Station for 1911–1912.* Madison, WI: College of Agriculture, 1913.

———. *Twenty-Fifth and Twenty-Sixth Annual Reports of the Agricultural Experiment Station.* Madison, WI: College of Agriculture, 1910.

Third Annual Report of the Wisconsin Dairymen's Association. Fort Atkinson, WI: W. D. Hoard Printer, 1875.

Thom, H. C. *First Annual Report of the State Dairy and Food Commissioner.* Madison, WI: Office of State Dairy and Food Commissioner, 1890.

INDEX

Page numbers in **bold** refer to illustrations.

ACKNOWLEDGMENTS

Many people helped with this book, from those who sent me stories, allowed me to interview them, read draft chapters, and checked facts to those who offered me encouragement and support for what proved to be an enormous task.

To begin, I want to especially thank Joan Sanstadt, *Agri-View,* for sharing historical materials, giving me several leads for interviews, printing a piece in *Agri-View,* and reading draft manuscript. Jim Massey, *The Country Today,* and Trey Foerster, *Wisconsin State Farmer,* also ran articles in their newspapers announcing this project and requesting stories and information about Wisconsin's agricultural history plus historical information about their newspapers. The results of this effort proved unbelievably rich.

The following people were especially helpful in supplying information and stories, and in several cases, reviewing material I wrote for errors and omissions: Chelle Calvert, Russell Miller, Karen Joss, Dale Seaquist, Linda Goldsworthy, Roger Huibregtse, Sandra Cleveland, Robert Kramer, Robert Williams, James G. Neu, Dennis Zeloski, Mark Martin, Glenn Lemmenes, Herb Magnuson, John Werth, Harry Erickson, Tom Borchardt, Tim Rehbein, Gretchen Grape, Fran O'Leary, Michelle Miller, Ray Antoniewicz, Walter Gojmerac, John Schoenemann, John Shutske, Brent McCown, Phil Dunigan, Ronald Schuler, Robert Cropp, Ed Jesse, Dwayne Rohweder, Robert Kauffman, L. H. "Bud" Schultz, Clarence Olson, Heidi Olson, Dave Shekoski, Jeff Rowsam, Clara Hedrick, Jean Brew, George Miller, Norval Dvorak, Nora Walnoha, Leo Martin, Bobbie Erdmann, and Allen Stea. I'm sure there were others as well; they know who they are, and I thank them profusely and apologize for not including their names.

As always I thank my wife, Ruth, who puts up with me as I scatter research materials throughout the house and sets me straight when I write something that makes no sense whatever. And I can never heap enough praise on Kate Thompson, my never-tiring editor, who wades through pages of manuscript and untold numbers of footnotes and clunky prose with skill and good humor—and then makes everything sparkle. Finally, producing a book like this is a huge undertaking, and I'm grateful for the exemplary work of Wisconsin Historical Society staff members Elizabeth Boone, John Nondorf, and Nichole Barnes.

ABOUT THE AUTHOR

Jerry Apps was born and raised on a central Wisconsin farm. He is a former county extension agent and professor emeritus for the College of Agriculture and Life Sciences at the University of Wisconsin–Madison. Today he works as a rural historian, full-time writer, and creative writing instructor.

Jerry is the author of more than forty fiction, nonfiction, and children's books with topics ranging from barns, one-room schools, cranberries, cucumbers, cheese factories, and the humor of mid-America to farming with horses and the Ringling Brothers circus. He and his wife, Ruth, have three children, seven grandchildren, and one great-grandson. They divide their time between their home in Madison and their farm, Roshara, in Waushara County.